Topless Prophet

Topless Prophet

The True Story of America's Most Successful
Gentleman's Club Entrepreneur

Alan Markovitz
with Thomas Stevens

AM PRODUCTIONS

Published by AM Productions
Detroit, MI

For ordering information or special discounts for bulk purchases, please contact Emerald Book Company at PO Box 91869, Austin, TX 78709, 512.891.6100.

Publisher's Cataloging-In-Publication Data
(Prepared by The Donohue Group, Inc.)

Markovitz, Alan.
    Topless prophet : the true story of America's most successful gentleman's club entrepreneur / Alan Markovitz with Thomas Stevens. -- 1st ed.

    p. ; cm.

    ISBN: 978-0-9840855-0-7

1. Markovitz, Alan. 2. Businessmen--United States--Biography. 3. Men--Societies and clubs--United States--History. I. Stevens, Thomas (Thomas Daniel), 1957- II. Title.

HC102.5.M37 M37 2009
338.7/092/073 [B]   2009930902

Printed in the United States of America on acid-free paper

12 11 10 09   10 9 8 7 6 5 4 3 2 1

First Edition

Dedication

This book, my life story so far, is dedicated to you, Dad.
Without your strength and will to survive, I would not be here.
You made it through that hell on earth known as the Holocaust and came to America, where you worked hard to achieve the American dream of owning your own business. In so doing, you and Mom gave me the foundation of a good upbringing in the proud middle class of Oak Park, Michigan. In spite of my sometimes rebellious nature, you nonetheless gave me the tools and the self-determination to build a business of my own, a business that I am fortunate to love and have prospered in. Ultimately, you gave me the gift of a solid beginning, instilling in me the importance of having goals and achieving them, and with the rewards that have poured forth, the ability to live life to its fullest. For this, I can give no greater thanks than to honor you by dedicating all that I have created, my story as well as yours, as told within these pages, to you.

With much love,
Your son

CONTENTS

Shot in the Head.. 1

The Setting of The Booby Trap............................ 11

The Springing of the Trap 49

BTs Dearborn 71

Booby Trap FLA 85

Tycoons Are Made, Not Born............................ 107

Trumpp Card 121

Assassin.. 151

Justice Redux/Hit 'Em in The Wallet................ 189

The Girls.. 203

747 Engine Failure on Takeoff 227

Friends, Scoundrels, & Cheats.......................... 263

Back to the Future.. 281

You Are Invited! 305

SHOT IN THE HEAD

The .40 caliber round from the cop's Glock hit me like a baseball bat to the face. I had no idea I was even shot, at first. It was the night of January 9, 1997, around closing time at 2:00 a.m.

Earlier in the evening the off-duty Inkster cop and his buddy (another off-duty cop) had come into 747, my latest and greatest incarnation of what premium topless entertainment should be. We'd been open only about two months on Michigan Avenue just west of Middlebelt under the landing pattern for Detroit Metropolitan Airport, in Inkster. The building used to be a decrepit former country bar called the Mustang that my partners and I had razed and poured a couple million into rebuilding as the slickest, swankiest gentleman's club in Michigan.

It's not that unusual to have police as customers. Hey, they're guys, right? And guys like naked, young women with gorgeous bodies doing the humpty-hump right there in front of them, on a beautiful stage that rivals anything Las Vegas (or anywhere else) has to offer.

The problem was, the one cop either had something for or against one particular dancer that night and had been arguing with her off and on for hours, while drinking and being a general macho prick. But when police come into the club, off-duty and prepared to spend money enjoying themselves, we accommodate them. Their sidearms, however, are taken from them and checked securely into the club safe, returned to them when they're ready to leave.

My bouncers had to intervene several times that night, trying to keep a lid on the rookie cop's behavior. But trouble kept flaring up. It's not that unusual. Worse comes to worst and you have no choice but to ask—or tell—the offending parties to leave. Usually they do and that's the end of it. But this night, trouble spilled out into the parking lot. One of my people had stepped back into my office to tell me the cops were out in the parking lot, waving their guns around and refusing to leave the premises. I walked into the vestibule to the club and had just opened the outside door when the shot that found me cracked through the air.

Getting shot is not like it is in the movies where you just go down, dead and gone—unless you've taken one right to the brain or the heart. The .40 caliber slug that had my name on it crudely removed half my face, ripped into my cheek bone, tore through my upper palate, taking out and loosening several teeth, and plowed itself to rest in my neck between my carotid artery and jugular vein, breaking my jaw in six places along the way. If it had cut the carotid, I would have been a goner in just a few minutes, my heart pumping out all that valuable red fluid, spurt after ugly spurt, till I simply expired.

As it was, I actually turned around and walked back into the club. My valet was saying, "Alan, you've been shot, your face looks like hamburger—you need an ambulance." Stunned but ambulatory, I continued inside, instinctively running my hand down the side of my head to see if something had come out of there. I came up with blood on my hand. It hit me. "Shit!" I thought, "I've been shot, all right!" Then all hell broke loose as I crumpled into a heap on the floor beneath the strobes and black lights. Everything began to turn to a blur as people were all over me, talking, screaming, somebody calling 911 for an ambulance.

In the meantime, the freaking lunatic cop and his partner just got into their car and took off. See ya later!

Pluck

I was the only Jewish greaseball at Oak Park High. My father is a Holocaust survivor—he was liberated from Auschwitz when he was 16—and emigrated to England, met my mom, and swept her off her feet when she was just 19. He lost one younger brother and his parents to the gas chambers, but four other siblings survived that hell on earth. Maybe that's where I get it from—pluck, perseverance, determination, balls, a little excess now and then. How else are you going to make it in this business? I mean, I wasn't class valedictorian, though I did pull down a fairly impressive GPA.

My parents wanted me to be a doctor or a lawyer, the typical young-Jewish-guy-does-well-for-himself success story. Instead I wanted to ride my Triumph Bonneville down the hallways of my high school—and I did! What a hoot. Got suspended for a week.

In response, my old man kicked my ass. He was only five foot seven and 145 pounds, but he used to get me good, often chasing me under our dining room table while doing his best at kicking the crap out of me like some outtake from *The Sopranos*. But let me be the first to say, I'm sure I deserved a lot worse than what he was doling out. These days, kids sue their parents for child abuse, or even threaten to call the cops on them because they've heard all the stories in the media about other kids getting away with that. The pendulum has definitely swung to an extreme, where responsible parents are being punished for the outrageous behavior of a handful of wack jobs. But my father was actually doing me a favor, was only trying to keep me in line, scare the hell out of me, and straighten me out. When I was getting out of line, hey, I knew it, he knew it, and any responsible parent would do anything he could under the circumstances. I was always getting in trouble for something. But when Dad was really and truly pissed at me, he did something far more horrible than kicking my ass: He chained my motorcycle to a tree we had in back of our house. A real King Kong chain and a padlock the size of your fist. I tried cutting it in vain with the biggest bolt cutter I could get my hands on, but Dad was no dummy. He anticipated my attempt at liberating the bike and took no chances with cheap chain or a flimsy cable lock.

I'm pretty sure my parents saw trouble coming even when I was in grade school. I was basically a smart-ass kid from the word go. An old childhood buddy that I ran into at a class reunion in Las Vegas a few years back reminded me of a verbal exchange I had with my fourth grade teacher, Miss Clayman, who declared, "Alan Markovitz, you have a big mouth!" I laughed as I was reminded that my reply was, "That's all right, because you have skinny little legs!" I'm sure it was Mom who reported it to my father that night when he got home from work at his TV repair shop. And I'm sure Dad gave me a licking that he hoped would drive the devil from my soul. But I needed the discipline and I know that it served me well later on in my ambitions to get out of school and start making money on my own. I think, in retrospect, that my father actually cut me more slack than I gave him credit for at the time, because I didn't drink and didn't do drugs, like quaaludes, which were popular in the mid to late 1970s even among my classmates who later became doctors and lawyers!

When I was growing up in Oak Park, which is a working- to middle-class suburb only a few miles from Detroit proper, we lived kitty-corner to the Milan family, who always drove Cadillacs. The Markovitz family, on the other hand, drove Chevys. I liked the idea of driving a nice car, but you needed real cash to be riding in Cadillac cars and the neighbors got theirs from the bar business. I imagine it was my first realization—or simply putting two and two together—in terms of what kind of business makes the kind of money that would allow me to live the kind of life I wanted.

My first job, however, while still in high school, was pumping gas at Sol and Ziggy's Mobil station at the corner of Ten Mile and Greenfield. I worked up to driving a tow truck and became the weekend manager, too, so the money was pretty good for a kid my age. I was also working part-time for my father, fixing televisions, and even took electronics classes, thinking there might be a future for me there. But electronics repair, I soon realized, was a dying business with everything becoming a throwaway. I wanted more.

The summer after high school I could've goofed off like a lot of my friends, working part-time, riding my motorcycle, chasing girls, and preparing for college in the fall, as my parents expected. But I had an idea. Because I've always liked things that go fast, my eye was caught by a newspaper story I'd read about the Israeli Air Force. In the decade following Israel's spectacular success in the 1967 Six Day War, their military was considered among the best in the world. The IAF shoot-down record at the end of the war was a claimed 451 enemy aircraft downed versus 10 downed of its own. Israeli fighter pilots were esteemed as some of the best trained, most aggressive jet jockeys flying. And, it turned out, they were always on the lookout for dedicated young Jewish people to join up. It seemed like a dream, but the chief advantage of youth is being unafraid of dreaming . . . and doing. With relatives living in Israel, I figured I had a leg up on going over there and getting the wheels turning. When I told my parents what I wanted to do, I wasn't sure they would go for it, but to my surprise and satisfaction they said that if I wanted it badly enough they'd support me 100 percent.

I began the process by writing a letter to the liaison officer of the Israeli embassy in Washington, D.C. In response, I was told to send in my academic record along with information about my background and family history. It didn't take long before I got the response I'd been hoping for. I was qualified to make a formal application to the Israeli Air Force, and I would be required to travel to Israel and stay for about a month to meet with representatives from their recruiting office and take certain tests that would determine my ultimate qualifications to become a pilot.

I was off—my first ever trip abroad—on the way to Rehovot, a city about ten miles south of Tel Aviv. I was very excited and somewhat nervous. I had learned that recruits are screened not only for their ability to perform assigned tasks, but also for their attitude in performing them—such as how they take hardships and unexpected problems, how well they work as part of a team, and how they approach problem solving and disaster management situations. As many as 90 percent of those who commence the testing—called *gibush*—are dropped from further consideration at its conclusion.

The experience was amazing. I did well on all the tests I was given, enjoyed the camaraderie of being among other young, aspiring pilots, and even had the opportunity to take an orientation flight on an F-21 Kfir, an awesome fighter based on the French Mirage design. I thought that having that control stick in my own hands would be the greatest feeling—and accomplishment—on earth. The rest of the month flew by, and soon I found myself sitting down across the desk of an Israeli Air Force commander who very patiently explained what came next. I was told that I had passed all the tests and tasks that I had been given and that I was qualified to be inducted and begin real training in the IAF. But . . . and there were a few BIG buts. I would have to learn Hebrew. I would have to take a full academic load in addition to my pilot training and, in spite of how well I performed, there was a 90 percent washout rate for new pilot recruits. The IAF wanted only the best of the best, he explained, and by making their program more progressively difficult, they guaranteed themselves that result. If I did not make the cut, I would still be required to spend two years in the service, which may or may not have kept me in the Air Force. There was a possibility that I could be assigned to the infantry. The commander told me that he didn't want a decision immediately—go home, he said, and think about it for a month, then decide. They wanted to be sure I made a decision that I could live with.

I left Israel feeling both elated at the extraordinary experience I had just had but also troubled by the very real possibility of washing out. If I were going to join the Israeli armed forces, I wanted to fly, nothing less. I was now forced to weigh the possibilities and make a pragmatic decision. I talked it over with my dad, who put it in blunt terms. He asked, "If you don't make the cut, are you willing to spend two years in the army?" That sure framed it for me. I was confident in my abilities, but 9:1 odds were tough to beat. When I thought about living in a barracks and marching in the hot Middle Eastern sun, the opportunity suddenly seemed a lot less appealing than flying a technologically advanced fighter jet. I rather reluctantly wrote back to the Air Force that while I was grateful for the chance to serve Israel, I honestly had to take a pass. It was simply not to be.

I decided to go back to school. The time had come for my first and last act in the world of academics. I did what Dad wanted me to. I started premed at Wayne State University, which I hated. The last thing in the world I really wanted was to be immersed in carving up cadavers and diagnosing diseases. After a semester of hitting the medical books, I was frustrated and bored. So, I switched to liberal arts and business, which was much more pleasant and easier for me, but all I could think about was getting into business for myself and making some real, serious money. I didn't realize it at the time, or maybe I did, but I was about to make my very first actual career move. Maybe it was fate, maybe it was desire, and just maybe it was the neighbors.

It's often said that you grow up and marry the girl next door. Or, you go where she dances topless and marry the business she's in! In my case, it was a little topless bar called La Chambre nestled happily in the middle of a strip mall at Telegraph and the I-96 freeway. It had been there forever, and it's still there today, coexisting with a nail salon, a check cashing service, and a Dollar Store. It used to be anchored by a cavernous nightclub called Uncle Sam's that was hugely popular in the mid-1970s when Michigan's legal drinking age was only eighteen. Uncle Sam's faded away, but the bouncing bosoms of La Chambre survived. And thanks to longtime owner Sol Milan, I had my first gig bartending, managing, and soaking up everything there is to learn about running a successful topless enterprise.

Flash forward. There I am, lying on the floor of The Flight Club with a face that's been half pulverized by the shot from a cop's automatic. A lot of things fly through your mind, chief among them the questions, "How bad is it? Am I gonna make it? Where the fuck is the ambulance?" Before I knew it, I was picked up, put on a gurney, and delivered a mile down the road to the closest available hospital, Annapolis. The doctors there took a look at me and apparently decided they didn't know what to do with me for the very basic reason that they didn't know where the bullet had gone. Maybe if I had gone to medical school like my parents wanted, I could have told them where the bullet was and saved everybody the hassle. Instead, thank God, they decided to put me on a beautiful maize and blue medevac chopper that whisked me another 15 miles to the University of Michigan, whose trauma specialists are the best in the business and did in fact save my life that cold and miserable January night.

It was a long, long haul back to what you'd call normal. The doctor who headed up my case, Steven Buchman, later testified in court that the bones in my face and jaw were not only broken but were riddled with hairline cracks similar to what you'd get if you poured boiling water over ice. My face was pretty much shattered. It took almost a year, in excess of half a dozen separate surgeries, plastic reconstruction, and close to a quarter of a million dollars to put me back together. Getting through the recovery mentally is a story unto itself, and now, although you can look at me and never guess what I've been through, the bullet is still lodged in my neck between my carotid artery and jugular vein because it was deemed by my medical team as too risky to remove. It remains a constant reminder of just how close I came to buying the farm; or should I say, gentleman's club?

Running a successful topless establishment is the consummate dream of a lot of businessmen. It's the obvious allure of fantasy meeting reality, your own private Neverland, and getting paid to boot. What honest heterosexual male among us hasn't at one time or another entertained fantasies of his very own harem of gorgeous young women who bring him pleasure, prestige, and wealth? All you have to do is find a location, get a liquor license, appease the police and the city fathers (and mothers!), and the money (and fun) will come gushing in like an oil well. Yeah, right.

The real story reads more like something out of *Fortune* or *Forbes*, if you run it right, which is to say, run it like a business. I won't tell you that I haven't had more fun than rolling downhill in a giant barrel of . . . make that exotic entertainers . . . but I will also tell you things about business, politics, justice, sex, and human behavior that you won't find in any college textbook. Running a top-flight gentleman's club full of exotic entertainers (i.e., women) is not a helluva lot different than piloting a very fast jet airplane. They are very costly to operate and maintain, things happen very fast, and if you don't have qualified personnel at the controls you can crash and burn just as quickly as you can take off and climb high above the clouds, where the sun always shines.

It's been an incredible ride so far, and at this stage of my life, I'm ready for bigger, better, and greater accomplishments than ever before. It's always about the next move, the next phase, the next big thing. Because as long as there are men and booze and beautiful women, there's a fine future to look forward to.

Come on along, have a cigar, order a great steak, kick back in the company of a beautiful lady, and enjoy!

THE SETTING OF
THE BOOBY TRAP

Eight Mile, the east/west boulevard that divides Detroit to the south from Detroit's tony suburbs to the north, is like no other strip on earth. For the last forty-odd years from the 1960s through the new century, descriptors such as *gritty, seedy,* and *crime-pocked* come to mind. It's a busy boulevard, nonetheless, and thousands upon thousands of people use it daily, always racing to beat the next red light, yellow being Motown shorthand for "Stomp on it." By day, it's just another humdrum four-lane highway—at night it comes alive.

Today, Eight Mile remains a mishmash of both greater and lesser topless bars, liquor stores (we call them party stores in Detroit), office buildings, brake and muffler joints, used European luxury car lots behind chain-link fencing, and the trailer park Eminem made famous in his eponymous hit movie *Eight Mile*. When Detroit Mayor Coleman Young was reelected, hizzoner infamously declared war on crime and told all the thugs, criminals, and rapists to "hit Eight Mile!" quite to the anger of the predominantly white suburbs they'd be hitting the road to.

Just to the east and north lies what is acknowledged as the country's first modern suburban shopping mall, Northland, built by local boy and developer Al Taubman in 1959 and serving the first wave of white flight from the city. Up till the late 1960s, what was once a white, middle-class and mostly Jewish environs is now a mix of black and white urban working class and some old folks who never moved further north or west, and, all in all, is an area that retains a distinct street vibe. Rich doctors, business owners, players, and the blue-collar men and women are all loosely tossed together in thousands of tract homes running between the mile roads and the occasional fancy high-rise apartment building.

The million-dollar homes don't begin to pop up for another ten miles or so, heading north into Birmingham along world-famous Woodward Avenue, heavy street racing and cruising scene in the late sixties, now host to the wildly popular and nostalgic Woodward Dream Cruise that draws millions of participants and spectators every August. Eight Mile is Woodward's hick cousin, if you will. Eight Mile may not have the plastic surgeons and mortgage bankers, but there is always the whiff of action on Eight. Maybe it's solely because of the dozen or so strip clubs scattered along it, from the east side's Tycoon's all the way to the west side's Trumpps—both my creations—and all the others in between running the gamut from tacky to glitzy, posh to poor. A guy can go into one after a day wrenching transmissions in his work shirt with his name sewn on above the left pocket and spend six or seven bucks on a cold one while geeking on a tangle of rowdy-looking dames with serious rackage. Or he can wear his three-piece suit and slip into the posh folds of a dark yet dazzling cavern of carnality for a twelve-dollar Bombay martini and a Dominican smoke grown from Cuban seed. Here, the girls will be more polished, but they'll still possess the unabashed sexuality, luscious breasts, and firm, well-rounded bottoms that draw the customers in as moths to the flame.

It's my preference to run the latter type of club, but in my business philosophy, I believe that there's room for everyone. And I will compete with complete and utter determination, no matter who the competition may be. That is the only way to make it to the top in this business of toplessness, as you will see for yourself.

Back in the day when I was just twenty and still working for my dad in the TV repair business, I listened to "Dust in the Wind" on Top 40 radio like everybody else. But I had an idea, just a tiny crystal of an idea, that I could form my own business and make a name for myself. Looking back on it, as a kid, I was always looking for what you might call my own niche, or maybe an angle that would put some cash in my pockets. Maybe it was buying a beat-up bike cheap from a neighborhood kid, fixing it, improving it, and turning it for a profit. And, like P. Diddy and Warren Buffett, I had a paper route, delivering *The Detroit News* to 150 tidy little suburban homes every afternoon. Seems like some of the highest rollers in business and entertainment started out this way because it's the soonest an ambitious boy (or girl for that matter) can get into a business that can be expanded as far as the energy and drive of a young person will take it. Hey, even a lot of adults eke out a living flogging the family car or truck on a paper route, except that today circulation numbers are down across the board for newspapers, making it less attractive an option than it used to be. For a kid, the green is pretty damn good, especially without having to buy gasoline!

The Markovitz house was located on Avon in Oak Park, which borders the city of Detroit proper. As I've already hinted, this heavily white and Jewish enclave was in the 1960s the idyllic, safe, all-American suburb where everybody knew everyone else in the neighborhood and we kids went to elementary school by walking a few blocks down the street. It was the era of Camelot and the Cold War, when "duck and cover" was not sports terminology but an emergency drill for surviving nuclear attack by ducking under our little school desks if the Russians or Cubans lobbed missiles at us. But we were really more concerned with getting together after school for a sandlot baseball game, hanging out and riding our bikes, and dropping in at our friends' houses for lemonade or maybe listening to the latest hit 45s when we got a little older and started noticing girls.

Aristotle, had the groovy Greek sage and philosopher lived today, might have posed the question: which came first, the girls or the entrepreneur? It's another way of posing the cocktail party question, "So, how in the world did you ever get into the topless bar business?" To which the proverbial smart-ass that I still occasionally am would probably answer: "By walking into a topless bar!"

Which brings us back to Sol Milan, and his Cadillacs, kitty-corner from me, Sis, Mom and Dad on Avon. Maybe it was the combination of my wild streak—I loved racing around on my Triumph Bonneville in high school—and my need to belong; though a bit on the scrawny side I managed to join the Saboteurs MC (motorcycle club) as a "guest rider." It was ironic, actually. The other club members were wannabe gangsta types, and here I was this Jewish kid, but I wore greasy leathers, slicked my hair back, and cultivated the perception that I was a real scrapper, that if you provoked a fight with me I wasn't going to back down and would do as much damage as I could even if I got the worst of it! As a result, I got into very few fights, which reinforced in me the truth that perception is often more real than reality itself. In the club business, I would find this axiom to come in handy again and again.

So l had been running his topless club Le Chambre, in a strip mall (no pun intended) at the corner of Telegraph and I-96, for some years before I walked in for the first time. I remember it as if it were yesterday. It was dark, as most gentleman's clubs are, traditionally. But there was an elevated stage running the length of the deep, narrow space, with blinking lights along the perimeter. The music was loud, and since this was the disco era, the infectious dance beat of songs like Donna Summer's "Love to Love You Baby" throbbed as topless dancers writhed and shook to the music. The atmosphere was intoxicating, a world unto itself. For a young guy, it was like walking into some kind of sheik's harem. It was easy to forget about the din of traffic on Telegraph and I-96, which bore commuters going to and from work, trucks delivering milk and bread and steel to the auto plants, and a thousand other ordinary daily errands. Inside, where the women were nearly naked and the booze flowed, that was where extraordinary life was lived. And where extraordinary amounts of money were generated. I bought a beer so that I could hang out for a while and soak it all up. Soon, I was in the middle of a daydream; I knew I wanted to be part of it, somehow. It all seemed to be right there within my grasp . . . but how?

On a subsequent visit to Sol's place, I remember talking with him in his cramped, paper-strewn office. He was interrupted to go out on the floor for a few minutes while I found myself gawking at his six-foot-tall cast-iron office safe, with a wheel that would look at home on an attack sub and a handle like a billy club. I could only imagine what kind of cash a club like Sol's was generating.

My appetite was definitely whetted. Man, I was impressed! I had to get into this business! Thus, it turned out that the smell of money mixed with the illusion of sex synthesized my youthful ambitions from simply hanging out at Le Chambre into "I'll do anything if you give me a job, Sol!" I decided it was an apt moment to go to bartender school, a two-week course that I easily passed. However, the wheels of change in one's young life often turn slowly, especially for one who is impatient. Looking back, it now seems events were unfolding at a fateful speed that would gain incredible momentum through the years.

Charlie was Sol's bartender, a rather unassuming guy who didn't say much, wore dark glasses all the time, and somehow reminded me of a professional sax player. One day, Sol informed me that Charlie wanted weekends off and asked if I'd like to tend bar on Saturday and Sunday nights. Of course I jumped on it—it was a dream job! And I clicked behind the bar, got good at making small talk with the customers, keeping an eye on everything that was going on around me. Which came in handy, as I was soon to discover. Problem was, Charlie liked his vodka, which as you might imagine doesn't blend well with keeping track of cash, customers, and other little things that add up to big things if you don't stay alert.

One day, Charlie goes on vacation and Sol asks me to tend the bar Friday through Sunday and keep an extra close eye on things—the regular weekend manager had been goofing off, too. Well and fine, I'm up to it. I'm learning everything about the business that I can, soaking it up like a sponge, enjoying the scenery at the same time but definitely focused on the business end. Until one night, a dancer named Connie caught my eye. Or perhaps, truthfully, I caught hers.

Connie was tall, maybe five foot eight and slim, with gorgeous full breasts, a washboard stomach, and a cascading bounty of curly brunette hair that owed its origins to Charlie's Angels. She was sweet, she was single, and apparently she was interested. I remember Peter O'Toole once said that when it comes to women, all men have to do is pretty much show up and let them run the show. They seem to know what they want more than the guys, so why not let nature simply take her course? By the way, this is still the best pickup advice I can give to fellas reading this book. In all my years around women, through intense observation and experience, I have found it to be true. Granted, sometimes you've got to bust a move to get the ball rolling, as many women want to be pursued. But if you keep your eyes and your mind open, they will give you plenty of signs. All you have to do is recognize the body language and let the good times roll.

That night, I closed the place and went home with Connie to her one-bedroom apartment a few miles north on Telegraph. To make a long story short, Connie rocked my world to the core. Even though she was only a couple of years older than I was, she knew what she was doing and ran the show like a world-class seductress. She did things that I had only read about in magazines like *Penthouse*. I felt as though I had been given the keys to the kingdom. The young Alan Markovitz truly, and in more ways than one, lost his virginity that glorious night.

Before I knew it the weekend nights at the club became weeknights too. I was also working for my dad during the week at his thriving TV repair shop—two trucks on the road and plenty of walk-in business—and going to Wayne State University taking a crack at premed. You've gotta please your parents, right? Plus, I was spending the night with Connie every chance I had. Along with clocking seventy to eighty hours a week juggling everything, something had to give. It did.

Of all things to go, it was my gig at La Chambre. I was conflicted trying to reconcile my family's desire that I get a profession—the proverbial doctor or lawyer—with my drive to make it on my own, in my own way. But I did not want to disappoint my father, so it was time to get practical, recalibrate, adjust. I was back to square one as I reluctantly said goodbye to Sol, picked up more hours at Dad's shop, changed my major to business and liberal arts, and soldiered on.

But Eight Mile was about to call . . . because I never could get the taste of the club business out of me. It was in my blood now and one way or another I was going to get back into it, on my own terms. As far as I was concerned, the die was cast. It has been said about successful business people that there are those who take their time making a decision but stick to it until they succeed . . . and those who are quick to change their minds but don't stick with something long enough for success to come. I knew there was money to be made in the topless business, but to make it I had to get in. Yet I didn't want to work for somebody else. I knew that the city of Detroit wasn't handing out any new cabaret licenses, so I had to find an existing operation that I could take over. If I had known what a huge proposition this was, maybe I would have been too intimidated to try. But it seemed straightforward enough—find a club that's on the skids, get it as cheaply as possible, and build it up. Today, it would be the monetary equivalent of buying a vintage Ferrari and restoring that ride into a showstopper. Only then the stakes were a lot higher.

How does one become the owner of a topless club? For me, in the dawn of the 1980s, it was simple: You look in the newspaper's classified section under Bars, Taverns, and Restaurants for Sale. I had become preoccupied with scanning the listings almost every day. I was making good money working at the TV shop, but I found that going to classes at Wayne State was a real drag. My heart just wasn't in it—I wanted to follow my dreams, to make it on my own. And I didn't want to wait. Impatience is the first cousin of ambition, and ambition doesn't rest . . . it can't afford to. The painter Pablo Picasso, when asked why he hadn't ended up a starving artist like so many thousands before him, reportedly quipped, "I can't afford to be poor!" It's a mentality, no doubt. But thoughts must become actions, or starvation does in fact become a real concern. I had kept both the dream of my own business and a connection to Sol Milan alive. I had casually asked him, months before, if I were to find an opportunity to buy a club, would he be interested? His muttered answer, something to the effect of "Yeah, maybe, depends on what you come across," was all I needed.

One day in 1980 I was flipping through the ads in *The Detroit News* as I had been for the past several months when one ad in particular grabbed me. It was placed by a broker named Jerry Gora, who had a company called Realbus, short for real estate and business. The listing said there was a property available that had the necessary cabaret license to provide topless entertainment along with liquor. I picked up the phone and made an appointment to see Jerry the following week.

Now, here I am, basically an inexperienced college kid going to see this broker. What credibility did I have? Sol Milan. And my experience working for Sol at La Chambre, enough to get my foot in the door. So, I took the meeting on my own, describing what I was looking for. Which turned out to be two things essential in real estate: location, and the big one—can I swing the deal? Good old Jerry Gora, who later went on to do five years on escrow embezzlement, had just the deal for me. It was a shuttered, broken-down topless biker bar with back taxes owing, a block down Eight Mile from the headquarters of the Renegades motorcycle club. If I could come up with $135,000, I could have the whole thing—lock, stock, and barrel. It had been called Vince's Blue Heron, but I thought it needed a clever new name. First, however, was the question of how a twenty-something college student working for his father was going to raise such capital. I was pretty sure Sol would go for it.

Looking back, I sometimes think I would have passed on the deal if I had really understood what I was getting myself into. Sol had looked the building over, a simple concrete block structure of about three thousand square feet with a gravel parking lot that would hold no more than a couple of dozen cars. It was in pretty funky shape, having survived God knows how many biker brawls, clubbings, shootings, stabbings, and bottles smashed over heads or against its black walls. In short, it was a wreck. But beyond the name, I already had a vision for the place—TGI Friday's: polished brass and hardwood accents, artfully tiled floors, and moody, low-key lighting, with hip decorative objects punctuating one's visual impression. Except we would be serving something hot definitely not on TGI Friday's menu—beautiful, bare-breasted dancers who would attract a moneyed, upscale clientele.

You want to know what really happened on the way to the forum? Bikers. Badass bikers. Not exactly a dovetail with the image we aspired to, and in fact attained. But damned good entertainment for folks who watch the eleven o'clock news or reporters who follow the police blotter.

Jump Start

In business, when a thing is right, you can feel it in your bones. When the right opportunity comes along, at the right time, the pieces practically fall into place by themselves. Then, once you sign on the dotted line, it's ass-busting time, sweating the details and putting your plan into action. Sol Milan, with his years of experience running Le Chambre (and my couple of years of working there) was the key to the whole thing. Our business relationship was simple and straightforward. We paid as we went, whatever was needed, beginning with the purchase of the property.

Sol was in for a 50 percent share—about $67,500. I was on my own. I kicked in everything I could come up with, all my savings, even cashing out of my beloved Triumph Bonneville to make the down payment and secure the note. But then the REAL bills began coming in—those that had to be paid to refurbish the building, turn it into a swanky club, and allow us to open the doors and begin to actually make money.

Architect's bill? Split it and pony up. Pave the parking lot? Another couple of thousand apiece. New bar? Get out your checkbook. Bam, bam, bam! Sol had cash flow from Le Chambre to cover his end. I didn't, and it wasn't long before I was tapped. But there was no way I was going to let the deal sour this close to getting the club finished. Sol was complaining that I was slow to kick in as the expenses kept coming, and he was right. So, to whom do you turn to when you don't have credit? Family, of course.

Dad knew I had taken the plunge, and he wasn't exactly crazy about the idea. But, being over eighteen I was legal and able to sign on the dotted line. I had committed and that was that. Whether I failed or triumphed, I had taken the critical first steps and I know that my father respected the guts it took to make such a move. At the same time, there was no guarantee that he would be willing to invest or loan me what I needed. I picked the time to approach him carefully, however, making sure he had had a good day at the shop before I approached him after dinner.

"Um, Dad . . . I have a business proposition for you," was my opening gambit.

"OK, vot izzit?" he came back, straight to the point in his Czech-accented English.

"It's the club, dad . . . we're really getting close to getting it done. I think we can open in a few months . . . but I'm tapped."

"You got a name for it yet?" he asked. "Something clever?"

You know how when you're a teenager and you need the car for a big date, and you've gotta ask your father for the keys . . . and you just know when you've got him and he's going to say yes?

"Yeah, I'd like to call it The Booby Trap." (I had been thinking about the name for months and thought I had come up with something both catchy and rather descriptive of the kind of business we were getting into.)

"OK," my father said, "how much do you need?"

It may sound like my dad simply rolled over, but there was a lot of subsequent discussion about the challenges ahead. Having my father on board reassured Sol, too, in more ways than one, so it was a win for everyone. But, never having been in such an unusual business, it was with some degree of reluctance that he became my partner. "Who could have imagined such a thing?" he remarked to me at the time. A survivor of Auschwitz who came to Oak Park after the war and made good raising a family in the TV repair business. And now he was about to be surrounded, literally, by dozens of topless women and hundreds of lust-filled guys who were thirsty for a cold one. Only in America.

Sol was priceless not just in providing his monetary share, but also in offering his practical and hard-won advice and successful business model for running a topless bar. But my father,

like all good fathers, really only wanted his son to be successful. Of course, he was staking his bet that the project would fly
because he was, bottom line, also a businessman who doesn't
throw money around without expecting profitable results. It
turned out that he had a lot more to contribute than just his
hard-earned dollars, as I was to discover when the shit truly
threatened to hit the fan.

We had all spent considerable time discussing what we would
need to take the shell of the former biker bar up to first-class
specs. It looked like another hundred grand would do the job,
which included hiring Paul Green, a young, talented, and ambitious uptown architect to design the club inside and out. From
the time we took possession of the property till opening night
in November of 1981, many trying months were to pass.

At long last, we were at that magical tipping point when all
we needed was the talent. As the Romans would say, "Bring
on the dancing girls!" In the topless business at that time, the
model was stone simple—you hired them and paid them an
hourly wage. You could either run classified ads in the daily
newspapers or deal with old-time "talent" agents who got paid
on commission, $25 of each girl's weekly take.

We'd run two shifts a day, eight or nine girls per shift at $9
or $10 an hour. It's simple math, and give or take, we expected
to pay eighty to a hundred dollars an hour for entertainers.
Ballpark eight or nine grand a week. You now understand (if
you didn't already jive as to why a beer at the topless bar costs
approximately what a six-pack does at the supermarket) that
topless establishments can be highly profitable but also cost a
helluva lot to run. It's a completely different business model
today, but we'll get to that part of the story in around the time
it takes for a few generations of dancers to come and go.

Itchin' for a Chain Whippin'

Now we get to the part about the badass bikers. You didn't think I'd forgotten, did you? We had only had The Booby Trap open about four weeks when we had our first run-in with the Renegades, the motorcycle club that practically owned the place when it was known as Vince's Blue Heron. Their concrete-block clubhouse was only a couple of blocks down Eight Mile from our location, and if you can imagine every stereotypical cliché of a scary, intimidating urban fortress—broken glass strewn over a crumbling parking lot, razor wire adorning the boarded-up windows, and a jumbo-sized, rusty iron door with a Frankenstein-sized ring welded to it for a door knob—you've got it. I don't know how some of these guys managed to ride their hogs on a head full of home-cooked PCP and a case of Mickey's wide mouth, like many did, but they did it with the style and aplomb of the modern Huns that they were. Of course, they expected to saunter, strut, or slither into the newly glitzified and highly polished Booby Trap just as they always had . . . adorned in grease-caked leathers, T-shirts that had bonded to their skin, and shit-kickin' biker boots with, shall we say, a bit of an attitude.

I was known as a scrapper, but some of these guys scared the hell out of me. I wasn't about to go toe-to-toe with any of them, and I was freaked that the menacing vibes these bikers brought down would soon lead to an explosion of nastiness and skull cracking in the middle of my enterprise zone!

The first night the bikers invaded, I'll never forget. It was a Friday night and the club was packed. We'd been open less than a month and were doing great business. Things were humming, the liquor was flowing, and we had eight or ten girls bumping and grinding up a storm. In retrospect, things were going too smoothly. Ask anybody who has ever owned or operated a topless club and they'll tell you some pretty hair-raising stories. That's why it's not uncommon for an owner or manager to have a 9mm tucked in his belt or behind the bar where it's easy to get to. But it wasn't my style.

This particular evening, around 10:00 p.m., a half dozen of the Renegades, wearing their club colors emblazoned on the requisite black leather jackets over grimy leather pants or blue jeans, sauntered in like they owned the place. When it used to be the Vince's Blue Heron, it was effectively their second clubhouse . . . the previous owners didn't give two hoots in hell who came in as long as they paid cash and kept drinking. If they started fighting and busted up the joint, nobody cared because the décor was basically black-painted concrete block and the cheapest tables and chairs money could buy.

But with my precious TGI Friday's architect-designed club on the line, the one with prominently posted NO COLORS, NO LEATHERS, and NO MOTORCYCLES IN THE PARKING LOT signs, I was put immediately on edge. The atmosphere became electrified as some of the bikers bellied up to the bar and the rest slumped into position at one of the tables, surly sneers writ large on their unshaved faces.

My head waitress came over to where I was eyeing the scene from the corner.

"Alan, what should we do? Do we serve them?"

"No," I said, resolutely, "we do not serve them. Call the police from the office. Now. I'll talk to them."

I walked over to the three at the bar, approaching them from behind. They turned to face me. Remember, I was 22 years old. Even if these guys weren't that much older than me, they looked like the proverbial wild bunch, like they'd been through a couple of wars, busted a few heads, and swung some mean cycle chain.

"Guys, listen, I'm sorry, but we can't serve you. No colors are allowed and—"

"What the FUCK?!?" growled the biggest one, a six-foot-four hulk with a do-rag and and a belly that looked like it was grown on a case-a-night beer habit. One of his front teeth was missing and I thought I was looking into the black maw of hell as he bellowed at me.

"This is OUR goddamn bar!"

Gee, I guess he didn't know who he was talking to. It was me against the giant. Sol was back home for the night, and other than my head waitress and my two doormen, Terry Thomas and Bob Crowell, I was the law. Even though my doormen were big dudes who knew how to intimidate, the odds were stacked against us. We didn't know if the bikers had weapons, so I really wasn't sure what my next move would be and I was definitely at a loss for words. Seconds that felt like hours ticked by. Then, suddenly, at that very moment, the real law came piling in, a dozen Detroit police officers bristling with service revolvers and 12-gauge shotguns cocked and locked. Now it was a whole different story, as the bikers, though being tough mofos, understood double ought buck and the sound of a pump action Mossberg pointing their way. The DJ cut the sound and the club got dead quiet.

One of the cops, keeping his gun pointed at the biggest biker, turned to me and asked, "You're the owner?"

I nodded.

"What do you want to have happen here?"

What do I want to have happen? I thought to myself. Uh, right. Gotta think for a second.

"I want them to leave. They've gotta leave, they don't meet the dress code and there are no bikes allowed in the parking lot."

"OK," the cop said as he turned back to face the three bikers at the bar. His partners were covering the other three at the table, who were now standing and staring at the cops with venom in their eyes. "You heard the man. It's time to go. You got a problem with that?"

The Renegades didn't say a word, but they knew the score had tipped out of their favor. There was no arguing with a dozen street-hardened Detroit cops and the firepower they were brandishing. They hesitated just long enough to convey the message that they were leaving when they were ready, not before, and then they began to walk slowly toward the door in a loose formation of loathing and contempt. Half of the cops followed them to the door and out into the parking lot with their guns still drawn, while the rest relaxed their weapons but kept them at the ready in case the action required them. Shortly, we all heard the sound of motorcycle engines roaring to life, and listened as the Renegades goosed and blasted their hogs off onto Eight Mile in a 120-decibel snarl that seemed to say, "Screw you and your titty bar, asshole. We'll be back."

I hoped that was the end of it, but there was much more to come before there could be any kind of peace with the Renegades.

For a time, things quieted down at The Booby Trap and life became a party . . . a very profitable party. Occasionally, one or two bikers would come in and manage to order a beer before my manager or I could get around to them and ask them to leave, which they tended to do when they were onesies or twosies. My bartenders didn't want trouble, so they generally served them or alerted one of the bouncers to their presence, which was also effective in getting them to leave. But with most of our trade coming from businessmen, workingmen, and young guys with a few bucks to spend, it didn't contribute to our upscale vibe. It's like cancer . . . a few malignant cells won't kill you but if you let it go, it'll take over the whole body.

It wasn't long before we had another major incident. This time, maybe a dozen bikers decided to make a show of force and teach Markovitz and partners just who was boss on Eight Mile. It was like a replay of the last confrontation, only meaner and uglier. You could hear the mob of bikes rolling in, even from inside the club, the bikers deliberately revving their engines to the max in an attempt to menace and intimidate anyone within range. They barged into the club like pirates in a raiding party, all of them pushing their way up to the bar and elbowing aside several patrons who weren't quick enough getting out of the way. I locked eyes with my bartender from across the room, waving my hands and drawing my finger across my throat to indicate I wanted these thugs cut off even before they tried to order drinks. My bartender just looked back at me like a man who was condemned to the gallows as I quickly dispatched one of my bouncers to tell him I was calling the police immediately, to just hang on and stall them. I picked up the phone and called Commander John Henry of the 11th Precinct, whom I had come to know through my previous encounters with the bikers. He liked the fact that I had upgraded the club from the nasty place it used to be and he was very cooperative and supportive.

True to their word, the Detroit police of the 11th Precinct were there for us. Within three or four minutes of getting my call, at least ten cars had careened into our parking lot with sirens wailing, blocking the bikers in and spilling out onto the street, lights flashing. They also dispatched a SWAT vehicle, and half the cops sported assault weapons, body armor, and shotguns. The police poured into the club and several took defensive positions at the door in case the brouhaha erupted outside.

Inside, just as the cops were arriving, one of the bikers had grabbed a bottle of beer off the bar and flung it violently into the wall after being told he would not be served. Two of his buddies were starting to come around to the back of the bar when two cops grabbed each of them by the collar and jerked them backwards, resulting in one biker falling to the floor, cursing, while the cop who had the other one released him and trained his shotgun on both perps. They got the idea and froze, muttering under their breaths.

"We just want a fucking drink like anybody else," the one on the floor said, eyeing the cop with bad intent.

"It doesn't look like you're wanted here, and smashing that bottle against the wall qualifies as drunk and disorderly. You all want to go into lockup for the night?" barked cop number two. The other police all had bikers in their sights and nobody was moving. The biker who was doing the talking was obviously the alpha in the bunch.

"Hey, man, we got a right—"

The cop cut him off. "You gave up your rights when you came in here on your bikes contrary to the no-bikes posting and the dress code. The proprietor has the legal right to refuse service, and you're both in violation and being refused."

"Yeah, well, listen man . . . "

"You listen," the officer shot back. "You either leave, or you're under arrest." He turned to me and asked, "You want to press charges for trespassing?"

"Not if they leave," I replied.

"OK, assholes, you know the way out," said the law. With that, a whole bunch of pissed-off bikers began shuffling outside with enough firepower to storm Waco at their backs. But as the alpha passed me, he quietly made a threat, "We're coming back to kill your fucking ass, hear?" I said nothing but took a deep breath and exhaled as the last of them tramped out.

Before leaving, the head cop told me they were making a detailed report on the incident, and I told them about the biker who had threatened my life.

"There's not much we can do about that until and if they actually try something. But we have all this on record. If I were you I'd think about getting a 12-gauge just in case.

"I would prefer avoiding that," I said.

"Just a friendly suggestion," added the officer.

A couple of months went by and there were no more bikers, until one fine day in May when my father happened to be in the club helping out with some new lighting we were installing. It was déjà vu as two more Renegades walked in, sauntered up to the bar, and ordered beers. It was early in the day, we had just opened, and I gave the bartender a nod to let them drink their beers while I decided whether or not to get the police involved once again. I was, to be honest, worried about the death threat I had received. I wasn't sure I had the stomach to go through yet another confrontation. My father pulled me aside and lit into me.

"Alan, what is the problem here? We have a business to run!"

"Dad," I said, "These bikers are going to start something that isn't gonna stop till someone's head gets smashed in, someone gets knifed or shot or all of the above, and we're gonna lose our business . . . if not one of our lives!"

"What about the cops?"

"The cops!?! We've tried that! They came and busted these guys three times already, came up with half a dozen cars with all their guns out, and we've still got trouble brewing."

"Well, maybe I should have a talk with them, Alan. Which way is the clubhouse?"

"You know where it is!" I shot back. "Two blocks over on the left there, right next to the party store."

"You can let these two drink their beers if you want. I'm going over there right now."

My father is the type of guy, you understand, who makes up his mind and doesn't change it easily. He is not easily frightened, intimidated, or spooked. After all, this is a guy who at fifteen years of age walked off a cattle car from Svalyava, Czechoslovakia, and through the gates of Auschwitz, the most notorious death camp in Nazi-occupied Europe, and walked out again eighteen months later. He'd seen prisoners get a slug in the head point-blank from the Luger of an SS man. He'd seen others hanged and left hanging for days to be made examples of. What are a bunch of Detroit motorcycle guys going to do to this guy, who has seen it all, lived through it, and feels like he has nothing to lose yet everything to gain by putting down some moves? Still, I was sweating bullets for the next twenty minutes. It was like watching a movie, in the sense that whatever was going to happen was already scripted and beyond my control.

What happened was this: My father calmly marched up to the big, rusty iron door of the Renegade's clubhouse and kept banging on it with his fist until someone inside heard him and opened up.

"WHO'S THAT?" my father later told me someone had snarled through the door.

"I own The Booby Trap!" he shouted back. And just like that, he was inside.

I will leave to your fertile imagination exactly what transpired between my dad and the Renegades who were inside that clubhouse that fragrant day in May. And I will say to you that my esteem for my father's ways, as well as my awe and disbelief, have wrought me in ways that make me who I am today. I was, and am, damned proud of my old man. He is not just my father but one helluva fine business partner who is not afraid to take care of business. Always has, always will.

Cut to the chase. My father came walking in less than half an hour later, like he'd just been to the dry cleaners. He went over to the two bikers at the bar and whispered something to them. They looked at each other and then they calmly got up, paid for their beers, and walked out without saying so much as a single word.

"Well—what the hell happened?" I stammered, the tension breaking in my voice.

"It's all taken care of," my father calmly replied. "We have an understanding."

"An understanding!? What kind of an understanding?"

"The boys over there will come into the club only if they adhere to the dress code. They will not make any more trouble."

"Yeah . . . and what else?" I inquired, warily.

"We will give them a keg or two of beer from time to time. And when they have their motorcycle convention every year, we will close for the day. And that is all."

"That's all, eh? Okay," I said. "I guess we're going to find out then."

"Yes, we will find out. But I don't think we will have any more problems from them."

"Dad," I pressed, "just what did you say to these guys? Seriously?"

My father replied, "I just told them some of my history in Auschwitz. They were interested to hear about it. I said I intend to run my business and that we will work this out now, and we will be done with it!"

I was amazed. Obviously, I had a lot to learn, and my father had earned a measure of respect from me that I didn't know I was capable of giving to him. Talk about steel balls.

I guess the Renegades had to respect my father once they realized he had no fear of them and that he wasn't backing down. Do not be surprised to know, then, that the Renegades did visit the club many times after that. They observed the dress code and there seemed to be a new level of respect between us and them. They enjoyed themselves in the club like any other customers and spent a lot of money, too. I wonder what we can all learn from this. Perhaps Theodore Roosevelt was right— speak softly and carry a big stick. Or, a big attitude—that's the real deal. Somehow people seem to sense when you're talking the talk that you know how to walk the walk, and decide they'd rather walk away than try you out. Draw your own conclusions; I've already drawn mine.

My Father's Trial by Fire

My father's story has so much to do with the story of my life, with my ability to persevere, to come from behind, or underneath, no matter the rough odds in this business, that it bears telling . . . for its inspirational as well as instructional nature.

I am the proud son of Max Markovitz, born in the region of the Carpathian mountains of Czechoslovakia in a small town called Svalyava. In the early months of 1939, after Adolf Hitler had come to power but before World War II had begun with the invasion of Poland, the area around Svalyava was partitioned to Hungary by Nazi Germany. There was a simple reason for this: the Hungarians would cooperate with the Nazis—the plans for the "final solution" were already being formulated. The Nazis were very thorough and systematic. It took a while for the deportations to reach my father's part of the world, but it was inevitable. In the spring of 1944 it was time for my father and his family.

It was around March that the Nazis came goose-stepping into Svalyava with the complete cooperation of the Hungarians. My father's father, Aaron, was the director of a wholesale leather goods firm which had already been "confiscated" by the Hungarian occupiers who functioned as an extension of the Nazi bureaucracy. Jews were not allowed to own or operate any kind of business, and Hitler's ruthless minions were well practiced at fleecing, coercing, and outright stealing whatever they wanted. Who was stopping them? It's why I don't believe in the appeasement of tyrants and madmen, on the international stage or in my own backyard. But that's a story for another day.

The whole family—my father and his father and mother, along with his two sisters and younger brother—were given just a few hours to pack; only one suitcase was allowed for everyone. They were told to assemble in the street and before they knew it they were being marched to the train station in the center of town. There they saw with their own eyes what they had heard rumors of: wooden cattle cars with their doors thrown open. My father was just fifteen years old.

They didn't know where they were going. About seventy-five people, more or less, were packed into each car. My father tried to think of a way to escape, but he didn't want to leave his parents and siblings. The situation was impossible. After half an hour, the train slowed and they soon learned that they were in the town of Munkach, east of Svalyava, at an abandoned brick factory that had been turned into a ghetto of sorts, a temporary prison where they would be held indefinitely with no inkling of what was coming next. But others who had arrived before my father whispered that they would soon be going to a labor camp. It was said that the Germans were losing too many soldiers in the fighting and needed workers badly. This gave them some hope, but the conditions were abysmal in the brickworks; little food—a watery kind of soup and a piece of bread were all the rations they got once a day—and sanitation was practically nonexistent.

After a month of not knowing their fate, my father and his family were put on yet another train. By now, it was April, and the passengers knew only that they were heading east . . . that meant Poland. After two days and nights with no food and water, they at last arrived at the worst possible destination for Jewish prisoners of the Reich. It was Auschwitz.

The train platform within the arched gate of the camp looked to be a half mile long to my father. It was well after dark when he arrived with his sisters Zita and Lea, who were eighteen and twenty-one; his younger brother, Henry, eleven; and his father and mother, Aaron and Ida, forty-three and forty-one years of age, respectively. There was chaos everywhere; passengers disembarking from the train were rudely shoved or jostled in one direction and then another. Gestapo and SS troops with snarling, barking German shepherd dogs, glaring floodlights, and the wailing of children as well as adults added to the madness of the situation. My father and his father were soon separated from the rest of the family. His mother and younger brother were selected and sent off with all the seniors, those over fifty-five. His sisters went in another direction. Children aged fifteen and younger were also separated. It was the last time my father ever saw his mother and younger brother. They went straight to the gas chambers, and then the ovens, of Auschwitz. The old, the infirm, and the young could not work, so to the Nazis they were useless.

Max and his father had one small advantage. Because my father's second language was German, he was at least in the position to understand what his captors were saying. Every little scrap of information he could glean could potentially help him—to know what the Germans were saying was at least better than not knowing! But in the barracks they met Polish Jews who had been in the camp for as long as two years; they pointed gravely toward the chimneys of Auschwitz, which were churning out smoke and ash twenty-four hours a day. "Grandparents, children," they said, "all up the chimney." The stench was horrible, the situation unreal—but it was real enough.

The situation at Auschwitz was fluid and chaotic. All new arrivals had to be processed, shaved, tattooed, and selected for either a specific work detail or disposition to another camp. Since the war in Europe was in its fourth year by this time, Allied bombing had crippled vital elements of Germany's industrial production and workers were needed for factories that the Nazis had moved to remote locations. Thus, it was after only a few days in Auschwitz that Max and his father were put on yet another cattle car and shipped to a camp in Austria. This was Mauthausen, a huge camp where my dad and his father joined perhaps 25,000 other prisoners—Russian, French, Greek, Norwegian, and Italian, as well as those from Hungary, Czechoslovakia, and other Eastern European countries. It was in Mauthausen that Max was separated from his father, never to see him again or to ever learn his fate.

But for my father, now alone and on his own, survival was the imperative. Yet again he was to be moved: next stop, Gusen, a sub-camp of the giant, sprawling Mauthausen. Both these camps were Category III, a destination the Nazis reserved for their most hated enemies; intellectuals, academics, and writers were among those who were to be subjected to the harshest treatment possible. The Nazis had a phrase for what they did in Mauthausen and Gusen. It was called *Vernichtung durch arbeit*. The translation: Extermination through labor. Max recalls the infamous quarry at Mauthausen, where the sadistic kapos whipped prisoners who were forced to carry roughly hewn stone blocks weighing as much as a hundred pounds up 180 or more steps to the top. Weakened by starvation rations of weed soup and a piece of bread, providing as little as two or three hundred daily calories when two thousand or more were required, the workers would sometimes collapse and fall, causing a domino effect of rock and men all the way down the stone stairs. Those who couldn't work any longer were beaten or simply shot where they lay. You didn't make eye contact in the midst of such a hell, however. You kept your head down and kept moving, because if you didn't you could be the next casualty. There were still trainloads of fresh prisoners coming in from the east, so it was either keep up or die and be replaced by the next victim.

Dad stayed out of the quarry, having been selected to work at Gusen instead. Nearby, high in the Austrian Alps, was the ideal location for the Nazis to build a huge warren of tunnels, carved out of the rock, in which to protect their production of Messerschmidt aircraft and V2 rocket bombs from Allied bombing. Every morning, at Gusen, my father and his fellow prisoners were awakened at 6:00 a.m., then transported to the location of the Bergkristall tunnels at a village called St. Georgen, where they worked nonstop until 6:00 p.m., before being returned to camp. Perhaps because the Nazis gave their engineers who supervised the workers the day off on Sundays, so too were the prisoners given that day to rest. But the work was brutal and the rations meager. Many of the prisoners had empty cans tied to their trousers, so that while they excavated they could collect worms and insects to eat later.

Every day my father worked hard and was still in relatively good physical condition owing to his youth. At night, up to four people were forced to share each bunk, and every morning, Dad, along with others, had to drag out those who died in the night. Every day there were fifteen or twenty more corpses, and the barracks and bunks had to be cleaned, hosed down, and made up again for the next night. For those who became sick, there was no alternative to death. There were simply no medical facilities, and if you became too ill to work, you were left to die on the spot, or dispatched with a bullet to the head. Though the camp had latrines, there was a sanitation barrel with steps into which inmates could relieve themselves; there was often a body stuffed into the barrel who had been a victim of Nazi sadism. Life went on for months in this manner, a mind-numbing, soul-wasting routine, and every day, more bodies to drag from the barracks. Max lost track of time, as there were no calendars in the camp. You simply endured and the seasons changed. In the spring, conditions were somewhat more tolerable, especially summer in the mountains. At least you didn't freeze! But then came the autumn of 1944, and with it the first chill winds that would bring with them one of the coldest winters Europe had seen in years—as well as Hitler's last great offensive, the Battle of the Bulge.

Now, the Fuhrer was becoming desperate. Engineers from Germany's top industrial firms had been dispatched to the mountains of Austria to speed production of the world's first fighter jet, the Messerschmidt Me262, along with the V2 rocket bomb that could reach London, and did, in horrendous numbers that killed and terrorized the population. It was on these super weapons—including the possibility of perfecting the atomic bomb—that Hitler was betting the farm. But time was getting short, and although the final offensive, launched with the Wehrmacht's finest Panzer tank units and many divisions of battle-hardened infantry, succeeded in punching through the Allied front that was advancing on Germany, the war was already lost.

It was the last, brutal winter that my father would have to survive digging and toiling in the rock tunnels in order to see springtime, and with it, perhaps some small glimmer of hope that there was a way out of that hell on earth. Max was entering his sixteenth year and the front was getting closer and closer. It was now April of 1945 and suddenly, without warning, came the day of evacuation. Every worker was to be moved from the mountains by forced march, deeper into Austria. Thousands of prisoners were pushed out onto the narrow mountain road, with escorts of German soldiers both on foot and on motorcycles and in trucks. The march was to take ten days to get to the destination of Dunskirchen, where the ragged throngs would be imprisoned yet again in another camp. Prisoners who could not keep up were summarily shot where they faltered, pushed off to the side of the road or trampled by the tens of thousands of feet advancing behind them. Rations were few—what little bread that could be carried from the start, and maybe a few more scraps and a thin gruel when the line stopped so that the German soldiers could rest.

Dad made it to Dunskirchen, but hundreds, perhaps even thousands, did not. No one counted the fallen. In the haste to keep moving, and to live, they were quickly forgotten. Only at the end of that road did one have a chance to look around for a familiar face. In my father's case, he was amazed to find his older brother, Arya, who had disappeared months before the family was deported from Svalyava. It was like a holiday, this special surprise, to learn that at least one other member of the Markovitz family was still alive! Given the horrors that he had witnessed over the last year, it was hard to imagine that anyone could have survived. The hell of it was that you just didn't know. Now, at least Max had his older brother, who was bedraggled and starved but very much alive.

The first thing a victim of a concentration camp does upon being liberated, if it is possible, is to eat. On May 6, 1945, that day at last arrived for my father. The American Army's 11th Thunderbolt Armored Division had arrived the day before. The Germans had fled just hours ahead of them, leaving their prisoners to wander around in a daze, at first not fully comprehending the fact that they were free. For what is that word, *free*, when hope has been pulverized by deprivation upon misery upon horror? It is, finally, the realization that one is alive. That one has somehow survived. Of a total of 70,000 prisoners, just 20,000 remained to be liberated. And then, the first order of business, to eat.

Dad's first meal, which consisted of canned Spam provided by the American army, had the immediate effect of making him violently ill. The rich food caused cramps and spasms, as his body could not digest it properly. He was quickly put into an army hospital in Dunskirchen, and for ten days he recovered, allowing his body to regain the ability to receive and digest food.

After more than a year of never being able to really rest, clean sheets and a real bed and food were the greatest of gifts. That, and discovering at the displaced persons (DP) facility there that both his sisters had also made it through the war. Zita and Lea survived because they had security at Auschwitz: They worked sorting out clothing from incoming prisoners, cutting garments apart to find jewels, gold, money, or other valuables that had been sewn into shoulder pads and waistbands. Every week, they later told Max, they produced a bushel basket full of jewels. They worked for over a year, until Auschwitz was liberated, and there was no shortage of clothing until the very end.

After regaining his strength, and putting on some weight, my father knew he had to leave the DP camp. He was rested, he was eating good solid food again, and he had received plenty of cigarets, chocolates, and nylons from the Americans, items he could sell or trade for good money. His intention, like many of those who found themselves newly liberated, was to go back home—where else?—to see who had survived.

In the spring of 1945, normal transportation networks did not exist. You had to find your own way to "get a ride" from here to there. What was moving, mostly, were trains. And in Max's part of the world, it wasn't the Americans that were moving the trains—it was the Russians. As they had rushed in from the east to meet the Americans driving toward Berlin from the west, they were overwhelming in both their sheer numbers (there were millions of Red Army soldiers on the move) and in their brutality and thirst for retribution. Anything that was of value in territory formerly held by the Reich, the Russians seized and loaded on flatbed railcars headed east back to Russia. Machinery, weapons, vehicles, raw materials, anything and everything became war spoils, and these trains ran day and night, relentlessly, to the east. There were also passenger cars, taking Russian soldiers back home. So, if that happened to be the direction you wanted to go, you were in luck. As long as you didn't mind the fact that there was technically "no room" for civilians, you could ride on the roof! The downside of traveling in such close proximity to the Russians, however, was that many of them were illiterate draftees from far-flung parts of the Soviet empire, such as the Urals, and some had never even seen a wristwatch before! When a drunk Russian soldier with a rifle demanded that Dad "Dav-eye chas!" meaning "Give me your watch!" he deemed it prudent to comply. All part of the price of going back home.

After several days of less eventful but exhausting rooftop travel, my dad made it back to his family's home in Svalyava, where he was reunited with his two sisters. Out of dozens of friends that Max knew, only three others had returned. His parents and younger brother he would, of course, never see again. And now, to add insult to injury, the Russians stayed in Czechoslovakia, setting up a communist administration—the area would soon become part of western Ukraine. The only solution seemed to be to keep moving. There was nothing now to stay for. The family home had been looted and trashed to such an extent that there was no sense in attempting to reclaim it. After a month of scrounging some money from the few items he was able to sell, my father was able to hire a horse and buggy in order to smuggle himself over the border into Hungary, with the intention of making it to Budapest. Ironically, he was to find himself in yet another DP camp until he discovered that there was a Raoul Wallenberg school that he could get into, affording him a chance to further his education and to have a place to live until he could figure out his next move. After some months in school, but still completely unsettled, Dad was itching for some kind of direction and opportunity for a new life. His sisters wanted to return home, or at least what remained of it, by attempting to take a train back to Czechoslovakia. They succeeded in getting as far as the Czech city of Brno, where one of his sisters married and my father and his brother were able to live.

In the new year of 1946, Max was becoming restless with the limited opportunities for life and livelihood in Brno and learned of an opportunity to join a refugee organization in Prague. He immediately traveled there and was successful in applying to the Jewish Refugee Committee, which had been created in affiliation with the British government to assist in the aid and relocation of the persecuted Jews of Europe. After several months working and living in nearby Birnau, waiting for some kind of a break, a splendid opportunity came along. The British government announced that it would admit up to 1,000 youngsters to England. Of Dad's two sisters, one would then stay with her new husband and the other was also to be approved for the British program.

So it was that several weeks hence Dad found himself among a couple of hundred other young people—Poles, Serbs, and Hungarians among them—on a British Lancaster bomber bound for Scotland's Prestwick Airport, final destination Edinburgh. For the following eight months Max received food, board and schooling. Though he knew some English, there was much more yet to acquire, and between study and working at the school, the time flew quickly. At long last Dad became qualified to take another step up—this time to an ORT (Organization for Rehabilitation through Training) school in London, sponsored by the Jewish Committee of Great Britain. Here, he found that his interest in and aptitude for technology qualified him to study electronics. He took to it immediately and advanced fast. Before he knew it, he was now able to work in his field, diagnosing and repairing a variety of electronic devices, work that had been supercharged by the rapid technological developments spurred by wartime budgets. The next four years would, in retrospect, go by in a blur. For the first time in his young life, Max was not merely surviving, but thriving. He was doing something he enjoyed and that he excelled at, and which with the recent advent of television provided excellent prospects for a prosperous future. To be able to repair as complex a piece of technology as a television set was an enviable skill. Life was good.

But still, my father had an itch for more, for something else, for something with greater opportunity—and not unlike millions of others around the world, that something else was the United States. Unlike millions of others, however, my dad was fortunate enough to have had relatives already living in America who had emigrated before the war. He had been trying to make contact with an uncle who lived in Pittsburgh, and despite the lack of an address he was sure he would find him and perhaps make arrangements to leave England. It took the Red Cross to find his uncle, and after extensive paperwork, including an affidavit that his uncle could provide the financial support that would prevent my father from becoming a burden on the U.S. taxpayer, his visa was approved. The year was 1951.

Upon his arrival in Pittsburgh, then going full tilt producing steel to fuel America's postwar boom, Max was stunned at the scale of industry—and the smell it produced! But the smell was sweet in the sense that it symbolized prosperity and progress. He quickly set about looking for work in his chosen field, writing letters to the largest electronics companies in the business. With demand for televisions going through the roof, and millions of GIs starting families and new households, the prospects for a good job were excellent. Of all the letters Dad sent out, one particular response interested him the most. It was from RCA, in Detroit. They wanted Max. And for Max, it was ideal, because he also had a cousin in Detroit who could help him get set up with a place to live and show him around. Detroit, too, was swinging in the early 1950s, cranking out new cars at a breakneck pace to satisfy pent-up demand from the war years when all raw material was for military production. After only six months Max was able to buy his own car, the first one in his life, and a fine ride it was—a gorgeous '48 Plymouth.

And so, this is how my father survived the Holocaust and made it to America . . . and finally, Oak Park, Michigan, where he would settle, open his own TV repair business, marry, and, with my mother Jackie, give life to me, my brother Paul, and my sister Marie. About a quarter century would then elapse, leading me, with the help of my father, to formulate and execute the plan for my first enterprise—The Booby Trap.

Moving On Up

A month after the Renegade problem was solved, we were rocking. With twenty-nine tables we were able to rotate as many as 150 customers in and out several times per shift, serving as many as two hundred lunches a day, more than many successful restaurants. Plus, we had another fifteen slots at the bar as well as some barstools along one of the walls to accommodate individual walk-ins. Our upscale image and positioning clicked . . . no one else in Detroit had figured out there was an almost bottomless market for businessmen who wore ties and also had expense accounts to spend. A lot of those guys had been going across the Detroit bridge to Windsor, where there were all-nude and decidedly fancy clubs, but it was hard to beat our convenience. By visiting my club on Eight Mile, guys could have a helluva fine lunch, maybe knock back a couple, and still be back in the office in jig time. Word definitely spread fast.

Other Voices: Dwight Fowler, Former Bouncer at The Booby Trap

On August 19, 1980, I was released from the Florida State Penitentiary after serving time for multiple counts of armed robbery, possession of illegal firearms, aggravated assault with intent to commit murder, and flight to escape prosecution. I needed a job, preferably something that would draw on my experience, yet not land me back in slam.

I made my way north to Michigan, where I had friends and family. I found a place to crash and started making phone calls. Pretty soon I was hooked back into the local grapevine and heard about a new topless club located on a bad stretch of Eight Mile, near the clubhouse of one of Detroit's most notorious motorcycle gangs. It used to be a seedy fucking dive with black walls, filthy mirrors covered with smoke scum and fingerprints, and a bevy of fat chicks with maybe a few teeth missing who could be found shaking their cellulite to the jukebox in the corner. But this young dude by the name of Alan Markovitz had come in and revolutionized the concept and turned what used to be a certified shit-hole into a very glitzy, very impressive topless club. But, because of the rough neighborhood, average bouncers would not do.

I got hold of the head bouncer, and he told me to come in for an interview for "doorman," a classier way of saying "face puncher," which is really what the job boils down to. I went into The Booby Trap the next day, and while I was standing near the entrance waiting for the head face puncher to interview me, a serious fistfight broke out. A couple of the "doormen" on duty pushed me aside and waded into the fray to put down the troublemaker. I figured, what the hell, there's talkin' about it and there's doin' it. I might as well show these guys what I got.

So, I charged in between the two doormen and shoved them aside in order to get my hands on the fuckhead who started the fight. I started wailing on the piece of shit left and right till I pretty much beat the clothes off of him. Then I grabbed him by the back of the hair and what was left of his Haggar's and torpedoed the asshole straight out the front door.

The valet brought his car around. I took the keys out of the ignition, dragged my man around to the trunk and threw him inside, slamming the trunk shut. Then, I drove about two and a half blocks away from the club, parked the car, walked back to the trunk, opened her up, tossed the keys inside, and slammed the trunk shut again. Then I hoofed it back to the club to see about finishing my interview.

When I got inside, I realized I was covered in blood, so I went to wash up, and when I came out of the men's room the head bouncer handed me a big-ass beer mug stuffed full of five-dollar bills.

"Take it, it's yours!" he said.

"What's up with this?" I inquired.

"Every time we toss a guy or bust up a fight, all the bouncers stick a fiver in the glass. Then whenever one of the guys steps in and breaks someone's nose, he gets the pot."

"Man, there's gotta be a few hundred bucks in here!"

"Take it out—it's yours. Now, let me fill that mug up with a cold draught. You sit down and drink it while I go back and talk to Alan."

I sat there drinking my beer in silence and five minutes later the head face puncher came out and handed me a polo shirt with "Booby Trap" embroidered on the front in bright green.

"You're hired, man!" he exclaimed, giving me a hearty slap on the back. "You're now one of Guida's Torpedoes!"

Dave Guida, now deceased—poor soul—was one of Alan's managers at the Booby Trap and he held all us bouncers to a high standard of mayhem whenever it was called for. Thus, we "torpedoed" the vile and deserving whenever necessary in order to maintain the safety and ambience of The Booby Trap for its patrons and employees.

That was day one of my employment, a career that lasted fifteen years, in which I punched a helluva lot of faces, saw all manner of human wickedness, frailty, and vice, and came out the other end somehow, a better man for all of it.

Alan is smarter than hell when it comes to foreseeing the future and leading the industry in quality control and knowing how to market gentleman's clubs. But I like to think that in my own humble way, along with Guida's Torpedoes, we helped to insulate Alan from some of the rougher aspects of operating a topless club so that he could do what he does best . . . excel.

When I'm in Detroit, I'll always stop in for visit!

THE SPRINGING OF THE TRAP

Now the fun begins.

After the initial flush of opening your very own topless club is over, it's nothing but work-a-day drudgery day after day. Not. Soooo not! Because there is nothing else on earth like running your own business, charting your own destiny. And when that business happens to be naked women and lots of cash, hey, ask Hugh Hefner what his ride has been like and I'm sure he'll tell you the same thing.

In the early 1980s, the timing had been right for a new kind of gentleman's club. The old-school topless clubs were run by the old school and they reflected that. The formula was simple: (1) music—even a juke box would do; (2) topless dancers—young, old, didn't matter as long as they were willing to drop top; and (3) up-charge for the beer and liquor. Sit back and rake it in, and if you wanted to get high on your own supply—breasts or booze—that was one of the big perks of the business.

To have topless dancers, you had to have a cabaret D license from the city of Detroit, however. These were relatively easy to get in the old days, and a lot of clubs from the golden days of burlesque (pasties on nipples, a boom bada-boom drum kit and band, and maybe some lame comedian) made the transition in the sixties to rock 'n' roll and the genesis of modern topless entertainment. But Eight Mile, where we set up shop with The Booby Trap, was right on the edge of many sweeping changes that I had the vision, guts, and perhaps recklessness to pioneer. This didn't go down too well with the old school.

Allow me to elaborate. As you have already read, in the beginning, the way you put dancers on stage was to simply pay them an hourly wage, like any other employee. This was the formula that had worked so well for Sol Milan at La Chambre for many years and had inspired me to get into the business in the first place. The major difference between "us" and "them" was that we spent the money to package The Booby Trap as a fresh, upscale destination with TGI Friday's as my inspiration. Polished brass, dark wood, tile floors, and nice lighting and décor were worlds apart from all the other topless clubs on Eight Mile, or anywhere else in Michigan or around the country, for that matter.

We had a high-traffic location, and in the early 1980s we also had a healthy, booming auto industry with tons of suppliers courting tons of buyers for the Big Three—Ford, GM, and Chrysler. It was still the heyday of the expense account, and The Booby Trap was the perfect combination of "class and ass" that attracted business suits by the hundreds if not thousands.

The Booby Trap was doing as much food business as liquor, whereas food has generally been a loss-leader for the majority of gentleman's clubs over the years. It was worth it (and remains a tool) for many clubs to sacrifice a New York strip steak for $6.95 if the customer will drink $30 to $50 worth of liquor, plus pay a cover charge and valet parking fee and maybe buy a $20 cigar to boot. The longer you can keep them in the club, enjoying themselves, the more they will spend, naturally. The key to this, of course, is to get the best-looking entertainers possible. But that ten bucks an hour that one dancer costs, multiplied by, say, ten girls per shift times two shifts a day, comes out to $800 per shift or $1,600 per day. For a six-day week that's a whopping $9,600, or close to forty grand for a month!

Fortunately, The Booby Trap was slammed from the git go. Don't be fooled—that thing about "build it and they will come" didn't come from the Kevin Costner movie—it surely originated with a well-conceived and executed gentleman's club. At The Booby Trap, we spent thousands on a state-of-the-art sound system, hired a hot DJ, and stocked all the premium brands in liquors, wines, and beers. We also threw down for heavy, well-made silverware, linen napkins, and the kind of service you'd expect at a four-star hotel. It all added up to an impression of class and prestige that makes for a true "destination" entertainment experience.

Six months in, Sol and my father were both very happy with their investment and to put it mildly, I was ecstatic. It was a dream come true for me, and I practically lived at the club so that I could keep an eye on everything. I am truly a hands-on micro-manager, but when I find good help, I trust them to hold everything up to the same standards that I do until they prove me wrong.

In those early days, it was hard work but it was also a non-stop party. I was always looking for ways to execute "kaizen," that is, like Toyota, constantly improve the methods we used to run the business and make The Booby Trap a superlative experience that would not only bring customers through our doors but turn them into solid repeat business.

Girls, Girls, Girls

Back to the girls. I am often asked whether there is any temptation to dabble in the merchandise, so to speak. Let me put it this way: If you work around throngs of sweet, sexy, half-naked women all day and all night long, sooner or later you get to know some of them rather well. I firmly believe that owners who lose control in this business do so for either one of two reasons, often both—they turn their brains to mush by drinking like fish or they get caught up starring in their very own sexual soap opera. Neither is good business, and I have always strived to keep business separate from pleasure. I rarely drink on the job. As for the talent, well, there is such a thing (even in the topless trade) known as "after hours."

Sometimes, though, no matter how objectively and professionally you manage your talent, you get a nut case. My nut case was named Susie Bufale, and it is no exaggeration to say that she practically blew me away with her crazy antics. Crazy antics with a .38 special, that is.

Susie was brought to me by a talent agent for an audition. She was nice, a very pretty blonde with a great body, and she knew how to move. She did a few songs that the DJ picked out for her and looked like she'd been on stage before. I hired her on the spot and asked her when she could start. "Tonight!" was her reply, so I grinned, pleased by her enthusiasm, and told her to show up at seven.

Susie worked out great and became a real draw at the club. When customers began calling to ask if Susie was there, I liked to be able to answer yes because I knew she was pulling in traffic and I wanted to build on it. Susie was generally quite reliable, and I was often surprised by how many guys were asking for her. I wondered what it was that appealed so well to our customers, besides her obvious knockout body and great dance moves. Some girls are really sweet and make their customers want to pamper and protect them. Others play the temptress to the hilt and have guys wrapped around their little fingers. Susie, I later learned, had a special talent that few men can refuse.

One night there was some kind of a ruckus going on in the women's bathroom. One of my bouncers, Terry Thomas or Bob Crowell, had come to my office to alert me.

"Susie's in there with one of her customers."

"With one of her customers? What's she doing?" I asked.

"One of the other girls says she's giving him a blow job."

I had one of the other girls go in to check on her and sure enough she was adjusting her top and the guy was zipping up when she looked over the top of the stall. As Susie hastily exited the bathroom, dancer two asked, "Hey, were you just blowing that guy?" to which Susie allegedly replied, "None of your goddamn business!" It was obvious what Susie was doing.

Hearing this, I immediately stormed into the small dancer's dressing room in the rear of the club and grabbed Susie's trunk and dragged it to the door, flinging it out into the parking lot. Coming back into the club, I came face to face with Susie, who was now screaming at me.

"What did you do with my trunk, you asshole? WHERE'S MY FUCKING TRUNK???"

"You're fired!" I shot back. "Get the hell out of here, you're never working here again!"

"Yeah, well fuck you, man!" she bellowed back as she pulled her coat on over her dancer duds and stomped out the door. It was all over in five minutes. It happens. You deal with it and you move on. C'est la vie.

The rest of the night was uneventful. But around 2:00 a.m., my parking valet came into my office and told me, "Susie's out in the parking lot; she says we stole her purse and she's pissed . . . she's acting real crazy, Alan!"

All right, I say to myself, let's just get this over with. I got up, headed for the door, stepped out into the cold winter night, and suddenly "BAM BAM BAM," I hear gunshots. I don't even see Susie but I hear those shots like the sound of a cannon going off and my body is slammed back against the wall of the club and then I'm down on my back on the cold and slush-covered pavement. I was a good five feet away from the wall but she hit me solid with her first shot and bounced me off that wall like a rag doll. All I remember was her standing over me pointing a .38 revolver in my face and people screaming "Hit the ground! Hit the ground!" She was wearing a big, black trench coat of some kind over combat fatigues and black army boots and that gun looked like a freaking Howitzer inches from my nose.

Somehow I managed to get my hands on the gun and was using my last bit of strength to push the barrel away from my face when my doorman and bouncers all jumped on her and threw her to the ground, pinning her. Somebody called 911 and the EMS got there fast, which was lucky for me because she had put one through my liver and out my back and another one collapsed a lung. I was losing a lot of blood, fast. Then, everything seemed to go into slow motion, as doctors explained later, due to a large amount of adrenaline flooding into my bloodstream, causing my central nervous system synapses to fire faster—like a high-speed camera producing a slow motion effect. Next, I began to lose my vision—everything seemed to be going white—as I began to go into shock from blood loss. I lost my ability to see temporarily and could not tell what was going on around me.

Minutes later, I was shoved into an ambulance with the world spinning crazily around me. The atmosphere in the parking lot was madness, with over a hundred people from the club all craning their necks to get a look at the crime scene and to get a look at crazy Susie who was being held down for the police. But Susie was the last thing on my mind. The ambulance passed three other hospitals to take me to Detroit Receiving, which has a great trauma team due to all the gunshot wounds Detroit is infamous for . . . lucky for me! The EMS crew blew up a special pressure pant on me to keep blood in my torso until we got to Emergency. The attending physician, Dr. Nelson, who ironically is now doing plastic surgery, including breast implants, later told me how close to death I was from blood loss.

"We're going to have to insert a chest tube into you, Alan," Dr. Nelson told me. "It's going to hurt because we can't put you under general anesthetic until we stabilize you."

I got a look at that two-foot-long tube out the corner of my eye and when they zapped it in I thought I was getting stabbed with a fucking samurai sword—I was screaming bloody murder at the top of my lungs from the pain. They typed my blood and I got a call much later (four years!) that I checked negative for AIDs and hepatitis . . . they simply didn't have the advanced testing that we do now . . . but at the time all I wanted to know was—am I going to live NOW?

Since I'm writing this, you know the answer. But getting blasted with a .38 will give you a real "out-of-body" experience, that's for sure. I was stabilized, my lung inflated, and I spent nine days in the hospital, stapled up, with a drain tube coming out of my liver. I lost 35 pounds and had to practice breathing into a little machine designed to build back my lung capacity. Every breath hurt like hell. But the best news I got was that one of the bullets fired into me missed my spine. By half an inch. That's how close I came to being in a wheelchair for the rest of my life.

It was a dancer who first claimed my innocence, although in a most pleasurable way. Now Susie Bufale, another dancer, had come along and blown my innocence, my body, and my mind all to hell in a matter of seconds. I later discovered that Susie was a junkie, and I had my first close-up look at how totally fucked-up our justice system is—she got only two and a half years for attempted murder. While still recovering from the shooting I had the pleasure of witnessing a judge who couldn't stay awake and I couldn't even have my own lawyer handle the prosecution—the system assigned the case to a green prosecuting attorney two years out of law school. They cut Susie a break because she was a poor, pitiful victim of society, hooked on smack. I kept telling myself to be grateful, grateful that I was alive, grateful I wasn't in a wheelchair, and grateful for my youth, which helped me survive the horrible trauma of being shot at close range. I was only twenty-six years old.

Post Doc

After getting out of the hospital, I was in rough shape. Getting shot has two components: the physical trauma of hot lead tearing through your tissues, wreaking havoc on your body, which is bad enough; then there's the mental aspect, the incontrovertible fact that someone was mean enough and crazy enough to want to kill you. That tends to destroy your innocence, hope, and enthusiasm for life. It can put you into a deep depression. You realize how fragile life is and how close you came to the big sleep and you do a major reassessment of your life. Had I just been lucky—or was it part of a greater plan? I often wonder if God kept me alive for my father, who had already been through more than enough hell to last several lifetimes. Questions and more questions—it's hard not to become philosophical when you almost die—and maybe someday I'll have the answers.

Fortunately, my dad and Sol took over at the club and kept things running. Without experienced help like theirs, there's no way you can keep a high-wire enterprise like a topless club running. Also, I was lucky to have a good woman by my side. My girlfriend Laurie Clark, who was a dancer at the club while attending college classes, lived with me at my apartment while I recovered. I couldn't even think about going near The Booby Trap for many weeks. During the day, when Laurie was out, I struggled to make myself get up off the couch, trying to follow my doctor's advice to walk as much as possible. I would walk up and down the long halls of my apartment building, often taking my cat Tiki along with me. He had an unusual talent for a cat—he fetched a ball better than any dog! I'd throw the ball all the way to the end of the hall, and he'd race after it like mad, running back to me with it and releasing it at my feet. I would throw the ball over and over until Tiki began dragging ass back, and by that time I was usually exhausted myself. On other occasions, I ran into one of my neighbors, a retired judge who was always up for a little conversation, and like others I've met in the judiciary, was intrigued by my business. I told him to stop by the club sometime.

In fact, it was four months before I was able to go back to work, and when I returned to everyday duties I was a shell of my former self. You could really say that I wasn't the same person I used to be. The period marked the beginning of a major transition in my life and business, which, as it turns out, was all for the best. But opportunities are often masked by periods of upheaval and despair.

Back at the club, business was good. I was still young, my liver was regenerating nicely, and the cash flow was excellent. Along with the brisk business trade that consisted of Big Three buyers and their myriad suppliers who stoked them with food, liquor, and dancing girls, we had a lot of foreign business executives, too. Among them, lots of Japanese, what with Ford having cut a deal to make cars with Mazda downriver from Detroit and with lots of other Japanese component manufacturers getting in on the market. The Japanese were and are some of my best customers—they never cause problems by getting wasted or out of control, they spend money freely enjoying themselves, and when they've had their fill they leave quietly. You might not be able to understand a thing they are saying because they tend to speak Japanese among themselves, but the look on their faces when confronted by a gorgeous, amply endowed dancer speaks a universal language: "Aaaah . . . velly, velly nice!" I love my Japanese customers and I want to say to them—*domo arigato*!

The Early Days

Now remember, in the early days, topless entertainment was a crude approximation of what it has evolved into today. The dancers at The Booby Trap would show up for work, get into their cute little costumes, and get up on our small, elevated stage for three songs at a time. The DJ's responsibility was to keep the girls rotating so there was always a fresh face and body for the customers to enjoy. If someone really liked a dancer, he would beckon her to the side of the stage where she would hook a thumb into her G-string, allowing a tip of a dollar or two to be slipped in. Some guys would occasionally lay a five or even a ten on their favorite, to impress her, or perhaps in some vague hope that she would decide to run away to Antigua with him. It's kind of like the Lotto for a few bucks you buy a little dream and while away an hour or three on the pleasant fantasy of scoring.

Once on stage, dancers typically do the first song of their set with a dress or gown over a two-piece costume, like a bikini, or something they bought from Frederick's of Hollywood back in those days. By the second song, the dress or gown was gone and maybe the top, too. By the third song the top was definitely gone and the dancer was doing some combination of strutting, bending over, writhing on all fours with her butt stuck in the air, or perhaps getting on her back while hooking her legs behind her head. Or she was climbing provocatively up one of the poles on stage, flipping over backwards or doing a combination of sexy moves designed to drive guys wild. And then, end of song, she was either back to the dressing room or maybe she spent a few minutes talking to one of the guys who tipped her, hoping for a little more folding money in appreciation for her exotic art. In an hour, a dancer who knew how to make eye contact and flirt it up could supplement her $8–$10 an hour with another five or ten bucks; $15–$20 an hour back in the early 1980s was pretty good green for a twenty-something girl who often lacked job skills and had not taken any college classes.

Then one day, the revolution began, in a quiet but powerful way that was to forever change topless entertainment in Detroit. It was also the beginning of my realization that there was an entirely new business model that could be applied to the club business, and it would be instrumental in setting me apart from and ahead of all other competition.

I remember a customer everybody used to call Pac Man who started it. He was a regular, and I mean he practically lived at the club. I don't know exactly what he did for a living, but he was rumored to be in the numbers racket and he always had one or more gigantic wads of cash on his person. I mean, these were rolls the size of your fist, you could choke a horse with one of them. If he wasn't pulling bills out of his pockets, he was getting them out of his socks. And Pac Man loved his Asti Spumante, which he ordered in splits, those little 6-ounce bottles. I remember we used to order cases of the stuff just for Pac Man.

One day, Pac Man is having a helluva good time sitting by himself at a table by the stage. These are little tables, by the way, maybe 24 inches in diameter on a flared steel base. One of his favorite girls is putting on a grand show and Pac Man is literally throwing fistfuls of dollar bills at her. Of course, she's loving it, she's hit the mother lode, and she's not about to get off that stage when the three-song set is up, but she has to. So, at the end of the set, Pac Man looks at her and she looks at him and he says, "What—you gotta go?"

"Yeah . . . " she says, and reluctantly gathers her garments and begins to step off the stage. But before she does, Pac Man picks up his Asti and pounds on the table with the flat of his hand.

"Come on, get up here and dance for me! Here's a ten!"

Our dancer looks around a bit nervously, and then you can almost see a cartoon balloon form over her head with the words "what the hell" in it, and just like that she steps awkwardly up onto the table in her four-inch CFM platforms and begins gingerly doing some dance steps to the next song, which has just begun. Pac Man is loving it, looking up not a foot in front of him, following the girl's long, lithe legs up to a tiny little G-string, and then, still climbing, up to a beautiful pair of all-real D-cups jiggling to the beat.

What happened next, you can probably guess. All the girls in the club wanted to get up on tables and dance for the customers. You know, "Hey, if you're letting her do it, why can't I do it?" All I could envision was dancers falling off the tables, breaking their legs, and not being able to work for eight weeks.

"No!" I tell them, "No, no, and no!"

But these are women, and women with determination who see dollar signs—cha-ching! They want that cha-ching as much as I do, so I decided that I would allow them to do personal dances for their customers on the floor in front of them—but no touching allowed!

Thus began the shift to more personalized gentleman's entertainment, which as we know was to become "lap dancing" or "couch" dancing, which occupies a very particular grey area in the laws governing topless and nude dancing. At The Booby Trap, it opened up a whole new income stream for the dancers, but it also helped to draw more customers to the club.

Let me be really clear about this: Getting the dancers off the stage and closer to the customers proved to be the catalytic event that revolutionized topless entertainment, not just in Michigan, but all over the country. This was bigger than even I had realized—it was the turning point from what used to be known as burlesque, or classical stripping, as entertainment that was passive, that is, meant to be observed only—to active, allowing the patrons of a club to participate in a close-up dance that may or may not allow actual physical contact between dancer and customer. This is that fabled "grey area" that truly revolutionized the gentleman's club. Along with it came another revolutionary idea—that instead of paying the entertainers to entertain, the entertainers should become independent contractors who would happily pay the club for the opportunity to generate income far in excess of what they had earned as mere hourly workers. I use the word "happily" with my tongue firmly in my cheek, for the changes that I would institute were not happily acceded to nor did they happen overnight. And certainly not without great turmoil and expense. But change, even positive change, is often catastrophic at best. Or, as the old saying goes: You can't make a great omelet without breaking some eggs.

There were to be many more changes to come, and my restless nature would be the impetus for most of them. In my business, if you're not leading the way you're going to get run over. That I was not going to allow.

Getting Restless

In retrospect, I can't seem to sit still for more than two or three years at any given enterprise without upping the ante or figuring out a way to expand. At The Booby Trap, I was constantly upgrading every chance I had. The lighting started looking a bit dated to me after a while, so I pushed for new wall sconces and additional exterior lighting that would make the club look more attractive at night. Rip out the old stuff and put in the latest and greatest . . . I was always checking out other clubs on my trips out of town and emulating the best of the best. Same thing when the carpeting began to look old—how about some fresh stuff with subtle patterns that would pop out when hit with additional black light fixtures? And maybe some art on the walls that would give the club a cool new feel? I never hesitated, calculating that the investment to keep The Booby Trap at the head of the pack in my market would always come back in greater revenues.

My partner, Sol Milan, however, was more on the conservative side than I was. His philosophy was "if it ain't broke, don't fix it," and he used to grouse when I asked him to pony up for improvements. Granted, Sol was very successful with La Chambre and comfortable with the way things were. He was also close to thirty years older than me and didn't have to prove anything to anybody. Sol would rather have squeezed extra profits by refilling the Absolut bottles with Popov if I had let him, but I firmly believed in a real premium pour for a premium price and applied this measure to everything in the club.

My father, on the other hand, was pleased with his return on investment and was content to let me run things the way I saw fit. He was happy for my success—hell, he was happy I was still alive!—but the fact remained, in my mind, that one had to grow or die. So, Sol went along with my passion for improvement for the most part, but it was clear to me that it was time to start looking for other, greener pastures. The business model for a successful topless club was already old hat to me. I took operations very seriously and ran a tight ship, but I needed more of a challenge. I was always looking around for new opportunities, and when you're in the business, you tend to keep an ear to the street.

By the spring of 1984 I had physically recovered from being shot, and the club was totally hitting its stride. I was making somewhere in the neighborhood of $75,000 a year, which was a lot of bread for a young dude new to his own business. Having Sol and my father helping me greased the skids enormously and provided me with backup and security in case anything got sideways, as it did when I was shot, so I had a comfort level that made me confident about pushing the envelope. I had just moved from my tiny but hip apartment at 555 Woodward in Birmingham to the high-rise North Park Towers, a real cool bachelor apartment on the border between Southfield and Detroit. But I'd been so busy and was spending so much time at the Trap that I didn't even unpack my boxes for a year after moving in.

I was still seeing Laurie, my dancer/girlfriend, who nursed me through the worst months after the shooting, but I have to admit it wasn't easy to turn away some of the other fine ladies that I was meeting by being in the business. Like a kid in a candy store, I couldn't resist, so I was not totally monogamous. I had money and I had girls; I didn't drink, so I thought, hey, I'm young so I might as well enjoy it while I can. After a while Laurie picked up on what was happening and got out of my life. I can't say I blame her. For a while I went completely nuts on bacchanalian sex. Two at a time. I've got to say, it's every man's secret fantasy—come on, you wonder about it, don't you? What would that be like? I'll tell you. It's incredible, it's like being on sensory overload. Imagine one set of hands stroking and touching you and kissing you down there. Now, imagine at the same time another girl kissing you on the mouth with your hands on her fabulous breasts. The feeling of utter ecstasy is absolutely exponential. And if you get tired and the girls are liberal you can kick back and watch them amuse themselves, which I guarantee will have a stimulating effect that will get you back in the game pronto.

Granted, this was just before AIDs became a nasty factor in all our lives, and I was lucky I never caught anything. But with the easy availability of hot chicks, I got truly addicted to two girls at a time and I had to wean myself off the habit. And, truth be told, it's very difficult to keep up such a habit when you meet a sweet girl that you really want to be with one-on-one. I mean, you just can't have it all. All right, maybe you can have it all, but it's not going to last. Every one of us has to pay the piper eventually. Just make sure you can write the checks.

Every night, after last call at 2:00 a.m., it's typical for the people working in the bar and restaurant trade to hang out after work to unwind. You'd think after an evening of nonstop rock 'n' roll, jiggling girls, and juggling customers, all anyone would want to do is crash into dreamland for eight hours. But the fact is, running a topless bar is a lot of hard work, so like anyone else we like to blow off some steam. And I'll let you in on a little trade secret here: Topless dancers can get as horny as any of the guys they're teasing and tempting with intimate table-side dances all day or all night. Even if they may be emotionally disconnected from the job they are performing, they are just as prone to erotic daydreaming or being stimulated from customers that they may find attractive. Not all dancers have a hot stud waiting for them at home, either. Like any cross section of the population, you have singles and sometimes even married girls, dancing for dollars.

Many girls, come closing time, didn't feel like going home and would frequently hang out with me, perhaps the bouncer, DJ, or shift manager for a few rounds. As I have already explained,

I'm not much of a drinker, but I am not averse to socializing with cute, scantily clad dancers. Vintners have to sample their vintages, so I reserved the same privileges. The psychology at work here is worth exploring. The plain truth of the matter is that owning a topless club gives you power, as well as prestige. Customers as well as dancers assume that since you have "the keys to the kingdom," you can supply them with anything their hearts desire. The two big motivators are, of course, money and sex. Or, more specifically, for the customers at least, the illusion of or the possibility of sex. Being an owner, I was like the rock star and everybody who worked at the club had back-stage passes. Why do groupies get off doing rock stars? The answer is obvious, isn't it? They think they're getting the fat end of the deal, having a thrill ride, and as long as the perception lasts, it's all good. As for the rock star, you can pick and choose, and the choosier you are, it seems, the more the fans want to be "the one" who scores with you. Hey, sometimes people are just lonely, and that goes for owners as well as dancers.

But, for all the fun, fast times, and business education I'd received at The Booby Trap, the trap had sprung tightly shut for me when Susie Bufale unloaded her .38 into me . . . every time I went to the club, my mind echoed with the sound of gunshots, and my still tender tissue ached along with my emotions. I knew that I wouldn't and couldn't leave the topless business, as it had become my raison d'être, the story of my young life, and a damned fine cash-generating machine. Plus, I was stubborn, focused, and determined to expand.

The way BTs came about was this: After getting shot by sweet Susie Bufale, as you already know, things were just not the same. Even when things are humming, like they were at The Booby Trap, and the money was rolling in nice and steady,

I was getting itchy. Itchy for a change. Itchy for expansion, itchy to do things more my own way. Itchy to sell, like a smart stock market player who knows it's time to unload while the stock is high, ready to walk away from the table with my gains and roll it all into a spanking new enterprise.

Naturally, when you've been in the business for a while, any business, a lot of information comes your way. What's going down on the street, the rumor mill, your customers, everybody's talking, and you just need to listen. A lot of entertainers, for example, often flit from club to club to liven things up a bit or when their earnings are a bit stale. They talk to the other girls, managers, owners, house moms, and others and the information comes back via the good ol' grapevine. Same thing with lawyers, cops, real estate people . . . they come in for a drink or two, you're on the phone shooting the breeze, and you hear all kinds of things.

So it came to pass that I heard there was a place for sale on Michigan Avenue in downtown Dearborn, a joint called the Pompeii, which was one of a total of three places in Dearborn that had grandfathered cabaret licenses that permitted topless entertainment. The other two were on the divey side of the equation and had been running for years. The Pompeii had been operated as a small topless bar in front and a restaurant in the back, opposite to what common sense would seem to dictate. The owner was an older gentleman who didn't seem to take a lot of interest in keeping the place up to snuff, much less upgrading the facility. If he was interested in getting out, scoring a tidy profit, and retiring to marlin fishing in Florida, it represented the kind of upside that I salivate over: plenty of square footage to improve, little direct competition in the way of quality, and tons of automotive and supplier business with

Ford Motor Company World Headquarters just a couple of miles east. I ran some numbers with Sol and my dad on what it would take to re-furb the location, talked to my lawyer, and had an offer drawn up which we duly submitted. Then, I waited. And waited. And waited some more. No response. Couldn't even get a phone call returned. I could only assume the owner wasn't interested in selling and had put the whole idea on the back burner.

Then, one day around six months later, I got a phone call from the owner's wife. She didn't sound so good. I quickly learned why—her husband had died suddenly just a month earlier. She had been cleaning out his office at the club and had found my written offer for the business from half a year previous. Since she was not a businesswoman and had neither the know-how nor the desire to operate a topless club and restaurant, she had simply called me up to see if I were still interested in buying! It took me less than two seconds to say, "Yeeesssss . . . that is something I would still be interested in. Let's get together on the details!"

Mrs. Owner informed me that she would have her lawyer and real estate broker get back to me on the matter and a week later we were in the middle of due diligence and finalizing a new offer for $160,000, which was accepted within 24 hours.

Other Voices: Max Markovitz

At the beginning, you know, opening a topless club was a completely new experience for both of us. I didn't really know what to expect, except that Alan had assured me from his experience working at La Chambre that it was a good business and that he had a basic grasp of the fundamentals. I knew he was very determined to make it work, and with Sol Milan as a partner, I figured we had a good insurance policy. But let me make this clear—Alan was taking the lead on the club, pushing hard to get the look right, create the proper ambiance, and look after all the hundreds of other details.

It was funny, though, when it came to be time to interview the employees—specifically the dancers. I thought, This is a very pleasant chore! But I said to Alan, you have more experience in this area so I think you should be the one to take care of it. Alan agreed, of course, and the process began. He was working at my television repair shop at the time, and I think maybe he was a little bored with tubes and transistors. Especially when it comes to 34C and 36D and all those curves that had to be, shall we say, negotiated.

We had our bumps, of course, dealing with the motorcycle club, which didn't scare me because I had dealt with a lot tougher situations in the war. What could they do to me? Kill me? I'm not stupid, but I wasn't afraid. I went into their clubhouse that day in May and I talked to their leader. People understand when you mean business and he listened to me. I told him we had a lot of money invested in our new club and we weren't going to put up with any nonsense. Follow the rules, I told him, and they were welcome in the club like anyone else. I think he liked that, and we sure never had a problem with the Renegades after that.

The worst part for me was when Alan was shot by a dancer. We both knew how close he came to losing his life and I was afraid for him. But he's tough. I like to think he got some of that from me. Neither of us is a quitter; we're going to do whatever it takes to succeed and hold onto our success. I'm very proud of my son—he has raised the bar on this whole business and set standards that other operators only try to match. He believes in making his clubs the best of the best and refuses to be dislodged from his position.

BTs DEARBORN

My theory is this—and it's not just a theory, because I practice what I preach: When you're on a roll, look for the next and best opportunity to extend your winning streak, or more accurately, project your formula, and capture as much market share as you can afford to. In the Detroit topless market, with something like thirty clubs competing with one another, owning one club represents almost 5 percent of the total local market share, and putting another club on line doubles that to close to 10 percent of the pie. The local pie, in Detroit, is conservatively estimated at being between $40–$50 million in gross annual sales. It's probably in the neighborhood of a $75–$100 million market, and remember, this gross tally does NOT calculate what the dancers take in as independent contractors.

Of course, just because your club (or clubs) represents a mathematical division of market share doesn't mean you are getting all of the available business, equally divided. You must do what any other business does—maintain your quality, keep your expenses under control, and maximize your sales per customer per visit. It was and is my nature to maximize my profit by offering not only the biggest selection of the best-looking dancers available, to draw customers in, but to provide a superlative and detail-oriented experience that keeps 'em coming back and spreads the word far and wide to other potential patrons.

I knew BTs had to be a quantum leap up the quality ladder from Booby Trap, although I had planned on naming the club "Booby Trap II" as a method of brand extension. Turned out that the rather conservative city fathers (headed up by the Orville Hubbard mayoral dynasty) didn't appreciate such a blatant name and in the end I was forced to resort to the initials "BTs" instead. It actually worked out better this way, as it served to differentiate the club from its namesake and predecessor and most of the people who patronized BTs thought it stood for "Big Tits," which, while rather coarse and obvious, nonetheless conveyed the nature of the business. Advertising is advertising. I remember growing up as a typical Detroit gearhead and all the other kids used to say that the STP stickers (for a then popular and still existing brand of motor oil additive) we used to see all around town stood for "sweet tasting _____." I don't know if that sold more STP or not, but it sure as hell assured that one would remember the brand name. I could only hope for as much for BTs!

A Clubs vs. B Clubs

The early to mid-1980s was a golden time. Detroit's Big Three had had some bumps, but as competition, Honda and Toyota were still in the rearview mirror and there were millions and billions to be made. Since all the cars coming out of Detroit's factories needed a lot of parts and components, and suppliers needed to woo buyers, it was the perfect time to be in the club business. Fat expense accounts were all the rage, and long, three-martini lunches were the norm for the legions of suits who kept the factories humming by striking deals for anything and everything from lights to locks, screws, nuts, bolts, you name it. What better place to strike a deal for 500,000 whatchamacal-lits than behind a rare steak with two pair of knock-out cuties gyrating inches away? The Japanese were here, too, remember, and they have been and continue to be among my best clientele. They are polite and professional and like to spend. In turn I like to make sure they have the best topless experience in town.

It may seem so obvious as to be unworthy of mention, but the key to running a number one topless club is the quality—and the quantity—of the entertainers. To ignore this is to for-ever condemn yourself to the ranks of "B" club operators. Yet it seems to be a perfect example of the classic chicken-and-egg question—which came first? The girls or the free-spending clientele to attract them? The short answer is that all the ingredients have to be present to bring the clientele in and to bring them back again: the best booze, the finest food, the crispest service, the most dazzling décor. It's the old "if you build it they will come" leap of faith that's called for here. If I am to take any credit for being a visionary, it's simply that I have always been stubbornly insistent on creating the highest quality gentleman's club on the market. So, naturally, clients as well as entertainers are attracted to what is "the best," and the rest of it is the arduous, ongoing task of managing your finely tuned machine to keep it from running off the rails. I guarantee you that if you take a spare $3–$4 million dollars and buy an existing topless club, pour another $1–$2 million dollars into groom-ing it to be a mind-blowing example of sleek, slick excess, and hire a European five-star chef, experienced management, and seasoned floor staff . . . you will probably fail miserably. Why is that? Because although the stunning quality of your newly minted topless club will probably attract throngs of customers, initially, if you do not absolutely master the herculean task of managing the wildly off-the-wall mix of extreme personalities who compose the bulk of your entertainers, or prevent yourself from dipping into and over-indulging in the Dionysian delights that surround you . . . well, let me put it in language you'll understand . . . you'll be well and truly fucked.

The most interesting thing about BTs, besides its great location down the road from Ford world headquarters, was how it became not only an "A" list club, but how it became a true scientific laboratory for the testing of the law that had been written to keep dancers up "on stage," as opposed to dancing in front of customers or on customer's tables. Over on Eight, it had been little problem to get the girls on stage down off the stage to do dances at (and yes, even on top of) the tables. In many ways, virtually anything was possible in Detroit in those early days, with a certain Wild West atmosphere that extended from the days when biker bars were the norm; unless there was brawling or gunfire, the cops pretty much steered clear. When The Booby Trap came along and upgraded the game, we were perceived as heroes, akin to Rudy Giuliani coming along and cleaning up New York's Times Square, turning it into a thriving commercial and entertainment district.

But back to the issue of "the stage." There could and would be no private dances in Dearborn—or anywhere else—until a legal method could be devised. The wonderful thing about laws, or city ordinances, which are in essence merely local laws, is that both the language and the intent can be creatively challenged if you have a smart lawyer or are smart enough yourself to interpret and circumvent that law. "Circumvent," put another way, is to meet the letter of the law while, shall we say, bending the spirit of the law.

No wonder it was such a hoot to come up with the notion, quite by accident, of slicing and dicing the stage. What is a stage, after all? It is an elevated platform, is it not? It keeps those performing upon it elevated above the floor. Now, unless there is language in the law that specifically defines the minimum or maximum dimensions of a stage, or states that it must be composed of a certain area, or square footage, then the legal definition of a stage contains quite a bit of latitude.

Stages, it must be noted, can also be portable. When the Rolling Stones go on tour, do they not take their stage with them? Yes, they do. It is clearly obvious that a portable stage can be either humongous, as the Stones' stage is . . . or, it can be smaller, and therefore more portable. Say, twelve inches by twelve inches? Now, it would be hard to get the Rolling Stones to perform on such a small stage, but a topless dancer, aaah— she would fit very nicely on a twelve-inch stage! I suppose in terms of modesty, I ought to point out that BTs did not advertise "two dozen separate stages for your entertainment pleasure!" Maybe we didn't want to tweak the noses of the city fathers. And the truth is, the issue was never contested. I just went ahead and had several of these small stages built, small and light enough that a dancer could easily pick them up and move them anywhere she liked within the club.

In practice, the idea worked like a charm. The portable stage brought BTs entertainers to within inches of their customers, raised their incomes by a substantial amount, and when the local police dropped in to say "hi" and be assured that BTs was complying with the law . . . well, they just took one look at a

dancer doing her number up "on stage" and smiled, or chuckled.

"We might have to run this by the commander, Alan," I was
told. "But that's pretty clever, you know?"

It was clever enough, and I gather the Dearborn powers
that be were as glad as I was to have a "legal position" that they
could stand on, because it certainly saved the city the hassle of
protracted litigation and kept BTs humming. Remember, we
were—and remain—a well-run, legitimate business that con-
tributes a lot of tax revenue to whatever municipality we operate in, as well as providing a lot of well-paying jobs.

The only time I can think of when we really had any kind
of problem on stage, portable or otherwise, was when I had the
brilliant idea of hiring a trained chimpanzee and his handler to
celebrate the one-year anniversary of opening up on Michigan
Avenue. It stood to reason that with folks appreciating wild
times with wild women, a little wild life would be just the thing
to create a memorable occasion for one and all.

Where do you find a trained chimp? In the 1980s, I looked
in the Yellow Pages. Now, of course, all you need to do is
Google "trained chimps" and all suitably entertaining primates
within fifty miles of your zip code will pop up for your perusal.
I called the number in the phone book and got a guy on the
other end who was the chimp's owner and handler. The chimp's
name was Bonzo, or Gonzo, or something like that. For the very
reasonable sum of $250, the handler would bring Gonzo into
the—beg your pardon, "Where was that you said you wanted
him to perform???"

"A topless club, BTs in Dearborn, to be precise," I replied.

"Um, gee, I don't think he's ever done a show in a topless
club before."

"Would there be any problem with that?" I asked, quite innocently.

"Uh, no, no, he's very friendly, I don't think there should be any problem."

"Great," I said, "Let's book it!"

Little did I know. When I was told that Gonzo had never done a show in a topless club, my antennae should have gone up. But why worry? There's a reason chimps travel with their handlers. That's who's getting paid to keep things under control. I figured the whole thing would be a blast, and anyway, you've got to try new things to keep the club lively. In this case, however, lively would be an understatement.

The following week rolled around, and at the appointed hour, a young dude and a chimpanzee came knocking at the door.

"Cute chimp!" I remarked.

"Oh, he's cute all right . . . but he also does tricks. Do you want me to go over our program with you?"

"Nah," I said. "We'll do a break after lunch and then you'll have the stage. By the way, is that a male or a female chimp?"

"Oh, he's a male all right."

I looked the chimp in the eye and he looked right back at me, as if, who was I to question his manhood?

The club was packed. BTs always pulled a strong lunch crowd, plus it was a Friday and everyone was in a mood to party. After most of the lunches had been served, the DJ did a few more sets and then made his announcement—and the cue for Gonzo—in classical speed-rap DJ patter.

"Allllrrrighteveryonenowwegotsomethin'reallyspecial, it's a really wiiiild act something you've never seen before!!! To celebrate the one-year anniversary of BTs we're bringing to the stage the incomparable, the entertaining, the one and only Gonzooooooo!!!"

On cue, the handler came trotting out from behind the stage holding Gonzo by the hand, the two of them leaping up the stairs to the stage, amid a roar of surprise from the club and squeals of excitement from the dozen or so dancers who had been assembled to give the chimp one of our birthday dances. The handler had apparently cooked this up as a special surprise that he thought would be more entertaining than the goofy tricks the chimp usually did at birthday parties. One of the dancers, topless naturally, brought a chair out to center stage where the handler seated him. The birthday dance, if you're not acquainted with the ritual, consists of dancers alternately straddling the lucky stiff and positioning their nipples inches from his face while the other girls cluster around, tickling, cooing and generally teasing the birthday boy with all their charms.

Gonzo got intoxicated all right—all the hot chicks swarming over him must have kicked in some primal instinct—because he started going bananas! In the blink of an eye, Gonzo screeched like a chimp possessed and started grabbing at the unfortunate dancer who was straddling him—grabbing her by her breasts and throwing his legs around her. The girl began screaming bloody murder as she reared back onto her four-inch dancer platforms, trying to stand and back away from the monkey, as the monkey did his best to hold on!

The handler rushed in and grabbed Gonzo by the arm and started trying to pull him off, but chimps, if you didn't know, are about three times stronger than the strongest bodybuilder. Gonzo wasn't about to let loose of what, I had to admit, was one of our most fetching brunette entertainers. Mind you, he wasn't hurting her, but he did seem to have a very clear determination of what he wanted. There was no doubt about it—the chimp knew she was hot and he wanted some!

Finally, with a valiant heave-ho, the handler disengaged Gonzo from the totally freaked-out dancer and started dragging the screaming ape off the stage. He looked desperately at me as he passed and I yelled out to him to take Gonzo back into my office and get him calmed down. After making sure that my dancer was OK and observing that the club seemed to think the scene was somehow part of the act—hey, everybody was drinking, after all—I made my way to the back to see how the handler was managing.

When I walked into my office I couldn't believe my eyes. Gonzo was splayed out in my black leather executive office chair, rocking back and forth like he owned the place. He looked at me with an expression, that I swear, clearly communicated "Who the hell are you and what do you want?" The handler just shrugged, with a rather embarrassed grimace on his face. "Don't worry," I said, "you're going to get paid." It was the first and last time I've ever booked an animal act in any of my clubs.

Pony Up

Another animal story from my early days, possessed of considerably more elegance than the chimpanzee episode, involves a beautiful thoroughbred horse named Allie's Flash Dancer.

You meet all kinds in my business and never know who's going to walk through the door. I've met all kinds of cool people . . . professional athletes, CEOs and entrepreneurs, old money and new . . . but the day a fella by the name of Richard Gray showed up at BTs, I couldn't image the delights that would be coming my way.

Richard was a distinguished and earthy guy in his fifties whose dad had started up a very successful tool and die business selling to the Big Three. He had money, he loved my girls, and he had good taste. Above and beyond that, however, he owned a million-dollar racehorse named Thumbsucker that he loved to talk about. He wore his passion for the ponies on his sleeve, and over his many visits to the club, I became intrigued by his stories.

One day, Richard suggested that I accompany him the following evening to the Ladbroke Detroit Race Course, a huge track and entertainment complex on the I-96 freeway on Detroit's west side, to see his horse race. It was a whole new experience for me, still in my mid twenties. I didn't know quite what to expect. But I eagerly jumped into my Jaguar XKE (fancy cars are so much more important when you're young than when you grow up, but I figured the hot English roadster would fit in perfectly with the horse racing crowd) and headed out to the track. Upon arriving, I informed the guard at the gatehouse that I was there with Richard, and I was waved through like a VIP. Nice start, I thought to myself, as I drove slowly through the paddock area, the equivalent to being backstage at a rock concert, looking for my party.

Soon I located Richard and his friends and was greeted warmly.

"Hey, Alan," Richard said, "the race is going to begin in fifteen minutes! Let's get some drinks and get situated here!"

Before I knew it, the stands were abuzz as a group of horses was led from the paddock to the starting gate—it looked like maybe a dozen horses would be running—and I could feel my adrenaline pumping. They were gorgeous animals, sleek and rippling with muscle, clearly anxious to do what they did best: run like the wind.

Suddenly the bell sounded and the crowd roared as thousands of pounds of thoroughbred horseflesh burst from the gate with nostrils flaring and hooves pounding, their jockeys in their colorful silks perched aggressively upon them as they hurtled down the dirt track. I was mesmerized. The announcer barked out their positions in crackly static over the loudspeakers and every eye in the place was riveted to the thundering mass now charging into turn one . . . but where was Thumbsucker?

"There he is!" Richard shouted. "He's in third place, but he's moving up! Lookit 'im go!"

Coming down the home stretch, sure enough, it was Thumbsucker pulling ahead . . . by a head, now by a length . . . running flat out for all he was worth. And then it was over—Thumbsucker by nearly two lengths! Richard was beaming, yelling; our whole box and the crowd was on its feet.

I was enthralled. Following the race, I tagged along to the winner's circle as Richard accepted a big, gleaming silver cup, not to mention the prize money for first place. What a rush. I thought that this was the kind of life I could get used to in a hurry. I wanted more. And not too many months later, with the excitement of the races still burning within me, I got another call from Richard that was the real topper—an invitation to the Kentucky Derby!

If you think you know what the Derby is all about—think again. It is an American institution dating back to 1875 that blends the drama of the finest thoroughbred horses in the world with the unparalleled gentility and pageantry of the American

South. Richard told me he was taking a date, his girlfriend Laurie, and encouraged me to bring a date, too. I chose Molly, a beautiful honey-blonde dancer whom I knew to love horses, and she jumped at the chance to go. It was amazing—Richard flew us down in his six-passenger Cessna and we had a car waiting for us when we arrived in Louisville. The Derby is run during the first Saturday of May, and the smell of honeysuckle and other spring flowers was as intoxicating as our female company. The day of the race, we all got to the track early to look around and get our share of mint juleps, the traditional drink of the Derby. Our dates were dressed to the nines in fabulous and elaborate dresses with big, fancy hats that evoked the antebellum South of *Gone With the Wind*. Richard and I were crisply dressed in white suits and ties, and we felt, sitting in our private box, like royalty, or better yet something out of the movies. Who says adults don't get to enjoy dressing up?

The race itself was electrifying—although I can't remember which horse actually won—and I was completely hooked on horse racing. The whole day was so much like a dream that I did something I don't usually do—I invited myself back for the following year!

"You're welcome to join me again next year," Richard told me, "but I have an idea I think you'll like even better."

I was intrigued.

"I know a trainer back in Detroit who has a three-year-old gelding ready to run. Her name is Allison Sinclair and I know she's looking for a partner. The buy-in is only $25,000."

"What's that get me?" I asked.

"You get a 50 percent share of her horse, you share expenses, and if the horse wins you share in the purse."

At that time in my life, I had maybe $75,000 saved in the bank—so, sure, I could afford $25,000—why not? Back in Detroit after one of the most fabulous weekends of my life,

I wasted no time in setting up a meeting with Allison and her jockey, a diminutive guy who looked exactly like what you'd expect a jockey to be. It was explained to me that the jockey gets 10 percent of any winnings and that the horse, named Allie's Flash Dancer—remember, this was the 1980s—would be ready to run in a mere six to ten weeks.

The night of Flash Dancer's first race it was the height of summer, hot and sultry, and there was electricity in the air. I had driven my new black Jag to the track again and was feeling lucky. We were scheduled for the seventh or eighth race of the night, up against all the premier horses, and on the track Flash Dancer was seventh of eight or nine horses running. After much waiting, wondering, and speculating, it was time. They were off! And Flash Dancer was fighting for position, all the way through the fourth turn, still in the pack . . . when without hesitation he suddenly exploded into the home stretch . . . and won by two lengths!

I was blown away! What were the chances of winning the first time out with a completely untested horse??? Everybody was ecstatic—particularly since we took a $12,500 purse! After the race, it got even better. I was treated like a celebrity, with the complete red carpet treatment every which way I turned. People were pumping my hand left and right and bookies were clamoring around me, picking my brain for hot tips. Pac Man, the bookmaker who famously jump-started table dances at The Booby Trap, instantly became bonded to me at the hip and was always approaching me at the track, offering to buy me a drink so he could talk horses with me—me, the instant expert!

Allie's Flash Dancer went on to win all six of his next races for seven in a row and was soon after named Michigan's number one gelding, estimated as worth $100,000. A lot of people urged me and Allison to sell him and take a big profit, but I was having way too much fun. Besides, winnings were covering all our expenses and we were even making a few bucks. We had our own box, we were treated like royalty, and I saw no end to the winning for Flash Dancer.

"Richard, we're going to take this horse to the Kentucky Derby, you wait and see!" I exulted one night after a particularly dramatic win.

"Cool your jets a little, Alan," Richard counseled me. "In horse racing, you never know. Enjoy the ride."

How right Richard turned out to be. It wasn't long after that ,coming around turn four at the Detroit Race Course, that Flash Dancer broke stride and dropped back, unable to even cross the finish line. I was devastated—what was wrong with my beautiful horse? We brought the vet in and the diagnosis was that Flash Dancer had hurt a leg and needed some advanced veterinary attention. Money was no object—I loved that horse. We sent him to a famous vet in Ohio who had treated Secretariat. The treatment went well, but Flash Dancer had to be laid up for months . . . and when we finally got a clean bill of health and ran him again, he came in third. The magic was gone.

"We can't run him anymore," Allison reluctantly told me. "He could get a catastrophic injury. I'm afraid his racing days are behind him."

I was crestfallen, but I knew it was the right call. I parted company with Allison and later heard that Flash Dancer was retired to a petting zoo somewhere. If I had it to do all over I would have followed up to make sure he was well cared for the rest of his days. It makes me sad to think such a beautiful athlete of a horse ended up in a petting zoo . . . but it's a lot better than a glue factory. It only goes to show, I suppose, that all glory is fleeting. I have some beautiful memories of those days, and now, let's just say I pay attention to taking care of my two-legged fillies. But I wouldn't trade those days at the track for anything.

BOOBY TRAP FLA

Florida has always held a certain charm for me. Like most snowbirds, I get plenty sick of Detroit's slag-grey slush and cold winters long before spring breaks. On top of that, by the mid-1980s, my father was seriously planning his retirement and relocation to Florida's east coast. As always, I could count on his support and counsel if I ever wanted to open a club there. After getting shot, I was a shell of my former self for a long time, even after opening BTs, and those warm breezes along with promising cash flow were more than enough to crystallize the notion of getting a gig going in Florida. With BTs chugging along like the little engine that could, I could well afford to invest for additional growth. Little did I know at the time, my plans for topless enterprise in the Sunshine State were to be circumscribed by a homicidal dancer in a kamikaze Fiero and a scary brush with the New York mob . . . replete with yours truly testifying against a couple of geriatric goombahs who were known associates of the now deceased Mafia kingpin John Gotti!

During the winter of 1987, on one of my sojourns to the Ft. Lauderdale area, I happened to be having lunch with an old buddy of mine. Over blackened tilapia and a couple of Coronas, it was revealed to me that a former NFL receiver by the name of Ray Abruzzi, who had played for the New York Jets and had been in business with Joe Namath, was looking for a way to turn a local bar/restaurant into a topless club. The place, called Bachelors Three, was located in Ft. Lauderdale on Sunrise Boulevard and had been closed for some time. It looked like Namath wanted out. There were at least half a dozen other places in and around Lauderdale that offered nude dancers along with liquor, so everything looked good. I reasoned that if I could turn Abruzzi's place into a topless venue, essentially make it Booby Trap South, it would be possible to sell the same number of drinks but triple or quadruple the profit margin. We only needed to do some redecorating, hire some new talent, and we'd be off and running!

Inside of a week, I had my first meeting with Ray Abruzzi. He was a very laid-back guy, greeting me in shorts and a tropical shirt. He carried himself with the confidence and accomplishment of someone who'd played pro sports, and he was hungry for some of the kind of money that was so conspicuously displayed those days in the Miami Vice–type atmosphere that was South Florida. Everywhere you turned there were dudes with ponytails and NikNik shirts driving around in Ferraris and Lamborghinis . . . strutting their stuff on South Beach, along with the full complement of hard-bodied babes who fed on their end of the food chain. The fact that all of South Florida was positively awash in cash was glaringly evident. Condos and office buildings were sprouting like mushrooms, along with extravagant new homes up and down the intercoastal, not to mention the insanely geeked-out boats (to me they look like small ships) moored everywhere.

Abruzzi was motivated. He could already taste the money and, perhaps more importantly, the cachet he would enjoy as an owner of a hot new topless bar. Between the experience I was bringing to the table, along with cold cash, and Ray's ready-to-rock location, it was a no-brainer! The deal was on. It was a straight 50/50 participation, involving my buy-in for half of what we calculated as the bar's current valuation . . . something in the neighborhood of a quarter million.

As I've indicated, nothing in the law in Ft. Lauderdale at the time, which is Broward County—Dade being Miami and a whole different story—prohibited operating a topless establishment. These other clubs were doing it, so it was apparent they were "grandfathered" into existing laws, like it was in Detroit. But, as I've come to learn, it's important to do your research. There's always a reason why things are the way they are, and therein lies the foresight (or lack thereof) for what will come. Some changes you can anticipate and plan for. Others smack you right in the forehead!

With topless bars operating unmolested throughout Dade County, there was every reason to suppose and believe Broward would be as tolerant to the trade. Florida loves its tourists, and large numbers of tourists love topless bars. But remember—there are a lot of senior citizens in Florida, otherwise known to city councils and politicians as an "important constituency." Nonexistent laws are a vacuum that can quickly become filled with new laws. And new laws, my friends, generally prohibit or restrict activities rather than permitting them. Write that down in your notebook; I promise it will come in handy for you.

After a few months, Bachelors Three was newly minted as The Booby Trap, which had been a terrifically lucky name for me, so I was hoping lightning would strike twice. We had a new canopy made up and affixed over the front doors of the club, along with upgrades to everything else from the bar to the sound system, including that staple fixture of all gentleman's clubs, a bona fide DJ booth.

We made a big splash with an advance radio campaign publicizing our grand opening and advertising for dancers at the same time. Because we were a new face in the crowd, it was no problem attracting a few girls from each of the surrounding establishments, and soon we were up to two to three dozen reliable girls per shift. Plus, there were always entertainers who liked to travel. With a full roster at BTs in Dearborn, I knew I could count on at least a few of them to come down for some fun, some sun, and some serious dollars.

Like any new club, initial buzz helps pull in the customers, and we had a solid opening night, followed by month after month of the increased receipts that come with selling $6 beers. I loved operating in Florida!

Things were good, but they were about to get a lot more interesting. One of the girls who wanted to spend some time playing (and working) in Florida happened to be a dancer by the name of Kim Boussner, whom I was seeing at the time. Kim was dancing at BTs and she was drop-dead gorgeous . . . a tall, lithe brunette with legs up to her eyeballs and a wildly unique form of dancing that led to her nickname, Spinner Kim. Plus, she had the most outrageous nipples I'd ever seen on a woman—they looked like .50 caliber machine gun cartridges that stuck so far out I swear you could've hung five Armani suits off of each one with no problem whatsoever. Kim also had the combined talents of smoking Marlboros like a chimney, drinking like an alcoholic sailor on shore leave, and going through pot like a Rastafarian. Oh, yeah, the nickname. Seems that when Kim got rolling good with her favorite beverage—Jack Daniels straight—and got up on stage, she would often culminate her routine with a spin, like those ice-skaters who rev themselves up into a blur for their finale. She was actually able to spin her dress—one of those flouncy skater numbers—up and off her body while she spun! The first time I witnessed this I couldn't believe it: Kim turned into such a whirling Dervish one night at BTs that she began traveling across the stage while she spun . . . just like a top! I watched in awe, as sure enough her dress shimmied itself up her torso, the skirt extending like the blades on a Huey helicopter as she picked up speed. Her hands met briefly above her head, allowing the dress to work its way up and off of her. But my amazement quickly turned to trepidation, as she spun closer and closer to the edge. Suddenly, like a trailer gives way to a tornado, all hell broke loose as Kim spun herself right off the stage, and her momentum carried her, still spinning, onto the top of a table and two patrons by the side of the platform! She hit that table like a bomb, sending drinks, food, and two guys sprawling onto the floor with her. Sitting on her ass in the middle of the carnage, and shaking off her dizziness, Kim looked up and innocently asked, "Wh-what happened?" We all had a gigantic belly laugh and the name Spinner was forever Kim's.

Naturally, I had the brilliant idea of moving Kim in with me at my new apartment on A1A, where I figured we could enjoy a pleasant domesticity together while I looked after my business. And after her. I really loved that girl and was willing to do almost anything for her. Besides moving her in with me, I cemented our togetherness by giving Kim a brand new, bright red Pontiac Fiero. She loved racing that car up and down Biscayne Boulevard at all hours of the night, often after hours of crazed partying at the club, doing shots of Goldschlager's alternated with Long Island iced teas and longnecks. You can see where this is going, can't you? Two words: Wild. Woman. I would soon learn that the true meaning of putting these two words together was, in Kim's case, like mixing gasoline and matches.

We had been together only a couple of weeks when the first episode unfolded. It was a weeknight evening and we were watching some tube on the sofa while my managers watched the club. Kim hopped up, put on her flip-flops, and breezily announced that she was going down to the 7-11 for a pack of smokes.

"I'll be back in twenty minutes!" she chirped as she bounced out the door.

A half hour later, no Kim. Forty-five minutes, still no Kim. An hour passed, then two hours. She must be taking a walk, I told myself, it's a gorgeous evening, still light. Not to worry. And then it was time for the eleven o'clock news. I started to freak. Called the club to see if she'd gone there. Nope, no Kim at the club. I jumped in my car and drove the three blocks to the store, hoping I'd find her there . . . where else could I look? But Kim was nowhere to be found. Not knowing what else to do, I went to work, thinking if Kim showed up back at the apartment, she would either call me or come looking for me herself.

Alas, an errant dancer is hard to find, much less corral. At twenty-five or twenty-six, Kim was just hitting her proper wild-woman stride. Suffice to say, she never came back that night, or the next day or the next night! In fact, just when I was about ready to file a missing persons report, Kim showed up at the apartment. It had been three whole days since she went out for that 20-minute cigaret run! I was flabbergasted, and livid.

"Where the hell have you been?" I yelled at her as she blithely stepped into the apartment, half in relief and half in genuine anger at having been put through three days of worrying whether or not she'd be found face down somewhere in the proverbial ditch.

"Oh, well," Kim replied, "there were these motorcycle dudes down at the 7-11 and they had really cool bikes, so I went for a ride!"

"For THREE FREAKING DAYS?!?" I shot back at her. "What—are you crazy??? You couldn't call me for THREE DAYS?"

"I lost track of time, I guess," Kim explained, before turning on me. "Hey, fuck you Alan! You don't own me! I can do whatever I want, whenever I want, so you can just go fuck yourself!"

"Thanks a whole hell of a lot!" I screamed. A fat lot of good it did me.

We ended up having a horrible fight that culminated in Kim turning around and storming back out the door, giving me the finger as she went. I was utterly dumbfounded at the fury, the capriciousness, and the insolence that Kim was capable of. What was it that kept me hanging on? I think it was the challenge of thinking I could tame a wild mustang. But honestly, I was young and simply hooked on the intensity of the relationship. Kim was nothing if not intense; then again, I was very full of testosterone and my relationship with her was a challenge as well as sexual awakening for me. But nothing can possibly prepare you for the trauma of being in a relationship with a full-blown alcoholic, and for what it's worth, take my advice: No matter how hot the girl is, if she exhibits any of the warning signs (out-of-control behavior of any type), walk away while you have the chance. Don't get sucked in. It's a hell you don't want to know. Unfortunately, some of life's most important lessons are not taught in the classroom and the only way we learn is through experience.

I went back to the club a few hours later and there was Kim, up on stage, doing her thing like nothing unusual had happened. I just shook my head and went into my office for a Perrier and some AC.

Mob Job

A couple months after opening up Booby Trap South, we were rocking. Not breaking any world's records, but doing good solid business. I was pleased. Abruzzi and I, along with general operating partner Phil Gori, who had relocated to Florida from Detroit, had carved out our own little niche in the greater Fort Lauderdale market, and a niche is all you need to grow an empire. Two or three "A" clubs can indeed constitute the kind of cash flow that makes for a nice little empire with all the toys and perks that go along with it. Remember, in Florida, you're selling part of a total lifestyle as much as you are breasts and $7 beers. Everybody wants to be a part of the action in paradise.

The only problem is, other people who own a piece of that paradise think that they have exclusive rights to it and wish to exclude others from "wetting their beaks," to use the jargon particular to certain Italian-Americans. Yeah, I'm talking about the Mob.

The New York mob, as a matter of fact. There was this other topless club across town called Solid Gold, one of about six or seven area clubs that were our competition. It was run by a guy named Mike Peter, the embodiment of the open shirt, gold medallion, coked-up cliché of that era. Plus, he had a real Napoleon complex. Peter had been into The Booby Trap a few times, checking us out, and I'd bought him a drink or two in the spirit of friendly relations. I always believed there's enough business for everybody and it's part of the American way to compete vigorously in the free market. So, as far as I was concerned, Peter and I were like-minded businessmen, until his actions proved otherwise.

One day, I showed up early to work and my partner Ray Abruzzi was at the bar.

"Hey, Alan," he said. "How you doin'?"

"What's up, Ray?"

"You know, Mike Peter was in here about half an hour ago."

"Yeah, what'd he want?"

"It's kinda funny, you know. He wants us to go over to Solid Gold tomorrow. Said there's a couple people he wants us to meet."

"What people are those—I mean, what's this about?"

"Something he and his investors want to talk about."

Now I was getting a little suspicious . . . whenever somebody you've never met wants to talk to you and they're vague about the subject, you have to wonder what their real motives are. But I wanted to know what was up—and there was no reason not to go over and check it out. So I agreed.

Walking into the office at Solid Gold the next day, I was mildly perplexed to find, frankly, a couple of old guys, indistinguishable from the legions of retirees you see all over Florida. Just after I arrived, some more old guys showed up and before the meeting started there was a whole round of the first two old guys kissing both cheeks of the new old guys along with a lot of hugging and muttering in Italian. It was like something out of *The Godfather!* Mike Peter did most of the talking, however.

"Thanks for coming, Alan," he began. "We wanted to talk to you about our business in South Florida. See, the thing is, we've got a franchise here. Do you understand what I'm saying?"

"A franchise? My understanding is that you own your club, and you operate independently . . . Solid Gold is trademarked, right?"

"Yeah," Peter replied. "But that's not exactly what I mean to say."

All of a sudden, one of the old guys piped up, in a gravelly sort of voice that was no doubt seasoned by eons of non-filtereds and booze. "It ain't right."

"Beg your pardon?" I said.

The other old guy chimed in. "It ain't right you opened up across town like you did."

I looked at Peter for some kind of an explanation.

"See, Alan, me and my partners here, we gotta protect our business. We have a lot invested here. We're sayin' it's not right you just opened up like you did without consulting us."

I was beginning to get the picture, but I was not about to start kowtowing to the crude overture these guys were making. And what was it they wanted of me, anyway?

"Look," I interjected. "There's plenty of business for everyone here. I opened up a bar that offers topless entertainment . . . that's my right, isn't it?"

Old guy number one started up again, a bit more insistently. "It ain't right you opened up!"

It was clear I wasn't getting anywhere with this bunch. They weren't happy, obviously, but they hadn't made any overt threats, either. I decided the smartest thing I could do was leave, which I promptly did, making the excuse that I needed to be somewhere else. Ray, who had been content to let me do the talking, followed.

"Al, what the hell—don't you think we oughta go back in there and resolve this thing?"

"I really don't think we have anything to talk about here," I said. "I guess the next move is theirs!"

I'll admit, I was a little shaken. I had heard rumors in conversations with others in the club business in and around Lauderdale that Mike Peter's Solid Gold was financed with mob money, and that he was suspected of laundering cash for the Mafia as well. Maybe that explained why he was able to afford a huge, fancy boat that he was famous for tossing wild parties on. I later learned that the two old guys in the club that day were, in fact, retired Mafiosi from New York who were partners with Mike Peter.

But, still, I wasn't about to be intimidated. If the Detroit Renegades couldn't stop me from doing business, neither could some geriatric wiseguys. I went back to work that afternoon and promptly forgot about the meeting and the vague threats that were made. I never heard any more about it. Mike Peter quickly became a stranger and I headed back to Detroit to take care of my core business. Charges against Mike Peter that ended up putting him in jail for a year were dropped on appeal and I never looked back.

Spinnin' Out of Control

Back at my apartment in Southfield, Michigan, the first thing on my mind, however, was what to do about my girlfriend Kim.

She was living with me in both places, and I had just kicked her out of my crib on A1A for ditching me for three days to go on an insane motorcycle holiday with some guys she'd just met. Although she was right back on stage again, I told her before I flew back that she had to get her own place or move back to Michigan. As soon as I walked into the apartment, my phone rang. Sure enough, it was Kim.

"Alan," she cried, "you've gotta let me come back. I'm sorry! I'm so sorry!"

"You say that now," I told her, "but when's the next lunatic episode gonna be? I can't live like this, Kim!"

"But Alan," she pleaded, "I'm so hot for you, honey! When are you coming back down to Lauderdale?"

"I'm coming back at the end of the week, and you're going to have to be out of my place, Kim! I'm telling you—I can't have it anymore!" Actually, I was thinking how I would love to have a little more of her. But I stuck to my guns. "So what's it going to be, Kim? Are you coming back to Michigan or are you getting yourself a place down there?"

"I'm staying here, Alan."

"What—you're staying at my place??? Is that what you're telling me?"

"It's our place, Alan! So you can just go fuck yourself!" she screamed. I held the receiver away from my ear to keep from getting a burst eardrum, and when I put the phone back to my head the line was dead.

What are you going to do? For all the passion, pleasure, and perks of being in the trade, you're guaranteed to pay with your sanity, I assure you. Still, I was only about thirty years old and willing to deal with the hassles of borderline cases like Kim for the thrill of it all. Yet I knew I had to make the call. It's one thing reading about the extreme behavior of alcoholics and addicts; living with it is a whole other story and a stripe of hell that I don't want ever to experience again.

I didn't hear from Kim for the rest of the week, and I'd busied myself with the myriad of critical details required to run multiple clubs. Honestly, with all the other girls dancing around me wherever I went, Kim faded from my mind. When I'm with someone, I am monogamous, but in those early days I was a confirmed bachelor . . . and running topless clubs practically requires some degree of "sampling," shall we say, in order to maintain quality control. What—you don't buy it? Then I guess I have to revert to the best excuse in the book: When you're running a deli, you don't have to make any excuses for having a corned beef sandwich whenever you feel like it. I'm human, and frankly, so would you.

By the end of the week, I was back on the jet from Detroit Metro to Ft. Lauderdale again. I was curious as to what was up with Kim. By not calling me, she guaranteed that I would be thinking about her. I didn't have to think long. When I opened the door to my place on A1A, it looked like a tornado had torn through. Empty pizza boxes, overflowing ashtrays and liquor bottles littered the place. The kitchen sink was filled with dishes that might have cultured anything from the bubonic plague to botulism. I could only shake my head; time to call the maid service and pony up the customary "natural disaster" premium to get the joint back in order. But first, I decided to call the locksmith and have the locks changed. I had made it perfectly clear to Kim that I'd expected her to get her own place or move back to Michigan. Things had gone too far, and I had to send her a message that she'd understand.

A few hours later the locksmith had come and gone, making quick work of changing the dead bolt on the apartment's single door. I headed for the club and the refuge of work, taking time to drop a duplicate key off to the maid service on the way. It was early evening, and another gorgeous day in paradise. When I got to the club, Kim was not there—a real relief! Ray Abruzzi told me she had worked the day shift and had left about an hour before I arrived.

"Do you know if she got herself a place, or if she's staying with one of the other girls?" I asked.

"How would I know?" Ray answered in his easygoing manner. "You know how these girls are, Alan, you never know what they're going to do next!"

"Ain't that the truth," I muttered as I flipped through the mail on my desk. Little did I know how true it would prove to be.

Not twenty minutes later, the office phone rang and I picked up. It was Kim on the other end, and she was hysterical.

"Alan," Kim sobbed, "you can't lock me out like this! Pleeeeease—Alan! You've gotta let me come back—I promise I won't do anything crazy!"

"Hey, Kim, listen to me! I've heard that before! I told you a week ago you had to get your own place or come back to Michigan . . . you gave me no choice here, you understand?"

"Alan, no! All my stuff is at the apartment—you can't do this to me!"

"I can and I am!" I retorted. "You can crash somewhere else tonight, and get your stuff in the morning, but you're not staying with me! I'll get you a hotel for tonight if you're short on cash and we can talk about it tomorrow—but that's it! That's as far as I go!"

"Goddamn you, Alan, please! Don't do this! You son-of-a-bitch!!!" she screamed as she hung up on me.

Sometimes you've just got to hold your ground. If I didn't draw the line with Kim then and there, I was only asking for trouble. She was as crazy as she was passionate, and you never knew when she would veer off into an insane direction and completely melt down on you—or disappear—or worse! I had had enough and was in no mood for more fireworks. I told the bouncers that if she tried to come back inside the club that evening that she was to be barred—no ifs, ands, or buts—and if she made trouble to call the police to remove her from the premises. It may sound harsh, but sometimes it's the only way to definitively nip trouble in the bud.

The evening passed uneventfully and pretty soon it was time for last call. It was 2:00 a.m. Ray Abruzzi and I shot the breeze as the bar staff closed out the till, and we did a final count for the night as the girls and everyone else meandered out. Soon, Ray turned to me and said, "I'm all in, Alan. See you tomorrow." I nodded, still shuffling through some liquor bills that needed to be paid the next day. I was in the mood to tidy up my desk and call it a night, maybe going out for a little breakfast before heading back to my apartment. I would have to deal with the mess until the maids were able to get in, hopefully the next day, when I would also be forced to deal with Kim and her stuff.

Five minutes later, I was all alone in the club, flicking off the last of the lights. I took a final look around to make sure I hadn't missed anything and made for the set of double doors that framed the entrance. I had just stepped outside and was in the process of putting my key into the lock when I heard the sound of a car engine racing wildly—I turned to look over my shoulder and not twenty feet away I saw two headlights bearing down on me at a high rate of speed.

"Shit! That car is coming right for me!" I thought, in a panic, as I instinctively pulled open one of the double doors that I had fortunately not had time to lock, and dashed inside. Without thinking, I scrambled deep into the club, making for the bar, as a bright red, late model Fiero, driven by none other than one Kim Boussner, plowed through the double doors and crashed violently to a stop into the steel pillar that divided both doors and supported the ceiling just inside the club's entrance. To this day I remember the sickening crunch of plastic, metal, and glass, all combining together into a deafening cacophony that lasted all of a second or two before an equally deafening silence enveloped me. I had managed to hurl myself over the top of the bar and was crouching like a scared animal, awaiting the certain fate of being squashed up against the far wall of the club had the Fiero not been stopped by one strategically placed steel pillar!

Kim, amazingly enough, was unharmed and was in the process of extricating herself from the wreckage, yelling at the top of her lungs. She was obviously intoxicated—drunk out of her mind—and I was in no mood to tangle with her. Fortunately, somebody had called the cops, and in minutes several patrol cars were on the scene. Kim was quickly handcuffed and placed in the back of one of the police cruisers, and a flatbed truck was called to winch the mangled Fiero out of the club entrance and haul it away. The impact had brought down the large lighted canopy from above the doors, and it had to be lifted off the remains of the Fiero in order to remove it.

"Do you want to press charges, Mr. Markovitz?" one of the cops asked me after I had managed to calm down enough to talk.

"Yeah, damn right I do," I said. "She was trying to kill me!"

The next day, Kim was locked up without bond, and I sat down with the Broward County prosecutor to sign the complaint. She was charged with assault with a deadly weapon, a felony rap that could have put her behind bars for years. While a case was prepared against her, she sat on ice for three weeks, calling me as often as she could to beg me to drop the charges. Maybe it was for old time's sake, maybe because I knew that Kim didn't really have a bad bone in her body—she was merely crazy from too much boozing—that I decided to drop the charges. The prosecutor was mighty pissed off at me for screwing up their case, especially after they had meticulously built it, fact by fact, witness by witness, with the endgame hanging on me alone.

My partner, Ray Abruzzi, was also furious with me for indirectly causing thousands of dollars in damage to the club by allowing my personal business to interfere with operations. We had to close down for a couple of weeks while repairs were made, and we lost a lot of money in the process. Finally, after two more weeks—five weeks in all—Kim got out of jail. I seriously hoped that she had learned her lesson and would never do anything so wacked ever again. She submitted, fortunately, to returning to Michigan, but the relationship was over. I never spoke with her or saw her again.

Sunset at the Club

Florida was never to be quite the same again, however, and it wasn't just the loss of Kim's crazy theatrics. After less than a year post-opening, the city of Ft. Lauderdale decided that it didn't want topless clubs serving alcohol and passed an ordinance prohibiting nudity and alcohol from enjoying the symbiotic relationship it had for years. The city fathers didn't give two hoots for the time-honored practice of grandfathering existing clubs under an "old" law, either, so our only choice was to pull up stakes and leave or wage a protracted and costly legal battle. Like the other half dozen or so clubs who were our competition, we decided to fight. There is supposed to be strength in numbers, and a common enemy is known for creating a united front, but it was a battle we were destined to lose.

Dade County was cool—they never fussed with their tax-paying topless clubs—but Broward County was a whole other story. Our lawyers tried everything, using arguments from freedom of expression under the First Amendment to equal protection based on like businesses in adjoining jurisdictions . . . but despite our attempts at injunctions, favorable rulings, or outright dismissals, we came up empty-handed every time. We appealed from local to district and then state courts, to the Florida Supreme Court, but it was no good. In the end, the ruling that the city of Ft. Lauderdale had the right to regulate liquor sales, and to outright prohibit booze from being poured where breasts were exposed, was upheld. We could either put tops on our dancers and become "bikini bars," or we could go out of business. Half a biscuit being better than none, we headed down the bikini highway like everyone else and watched our sales begin to slump. To try to pump up business, we had no choice but to lower drink prices to keep customers coming in. But with topless bars operating only a few miles away in Dade, the writing was on the wall.

To make a long story short, we tried every promo and gimmick there is in the bar biz, but there was no escaping what we had become—yet another bikini bar. In South Florida, let's face it, you can see all the bikinis you want down at the beach. Take along a six-pack and you've got it all. Add that to the fact that without the huge upside potential of a topless bar, the business got boring. It just wasn't much of a challenge anymore, and I thrive on challenges. Finally, around the end of 1988 we decided to pull the plug.

A Federal Case

Flash forward. It's 1989 and I get a call from my lawyer, Harold Fried, in Southfield. A couple of FBI guys have contacted him about my Florida days and want a meeting to discuss "cooperation." Interesting, I thought, wondering what it was that they wanted to talk about. Harold had assured me that they had no bone to pick with me but felt that I might be able to help them out in an ongoing investigation. I grew up watching TV shows like *Dragnet*, and have always enjoyed seeing bad guys get their comeuppance. I've always figured it's a good idea to help out law enforcement when you can, since you never know when you might need some help yourself. So, I agreed to a meeting in Southfield with my lawyer and the FBI, who, little did I know, would play a very important role in my life . . . to whom I, in fact, owe my life!

The meeting was with two Florida region FBI agents who had traveled to Detroit just to interview me. It was my first-ever experience with law enforcement at their level. I had nothing to hide, but I still couldn't imagine what they wanted to see me about. Curious as all get-out, I took my place at the table at my attorney's office in Southfield, with Harold Fried seated next to me and the Feds across the table with a nondescript manila file folder in front of them.

"Do you remember a meeting," the older of the two agents began, "that you attended in Florida at the Solid Gold Club with Mike Peter and some older gentleman?"

"Yeah, sure I do, " I said, thinking back to my strange encounter with the gravel-voiced septuagenarians a couple of years earlier.

"Here's the thing," he explained. "These guys are retired dons or capos—New York mob guys who have basically been put out to pasture in Florida. But that doesn't mean they've been sipping Chianti and playing shuffleboard. We have them on federal indictments for money-laundering, coercion, blackmail and racketeering . . . and we want you to testify against them in federal court in Florida."

"Whoa!" I exclaimed. "I'm not so sure I want to go on the record against the Mob. I don't need that kind of trouble! These guys looked at me like they could make one phone call and it's lights out!"

But the Feds can be very persuasive, I was about to discover . . . and it turns out that I wasn't going it alone.

"Look," the other agent chimed in, "we've got a hundred other parties we're tapping for testimony—you'll be one voice among many. Besides, one of the guys sitting in at that meeting was an FBI informant; he'll take most of the heat off of you."

"Then why do you need me at all?" I asked.

"Because we are taking no chances on nailing these guys. We need every scrap of evidence, every shred of corroborating testimony we can gather to solidify our case. All you have to do is point these guys out in the courtroom and answer a few simple questions. Can you handle that?"

What would you do? I agreed. "Well, OK . . . I guess it can't do much harm, can it?"

"It may do an immense amount of good," the agent answered.

Six months later, there I was, in federal court in Ft. Lauderdale. My father was there with me, and we watched, incredulously, as the two defendants in the case shuffled into the court
room—one with a cane and the second in a wheelchair with an
oxygen tank in tow. What a show. When my moment came, after
several dozen other witnesses, it was a piece of cake and over
in a matter of five minutes. Did I meet with the defendants on
or about a certain date? Yes, I did. Are those the persons with
whom you met? Yes, they are. Would I mind pointing them out
to the court? Yes, that's them right there, I said, pointing. The
disheveled defendants glowered back at me, probably thinking,
"If I were thirty years younger I would crush your head, you
punk." I got the hell out of there immediately after testifying
and never looked back. The Feds had their men and I was glad
to discharge myself of the obligation. It turns out the Feds and
I have had quite a history together, as the rest of this book will
tell. The geriatric goombahs, they're dead and gone now, part
of the tapestry of history. As for Mike Peter, he got one year
on the rap and lost his bar, even though all the charges were
later thrown out on appeal.

TYCOONS ARE MADE, NOT BORN

Nobody hands you anything in this life. You've got to go out and make your dreams happen. In the topless game, to grow, you have to constantly look for new opportunities for improvement and expansion. Owning one club in a given market is a lovely thing, but considering the unexpected kinds of things that can happen, it equates to having all one's eggs in one basket—and that's not enough baskets, in my opinion.

After plowing 350 grand into what turned out to be a big sinkhole in Florida, I had to come up with a winner. That was a big hit, equivalent to maybe twice the amount in today's dollars. On the other hand, I had recently sold my baby, The Booby Trap, for a very tidy profit—cha-ching! With BTs rocking in Dearborn I was now ready to come back to Eight Mile, and opportunity knocked with just the right property in a location that was ideal. Eight Mile had plenty of topless clubs, most of them all to the west, on the other side of the Southfield freeway that slashes north from Henry Ford's Greenfield Village in Dearborn up into the city of Southfield itself, where it turns into Southfield Road and runs up into Birmingham. If you follow Eight Mile east, past Woodward, and keep going . . . you'll come to Groesbeck Highway, which is exactly where a shuttered restaurant called Kavan's was calling my name. And this time, I was planning on going in without partners. It would feel good to really have one captain—me—in charge of the ship.

Kavan's was part of a small chain of Detroit family restaurants—burgers and booze. It was originally a Biff's, a workingman's restaurant—a handful of Formica tables, a lunch counter, and plastic laminated menus. Kavan's was more of the same. Its location was perfect for a topless club because it was on the proverbial main drag but it didn't have any residential neighborhoods nearby. If the city council could be persuaded to issue the first new cabaret license in decades, I would have an anchor on the East Side.

In researching the ownership of the property, I had discovered that it had been bought and was operated under a new name, Pal's, by two ladies who were in tight financial straits. Bad news for them, but good news for me, as it was more likely they would be happy to sell out for the right price, making everybody happy. The only fly in the ointment was the fact that the guy who actually owned the building, a guy named Gary Kotlarz, didn't want to sell . . . especially when he found out what I was planning for the location. While I was maneuvering, Kotlarz acted fast and foreclosed on the Pal's ladies, forcing them out. If I had known what was going on, I would have gone to the ladies and offered to float them while negotiating a buyout on the place. Lesson: If your competitors smell money, watch out. Your position has just been compromised. How badly compromised? Yup—he wanted to be a partner.

Kotlarz didn't want to sell or lease to me, despite my sweetening the pot a whole lot more than the location was worth as a restaurant. Kotlarz was betting on the long game, that I would be able to get the cabaret D license and turn the burger dive into a massive green generating machine. If I wanted Tycoon's to become a reality, I would have to cut Kotlarz in for a 45 percent share. I nearly choked on that one, but at least I wasn't forced to fork over several hundred thousand for the property, just a huge slice of the future cash flow. Still, it was worth it to establish the first truly high-end topless club anywhere on Detroit's east side. My only competition was a place called The Gold Door, a mile farther east on Eight Mile, now a club called Players. Kotlarz ended up getting his mitts on that location, too, but first things first. I had to secure that cabaret D license or there would be no toplessness to speak of, and hence no club.

Fortunately, there were only six or seven homes that were close by, but on the outside of the 500-foot rule for separation between adult businesses and residential housing. By talking to these neighbors, as well as others, I was able to get a majority of the homeowners to agree to go along with my plans to develop the property into a gentleman's club. I staked my reputation as a first-class operator into the bargain and reasoned that an occupied versus an abandoned property would inherently create less of an environment for crime to occur.

At the same time, I was negotiating with Gary Kotlarz for his share—what his financial responsibilities were to be besides putting the building on the table. His position was that it was up to me to get the cabaret D license and spend whatever it took to do so; until then he wasn't coughing up a nickel of his own money. I guess after foreclosing on the ladies, this fat cat was too busy digesting the killing he'd made to do anything to hold up his end. I had to throw in my half share of the building in cold, hard cash . . . but Kotlarz wanted his risk to be absolutely zero. It was either deal with him on his terms or abandon the deal. That I wasn't about to do. I can sometimes be tenacious even against my own best interests, but I know a winner when I smell one and Tycoon's was to be my brilliant encore to BTs, one way or another, whatever it took.

Turns out, Kotlarz had another partner I wasn't informed of who was in for 10 percent (making his end 55 percent) and was also pushing Kotlarz to rape me any way possible. To make a long story short, over the next year I got the club cranked up and running, and you know who had their hands out for their share. I told them, "Look, no way. I get paid back first for what I ponied up to make the place, then you start getting yours." I remembered back to my La Chambre days with Sol Milan, when I had to come up with half of every single expense as they occurred, and I wasn't about to become more of a patsy than I'd already been forced to. Always learning, I generally do not make the same mistake more than once, especially when it has been burned into me by the inevitable financial consequences of bad decision-making.

Consequently, I had yet again ended up with a partner with a controlling interest who was, at best, adversarial. Now all I had to do was get through the licensing process with the city. Because of the generally industrial nature of the area around Eight and Groesbeck, the number of neighbors I actually had to talk to was only six or seven—homeowners who would have to agree to the presence of a brand-new topless bar. At least I had it going for me that I was known for putting up gorgeous, high-end establishments. If any of the homeowners truly objected, I could always ply them with largess. In other words, cash. It turned out to be easier than I thought. Framing the argument for my new club as a great alternative to the now boarded-up, defunct hamburger joint, a dark building with weeds poking up through cracks in the parking lot, was the right approach. With activity, bright security lighting, and an enhanced police presence, I explained, the nearby homeowners would probably be safer than ever. To the credit of my new neighbors, they agreed. Plus, they were at least a quarter mile away from the property and some of them just plain old didn't care.

It was time to file a proposal with the BZA—the Board of Zoning Approval—to get a nonconforming use approved, that is, change the property from a restaurant into a club serving alcohol with the addition of a new cabaret D license. Surprisingly, the first time we went in, showed our plans for a fancy new building, and totted up the cooperation of the nearest neighbors, we got a yes vote! How often does that happen in this business? Almost never. I should have been suspicious, or superstitious, perhaps. Not a week later a hitherto unknown community group, with a name like Concerned Citizens for Clean Neighborhoods, came in with their own lawyer, who took their complaint against us back to the BZA in an attempt to reverse its decision. When that didn't happen, they went to court and got an injunction against our opening. They came up with an argument that the local community leaders and their constituents had been blindsided by us coming in under the radar. Hey, we'd gotten on the BZA's schedule, like anyone else. They just weren't looking for us, that's all. This hastily organized group, basically a neighborhood association, didn't get the decision flipped, but the judge did issue a "stay" of their call in order to study the matter further. "Further study," however, meant they could study it, or table it, for months or years and freeze us out cold.

Now I'm sweating bullets again because I'm carrying 100 percent of the weight on Tycoon's while looking toward only 45 percent of the profit after we're up—and the banks won't finance the construction or improvement of topless clubs! You come up with your own cash or you get investors or it's not happening. The only possibility was to get the matter in front of another judge. In order to do so, I had to hire another judge, an ex-judge actually, by the name of Samuel Gardner, who in private agreed with me that I'd been fucked. But don't panic, he'd advised me—I had drawn another now retired jurist who was to adjudicate my case. But the kicker is, he was running for reelection several months down the road in November. Judge Gardner puts together a sit-down with the judge and he agrees I got the shaft, and suggests he's inclined to see things my way. He politely advises me to vote in November.

By this point, I've sunk $400,000 of my own money into Tycoon's and I am pretty much tapped. If it doesn't go my way, I'm so far out on a limb that I figure I'll have to sell hamburgers for about a hundred years to make back my stake. All I can do is keep moving and get ready for a late fall opening and hope against hope. I know Tycoon's is going to raise the bar on both Booby Trap and BTs because I'd hired a fantastic new designer and builder named Ron Rea who went to town making the new club totally state-of-the-art. From the leather-upholstered, undulating, high-back booth seating that wrapped around the perimeter of the club on an elevated dais to the super-sized stage with fifty grand worth of high-tech lighting, Tycoon's was poised to knock the socks off every other club on Eight.

I thought November would never come, but it did, and with a gigantic sigh of relief, I watched my guy breeze back into office. My lawyer put in an immediate call, and we were told to cool our heels for another month. The judge pretty much conceded that he knew we were solid in our appeal, and he intended to make a favorable ruling, but wanted to wait a "respectable" amount of time before going public. I was about bust at this point, but it didn't matter—it was a colossal win. Let me be clear: I won on the merits of my case, but elected judges unfortunately have to be part judge and part politician. It is what it is, and if you want to play in the big boy's sandbox, that's the ante.

As far as my relationship with Kotlarz, that was to become sour as hell, but first, let me tell you what happened once Tycoon's got up to speed. Man, it was beautiful.

I remember, opening night in February of 1989, we were slammed silly. There's just something about the opening of a new club that brings out all the local celebs and topless club connoisseurs en masse. Maybe it's part see-and-be-seen, maybe it's the promise of an extra large helping of the finest female entertainment from not just my other clubs, stepping out for the night, but entertainers from other owners' topless clubs who can't seem to resist that intoxicating "new topless club smell"— something akin to that new-car smell we all know and love. Anyway you cut it, we must have had fifty or sixty drop-dead-gorgeous dancing girls on premise, along with luminaries such as Arthur Penthallow, the booming golden voice of Detroit's pre-eminent rock station WRIF-FM, and Wayne Fontes, the boisterous, cigar-chomping Detroit Lions coach at that time. The point was, we had the buzz. And we knew it. That intangible "something" is worth more than $100,000 a year in advertising. It builds from reputation and from word of mouth, and the only thing that can kill it, ultimately, is if you lose your license— or your dancers. And that's exactly what happened when I tried to "revolutionize" topless entertainment in the Detroit market.

Paradigm Shift

In the early days, as I have often lamented, I had to actually pay my dancers to dance. Even with a handful of girls and two shifts a day at The Booby Trap, it was easy to exceed $1,000 a day just to keep them boobies a-bouncin'. That's a helluva lot of beers and drinks, even at premium prices, just to make your nut before you can start counting a profit. The steaks and chops, as with most restaurants, are not income-producing. (Not unless you peg them at ultra-premium prices, say $59.00 for a surf-and-turf plate, such as I'm able to get at The Flight Club; even then, it's only possible if the club itself is ultra high-end.) Still, I'm not complaining about how much money I was able to generate even with the pay-your-talent model. But who could resist the temptation of a colossal paradigm shift? All I could think about was how to reduce or eliminate that massive outlay; doing so would capture a huge profit. A thousand saved is, after all, a thousand earned.

What had nudged me closer and closer to fashioning a new reality in dancer compensation were two factors. One, successfully moving dancers off the stage created a new income for them through table dancing—at a customer's table—or on a box or pedestal at their table—at first at $5 and then at $10 a dance.

The way it evolved was pure chutzpah on my part. As you may recall, at BTs the local Dearborn ordinance specified that dancers must perform on stage. But what's a stage? A stage is, by definition, an elevated platform. Nowhere in the ordinance did it say how big a stage had to be. That's what led to my quantum leap in thinking: What if you could make little stages . . .

that the dancers could actually carry with them throughout the club'? Portable stages. Eureka! I mean, why not? I had to try it. I knew of a local company that had done various types of metal work for bars and restaurants. I did a little sketch on a cocktail napkin of what looked more or less like a three-legged stool. Only I gave it four legs and specified some kind of nonskid surface on the top. I took it to the fabricator and it was agreed that they could make it out of aluminum, so that it would be both lightweight and easy to carry but also very sturdy. I had a half dozen of these things made up and took them into BTs to show them to the girls.

"You expect us to dance on that little thing?" one of the dancers said with a skeptical sneer.

"You just move around a little and keep their eyes at your hip level—hey, it's worth ten bucks for three minutes, isn't it?"

"I see your logic," she said. "Well, what the hell—I'll try it!"

"Just don't do too many shots, right?"

It was much later before the emergence of the VIP room, where customers could retreat in privacy for a more personal experience at a premium price—$20 or $25 a dance—with every penny going directly into the dancer's kitty. But even at $5 and $10 a dance, suddenly, some popular dancers were making $20–$30 an hour plus the $10–$15 an hour I was paying them, taking home up to $50 or more per hour. Some days a single dancer was taking more home than I was, with $300–$400 shifts becoming the norm.

Previously, no one cared if the dancer was making a killing. The longer you kept customers in the club, the more they drank, the more you made. Period. But to me, all that hourly cash going out was like squandering a natural resource. The more of that resource that could be devoted to keeping a club ahead of the competition, in both ambiance and amenities, would only lead to market dominance and more profits, which could again be deployed ad infinitum. Deployed as well as enjoyed.

After Tycoon's had been open for a few months, I decided it was time to implement a new model. Instead of paying the ladies up to $15 an hour to dance, I would pay $7 an hour across the board. My argument was that dancers' incomes had risen so dramatically with the advent of personal dances (not to mention the additional tips many dancers received on top of the price of the performance) that it was only fair that the club had a share of the booty. After all, the club was providing the framework—the very infrastructure!—that made their dancing profitable in the first place. This was the beginning, and even I didn't realize it at the time, of making the radical 180-degree change that would have the dancers paying the club for the privilege of making an income on the premises, not as hourly wage earners but as independent contractors. By cultivating regular customers, by learning how to sell more dances—serial dances—to each customer, by exploiting the system the club was providing to them, dancers would be able to take home incomes far in excess of an hourly wage. This is, of course, exactly what has evolved today.

But, instead of seeing my thoughtful, well-reasoned argument as an opportunity to make more money in the long run, what I had was a dancer insurrection. I thought they were going to bite my head off, chew it up, and spit it right out. Most of my dancers simply exercised their rights as Americans to work wherever they wanted—and since Tycoon's wasn't the only topless club in town, they all walked. That afternoon. Suddenly

I had a big, glitzy topless club with no topless dancers. They unionized among themselves, you might say, in the interests of teaching me a lesson. And they taught me one, all right. Not the lesson you may think: I realized that despite my shocking setback, the lure of the money from those private dances would ultimately pull them back . . . but only if I dug in and held my position. And it looked like it was going to be an expensive position to hold. In the meantime, I was looking at a pathetically empty stage and wondering how in hell I was going to pull out of it.

Fortunately, I had chosen a good day and a good time to make my announcement, a Monday afternoon. The weekend had been packed, the lunch crowd had cleared out, and I was looking at a traditionally soft week night. I could always pinch some dancers from BTs, pay 'em a little extra to fill in, but I had to be careful. If the girls who had just walked found out I was paying scale again—scale plus!—they would be even more pissed off at me. I had to explain the new deal to whatever temporaries I could scrounge up and start to improvise on my next move. But first I'd have to walk a very fine line. I knew that my striking dancers would try to go over to BTs, so I would have to preempt the move by cutting hourly pay at BTs too.

An hour later, I was off the phone with BTs and had arranged for several dancers to make the night shift. I told them the new policy, effective immediately, and agreed to front them some cash if they would work with me. If I was lucky, they would actually show up. Trying to organize topless dancers and get them to show up in a coordinated fashion was and is something akin to herding cats. In twenty-five years in this business, I've never heard a better analogy. My next call would be to one of the talent agents who specialize in recruiting girls to various clubs, for commission. These are the guys who also round up talent for amateur night competitions, as well as feeding some of the Detroit area's sundry bikini bars. Calling in some favors was sure to produce a few more dancers—enough to pull the fat out of the fire, anyway.

That Monday night worked out OK, and pulling girls from other clubs is always a decent gambit because of the old adage, a change is as good as a vacation. Fresh faces for the customers as well as the girls. What I was really sweating was that the quasi-strike of my regulars would turn into a boycott to force me to raise the hourly back to where it was. This I was determined to resist, because if I folded now, I would be perceived as weak and would be at the mercy of the talent. I had to hang on somehow.

The rest of the week was touch-and-go. A couple of the girls who came over from BTs went back, anticipating a solid weekend with their own regulars. I patched in with some more finds from the agents and worked the phone with other dancers I knew at some of the other clubs around town. Tuesday through Thursday kind of dragged by, and by the time I was looking at Friday I didn't have a clue as to whether the weekend would be a disaster or not. Word travels fast among the topless cognoscenti—dancers and customers alike—about which clubs are kicking the gong big-time and which are bleeding. When a club is hot, it tends to stay hot or get hotter and when a club hits the skids, it can mean a long, slow ride to oblivion. To be honest though, even a lazy and disinterested operator can milk a dive joint for a long, long time, just like some of those stores you see that have had "Going Out of Business" signs in the windows for years. But a top-performing club cannot be allowed to degrade, because once a club has acquired a reputation as being clapped out, you're stuck with it. Unless you plan to start over from scratch and begin pouring massive amounts of lucre into the mix.

Sure enough, the weekend sucked. Revenues were down 50 percent from average, and with a lousy half dozen dancers pacing the stage like sick cats, it was no wonder. I was beginning to think I had screwed up in a very grand manner, painting myself into a corner I would be lucky to escape from. Think, think . . . what was my exit strategy? I needed dancers, dammit, dancers who looked alive! I was in a miserable state of mind Sunday night, not being able to see the big picture . . . but I knew I had to start by getting more girls back in the club. I drove home and watched a rerun of *Bonanza*, my favorite show from childhood. Hoss was busy nursing the daughter of one of Pa's business associates. The visiting lass was bedridden with scarlet fever, or something. Hoss kept going back to the well to get cool water with which to mop her forehead. I saw a parallel with my present situation. If I could just manage to bide my time in order to let my regular dancers at Tycoon's cool off, I was sure they would come around. And once they saw that they would be making as much, or more, than under the old system . . . they would simply adapt.

Back in the club, the next day, I was reading a newspaper in my office when the fever broke, so to speak. Heather, a tall, willowy brunette with natural 36Cs who was one of my most attractive dancers, showed up unexpectedly.

"Hi, Alan!" she chirped, as if nothing nasty had transpired. "I decided to come back and see how things go with your new system. Maybe I'm a sap, but I kinda missed you."

"Yeah, sure," I joshed back, grinning. "Or maybe you had a notion Mr. X, your regular, was going to be here for lunch."

"Oh . . . is he?" she asked, innocently. "You know, he bought over $400 in dances from me last week."

"Then you'd better get dressed—or undressed—and out on the floor," I replied, trying to sound stern. I kept my nose buried in my paper and chuckled to myself as I thought that maybe, just maybe, there was a way out of the woods here.

Over the next couple of weeks, most of the departed dancers returned to Tycoon's, along with a bevy of new ones, upon hearing that things were starting to swing again. Nobody wants to miss out on a good thing. The loosely organized "strike" caused by the 50 percent reduction in hourly wages had shrunk club revenues for a few weeks, to be sure, but I was now convinced that I could soon make the final leap to dismantling the system entirely. The key was to simply bump up the price of personal, or VIP, dances and show the girls how to sell multiple dances to their customers. Then, it hit me like a bolt from the blue. Any new girls at Tycoon's, from this date forward, would have to come on board for ZERO hourly pay; I would announce to the current line-up that as of immediately we were going to a zero pay system and that would be that. Best get all of the collateral damage out of the way at once, if possible. Still, I was gambling big-time. It all came down to whether or not I could keep enough girls in the club long enough to attract a greater influx of customers.

Here I am, the self-confessed "Jewish greaseball" of Oak Park High with my bitchin' Triumph Bonneville.

My dad, still a teenager, in April of 1946 after going through Auschwitz, Mauthasen, Gusen, and Dunskirchen and being liberated only a year earlier.

My dad Max and mom Jacqueline around 1960.

Max with his sister Zdenka, one of his two sisters who survived WWII.

One of my proudest moments was giving my dad a fully restored '57 Chevy like the one he used to own, his all-time favorite car.

My mom Jacqueline when she was in her twenties.

That's me on the left and my brother Paul on the right hanging out with dad.

My dad with Sol Milan, who owned La Chambre and gave me my first break in the topless business.

My second club, BTs on Michigan Avenue in Dearborn, Michigan.

Posing with Detroit Mayor Coleman Young and Freddy Giordano, my ex-partner, who put a murder contract on my head.

This is the chimp that I "hired" to entertain at BTs first anniversary celebration. I'll never forget what a horny primate he was!

The famous "Spinner Kim" Boussner, who could spin so fast she put pro skater' to shame back in the 1980s.

My very first topless bar on Eight Mile in Detroit, The Booby Trap.

The Flight Club as it looks today . . . where I was shot in the head in 1997.

My latest, greatest creation on Eight Mile—The Penthouse Club, which opened spring of 2007.

With friends about to jet off to Houston for a bar mitzvah in my Citation III jet.

At home with Lea in Grosse Pointe, in a house originally built by the Ford family, which I have restored.

Hockey legend Wayne Gretzky is one of many sports stars I've had the pleasure of meeting.

NASCAR great Rusty Wallace mugs with me.

I got a big kick out of meeting the charismatic and entertaining Chazz Palminteri in late 2008 in Detroit while he was performing his one man show.

Two Detroit success stories—Tim Allen and me!

Here I am at Pike's Peak Raceway in Colorado getting ready to start the race.

I'll never forget my racehorse, Allie's Flash Dancer. Here I am after another win.

I met Ivana Trump at a fund-raiser in Atlantic City and found her to be a charming and cultured lady.

Yup, that's Jason Priestly and yours truly . . . can you guess which one got the most girls? He probably did.

James Caan and me in 2008.

Hanging out at Sinbad's restaurant on the Detroit river. Left to right: Alan Leaf, Robert Levy, Larry Oleinick, Richard Ovshinsky, Mark Jacobs, yours truly, and Greg Bernhardt.

Isn't she beautiful? My fiancée Lea.

Photo Section

P. 6

UNITED STATES DISTRICT COURT
EASTERN DISTRICT OF MICHIGAN
SOUTHERN DIVISION

UNITED STATES OF AMERICA,

                Plaintiff,

-vs-

D-1 FREDERICK GIORDANO,

                Defendant.

_____/

93-80897

CRIMINAL NO.

HONORABLE

VIO: 18 U.S.C. § 1958

INDICTMENT

THE GRAND JURY CHARGES:

COUNT ONE

(18 U.S.C. § 1958 -- USE OF INTERSTATE COMMERCE
FACILITIES IN THE COMMISSION OF MURDER-FOR-HIRE)

D-1 FREDERICK GIORDANO

On or about September 29, 1993, in the Eastern District of
Michigan, Southern Division, FREDERICK GIORDANO, defendant herein,
did knowingly and willfully cause another to use a facility in
interstate commerce, that is, Western Union Telegraph, from the
State of Michigan, to the State of New York, with the intent that
the murder of Alan Markovitz be committed in violation of the laws
of the State of Michigan (Section 750.316 of the Michigan Complied
Laws Annotated) as consideration for the receipt of, and as
consideration for a promise and agreement to pay, things of
pecuniary value, to wit: $12,000.

                1

EMS65.CLC

EXHIBIT

All in violatic of Title 18, United Stat. Code, Section 1958.

COUNT TWO

(18 U.S.C. § 1958 -- INTERSTATE TRAVEL IN THE
COMMISSION OF MURDER-FOR-HIRE)

D-1 FREDERICK GIORDANO

On or about October 18, 1991, in the Eastern District of Michigan, Southern Division, and elsewhere, FREDERICK GIORDANO, defendant herein, did knowingly and willfully cause another to travel in interstate commerce, that is, from the State of Massachusetts, to the State of Michigan, with the intent that the murder of Alan Markovitz be committed in violation of the laws of the State of Michigan (Section 750.316 of the Michigan Compiled Laws Annotated), as consideration for a promise and as consideration for a promise and agreement to pay, things of pecuniary value, to wit: $12,000.

All in violation of Title 18, United States Code, Section 1958.

COUNT THREE

(18 U.S.C. § 1958 -- USE OF INTERSTATE COMMERCE
FACILITIES IN THE COMMISSION OF MURDER-FOR-HIRE)

D-1 FREDERICK GIORDANO

On or about October 30, 1991, in the Eastern District of Michigan, Southern Division, FREDERICK GIORDANO, defendant herein, did knowingly and willfully cause another to use a facility in interstate commerce, that is, a telephone, from the State of Massachusetts, to the State of Michigan, with the intent that the

EMS65.CLC

2

The actual federal indictment in the case of The United States of America vs. Frederick Giordano. *At left, Freddy on the day of his arrest by the FBI outside BTs, Dearborn, Michigan.*

Photo Section

murder of Alan Markovitz be committed in violation of the laws of
the State of Michigan (Section 750.316 of the Michigan Compiled
Laws Annotated), as consideration for the receipt of, and as
consideration for a promise and agreement to pay, things of
pecuniary value, to wit: $12,000.

All in violation of Title 18, United States Code, Section
1958.

COUNT FOUR

(18 U.S.C. § 1958 -- USE OF INTERSTATE COMMERCE
FACILITIES IN THE COMMISSION OF MURDER-FOR-HIRE)

D-1 FREDERICK GIORDANO

On or about November 6, 1991, in the Eastern District of
Michigan, Southern Division, FREDERICK GIORDANO, defendant herein,
did knowingly and willfully cause another to use a facility in
interstate commerce, that is, a telephone, from the State of
Massachusetts, to the State of Michigan, with the intent that the
murder of Alan Markovitz be committed in violation of the laws of
the State of Michigan (Section 750.316 of the Michigan Compiled
Laws Annotated), as consideration for a promise and agreement to
pay, things of pecuniary value, to wit: $12,000.

All in violation of Title 18, United States Code, Section
1958.

3   EMS65.CLC

COUNT FIVE

(18 U.S.C. § 371 -- CONSPIRACY)

D-1 FREDERICK GIORDANO

1. That from on or about August 1991, and continuously thereafter, up to and including November 1991, in the Eastern District of Michigan, Southern Division, and elsewhere, FREDERICK GIORDANO, defendant herein, did knowingly and willfully combine, conspire, confederate, and agree with other persons both known and unknown, to commit an offense against the United States, to wit: to violate Section 1958 of Title 18, United States Code.

MANNER AND MEANS OF THE CONSPIRACY

2. It was a part of the conspiracy that the defendant FREDERICK GIORDANO, with the intent that the murder of Alan Markovitz be committed in violation of the laws of the State of Michigan (Section 750.316 of the Michigan Compiled Laws Annotated), and as consideration for the receipt of, things of pecuniary value, would cause another to use a facility in interstate commerce, that is, a telephone, from the State of Massachusetts, to the State of Michigan.

3. It was further a part of the conspiracy that the defendant FREDERICK GIORDANO, would cause another to travel in interstate commerce, that is, from the State of Massachusetts, to the State of Michigan, to accomplish the murder of Alan Markovitz.

EMS65.CLC

4

OVERT ACTS

4. In furtherance of the conspiracy and to effect the objects of the conspiracy, the following overt acts, among others, were committed in the Eastern District of Michigan and elsewhere:

    (a)   On or about August 1991, FREDERICK GIORDANO requested that Dean Thomas Tilotti, not named as a defendant herein, have Alan Markovitz murdered.

    (b)   On or about October 18, 1991, Alan Howard, not named as a defendant herein, travelled from the State of Massachusetts to the State of Michigan.

    (c)   On or about November 6, 1991, Dean Thomas Tilotti, defendant herein, and Alan Howard, not named as a defendant herein, had a telephone conversation.

All in violation of Title 18, United States Code, Section 371.

THIS IS A TRUE BILL

_____
FOREPERSON   8/31/93

ALAN GERSHEL
United States Attorney

_____
ERIC M. STRAUS (P38266)
Assistant United States Attorney

_____
KEITH E. CORBETT (P24602)
Chief, Organized Crime
Strike Force
Assistant United States Attorney

Dated: August 31, 1993

5   EMS65.CLC

TRUMPP CARD

The late 1980s was the era of big hair, big beautiful breasts, the big expense account, and the big deal. It was also the time when my previous experience and success had brought me to the point where I was ready to throw the dice on my biggest bet yet . . . Trumpps. It is not coincidental that the name I was set on was inspired by the mega-success of Donald Trump, who flew high and nearly drilled a hole in the earth in bankruptcy court when his Atlantic City casino holdings came close to going on the block to pull him free of nearly $1 billion in debt!

The same thing happened to me, although not to the tune of a billion bucks. Through a combination of politics, competition that was so determined to destroy me that they practically destroyed the whole topless business in Detroit, and headline-grabbing media manipulation by the authorities—not to mention police busts—I was on the verge of going bust. It's pretty sweet when your topless money machine is operating full tilt, but when somebody pulls the plug, all the oil—one's loyal patrons—drains out fast. One could almost see the headline: TOPLESS CLUB OWNER BUSTED FOR BUSTS!

But that's all hindsight. I was on a massive roll and could see nothing but blue skies ahead . . . when you're rolling, you've got to continue flat out and balls to the wall because you don't know what's coming next. What I did know was that if I could increase my share of Eight Mile I felt I could dominate the Detroit market. Since I had the cash flow, it was time to put it to use. You can only buy so many Ferraris . . . the real fun is pulling yourself up onto an unprecedented level.

When you're on the way up in the business, expansion is achieved by bankrolling yourself . . . banks don't like to finance risky ventures like restaurants, for example, and topless clubs are like poison to bankers. Too many crazies to screw up the recipe, too many authorities like the cops and the state liquor control commission to run afoul of, too many people who have access to the till and might skim the enterprise into receivership. But those same bankers, I have found, love to visit my clubs and enjoy the company of lovely ladies. I guess I can take comfort that few bankers would have the guts or the ability to borrow from their own kind, in order to open a topless club!

By early 1990, I already had my eye on the perfect location. It was another old and decrepit and shuttered topless bar called Basin Street. And it was cheap—$250,000. But the best part was that the property was zoned for two stories. The old bar was on the first floor and a dump of an apartment was on the second. By tearing out most of the second floor but keeping a mezzanine, it would be possible to dramatically open up the club and still have discreet areas up in the aeries, like some of the New York clubs. I had recently traveled to Manhattan for the first time and was mightily impressed by the interior architecture there, both in its topless establishments and in its mainstream nightclubs. I wanted something that would rival anything the Big Apple had to offer.

Meeting with my designer, Ron Rea, known worldwide for his commercial work, I told him I had a budget of one million dollars for the new club. His instructions: Max it out. Spiral staircases to the upper VIP level with a separate bar for high rollers, and a stage unlike any other. The stage, that was to be pure Vegas. I wanted a completely transparent Plexiglas shower box that rose from the center of the stage on its own hydraulics, big enough so two dancers could go inside and spray each other with hot, soapy water to the delight of one and all. And on the walls, giant Vargas Girl–type paintings. I wanted it to look like a freaking art museum of erotic and live arts when we were done. Nothing less than extreme was extreme enough for my tastes at the time, but everything had to be beautifully executed, utilizing the best materials: marble and steel, plush carpet befitting the boardroom at Morgan Stanley and massive doors that gave the impression that you were entering Fort Knox.

For the first time in the Detroit market, and unprecedented anywhere else in the country, I booked 30-second spots on ESPN and the Larry King show, as well as a massive radio blitz and outdoor campaign. Press releases about our grand opening in the fall of 1991 went to all news outlets, and I made sure all the VIP contacts we had with all the major sports teams got special invitations. It was all designed to redefine the marketing and positioning of a topless club as the ultimate mainstream entertainment. Whereas most operators want to stay under the radar, I was determined to make a full frontal assault on the public and spread the name Trumpps far and wide, establishing the moniker as the five-star brand of topless, exceeding all others.

The launch worked. In the fall of 1991, Trumpps opened to a string of limos a quarter mile long down Eight Mile, carrying everyone from Detroit TV news anchor Bill Bonds to Alto Reed, Bob Seger's sax man, to throngs of top brass from General Motors, Chrysler, and Ford, as well as many of their top-tier suppliers, friends, and sycophants.

Perhaps the best thing about opening Trumpps was that it occurred while I was enjoying a period of great peace and accommodation with the authorities. Tycoon's was operating without harassment, the Dearborn police had moved away from trying to enforce their arcane ordinance about dancers dancing "on stage," and the police were stopping into the new club to say hello, check that we had our license (I think they just wanted to get a look inside, like everybody else!), and, in some cases, to return off-duty for a drink. Of course, we have always welcomed the authorities, as it is far better to work with them than against them, and they are, after all, human. In business as in life, there is great wisdom in the axiom that it pays to take the path of least resistance.

After a few months, with the year-end holidays approaching, Trumpps was rocking like The Rolling Stones. The girls were making out like bandits, because, very quickly, private dances had evolved into a state-of-the-art profit center. I wonder if it had anything at all to do with the massive, over-stuffed couches and easy chairs that a guy would just about get lost falling into. The broad, upholstered arms were perfectly proportioned and placed so that dancers could use them for support as they swooned, leaned, and shimmied their perfumed curves within millimeters of their customers. With the bar up there on level two keeping everyone happily drinking, some girls were doing six, eight, and ten dance sets at the record high rate of $20 a dance. Entertainers were taking home $600, $800, and $1,200 a shift—one of my more popular girls at the time pulled a double shift and cleaned up north of $2,000. You can only imagine how much the club was taking in. It was nothing unusual to serve two hundred lunches alone on a Wednesday or a Thursday. Assorted executives, sports stars, business owners, celebrities, and media figures were having their secretaries call up to ten days in advance to secure reservations.

It was unreal, it was ridiculous—and it was beautiful. I had bet, along with several private backers, close to $1.3 million to get Trumpps built. With income from Tycoon's and BTs, I had pushed Trumpps into some highly rarefied air; I was making over $1 million a year. It blew my mind when I got a letter from the IRS telling me that that was "excessive executive compensation." Hey, I earned every penny of it, so blow off. Then my bookkeeper told me we had to start employing the same corporate accounting practices as Exxon, GM, and Chase Manhattan in order to maximize my tax advantages. Not a bad problem to have, I'll admit.

Everybody was making so much money at Trumpps that I was finally not only able, but compelled, to finish dismantling what I had started at Tycoon's—the old pay structure. Dancers had been taking their pay solely from private dances and tips—now was the time to do the previously unthinkable: to charge dancers to dance. When you're taking home over $500 a day, you do not want to give that up. Instantly, it becomes quite a reasonable proposition to pay the club, say, $20 per shift to work. The economics were quite delicious, considering Trumpps was running up to thirty dancers a shift . . .

30 x $20 equals $600 a day in guaranteed income for the house, two shifts makes $1,200 multiplied by seven days a week—and we're talking $36,000 a month!

In the space of only a few months, Trumpps had gotten so hot that we were sucking business away from every other bar on Eight Mile—except Tycoon's, which was far enough east of everyone else, including Trumpps, that we had a practical lock on the market. The other bars on Eight were nowhere near us in quality or execution. They ran the gamut from well-established dives (blue-collar topless bars) to more upscale establishments that, in their heydays, made great bank but had been neglected by their owners. Listen up, business students—in any enterprise, whether service or product, be on the lookout for complacency of any kind by your competition. People get fat and lazy and stop looking for the advantage, providing ample and numerous opportunities to exploit their weakness to your great profit.

This is what I have consistently done in the business, from my very first enterprise—managing Sol Milan's bar and making improvements anywhere he would let me—to modeling The Booby Trap on the up-market TGI Friday's look and feel. The businessman's market was completely neglected in favor of doing business the old way, catering to only the blue-collar end of the spectrum. Until I started moving the men's club in the direction of gentleman's clubs, you had to go across the Detroit river to Canada, where you could find very posh and tasteful establishments such as Jason's. Canada was all nude, to boot, but the ascendancy of the Detroit clubs with the birth of BTs, Tycoon's, and Trumpps practically gutted them. After 9/11, with the increased hassle of stringent border security, my clubs have done even better at countering the Canadian threat.

In the next couple of years, nobody could touch Trumpps. I had succeeded in creating the hottest club in the region, popular with expense-account executives, out-of-town conventioneers, and globe-trotting automotive executives from Germany and Japan. Rock stars, from Gene Simmons of KISS to Guns 'n' Roses to The Black Crowes to The Rolling Stones, made Trumpps a required stop when they were playing Detroit. Consequently, I began to be sought out for quotes or commentary and ended up on local radio and TV shows, as well as on the front pages of the *Detroit Free Press* and *Detroit News*. Success obviously breeds more success, and business snowballed.

As Trumpps continued to rack up record receipts, I began to fine-tune the system, which pushed profitability up even more. For example, many dancers typically arrive late for their scheduled shifts, because more money is made later in the day, following the lunch and dinner hours, when customers have had a few drinks and get into the spending mode.

Keeping in mind that quality control means having quantity control as well, I reminded the girls that the more of them that were on the floor at once, from beginning to end of shift, the more likely the customers in the club would be to select one of them for private dances. They would make more money and the club would make more money—a typical win/win. If a dancer protested that she didn't "feel like" coming in till an hour or more after her shift began, I suggested that we were both losing money and that there should be some sharing of those economic consequences. In the interests of fairness, too, the issue was becoming a sore spot. If one dancer wasn't penalized for coming in late, why should another have any incentive to show up on time? I could see how the discipline inherent in a well-oiled machine liked Trumpps would begin to break down, leading to anarchy.

In the interests of good management, I implemented a simple system. If a dancer scheduled for a shift arrived five minutes past the hour, hence an hour late, she would be charged, or fined, $10; if she were two hours late, $20, and so on. This new approach began to show dividends from the outset; girls were more often on time, and if they weren't, revenues to the club increased by a significant factor. Tipouts, as we call the collective fees paid by performers, were now $40–$50 per shift, or more. Surprisingly, many dancers took a perverse pride in being late and paying the fines because they were doing so well in just four or five hours on the floor that it was well worth some "chump change" for the privilege. Their prestige was enhanced, their position in the pecking order elevated. Who was I to complain?

So, what was driving our unbridled success—besides prime location, stellar entertainers, outrageous ambiance, buzz on the street, five-star food and drink—and a VIP area that approximated the best of an adult Disneyland and The Four Seasons blended together? In truth, it was the existence of a very simple grey area that draws a fine line between the closest proximity of female flesh to male bodies permitted by law, supercharged by the possibility of, the nuance, the obvious notion that you could reach out . . . and . . . just . . . tut, tut, tut! Why, she wouldn't permit it, would she? And what gentleman would be so bold? And most important of all, he isn't allowed to touch the dancer. And therein, dear readers, lies the rub.

The VIP area, ten years previous, was all but unknown. Without it, the grey area that began with taking dancers off the stage and putting them on "portable stages," or on or at the tables in front of their patrons, would not have had the potential to morph into the most amazing profit center that topless clubs, and their entertainers, have yet come to know. VIP rooms or areas, by themselves, however, are nothing new. Any upscale nightclub has always had a VIP room with an eye on attracting and keeping high-roller or celebrity guests segregated and specially treated. They bring cachet and prestige to the club, attracting the paying hordes that make a club become really hot.

Putting VIP rooms into the topless club was, at first, counterintuitive. The entertainment, plainly, was out front, up on the stage. That's where the action was. There could be no other action until a context—the creation of the personal dance— was brought into existence. Then came the "Aha!" moment, when suddenly the advantages of the VIP area became glaringly obvious. But back to that grey area: By its nature, it's a tricky proposition. If real contact was truly permitted in the VIP room, in exchange for money, what you would have is something awfully close to actual prostitution. That is obviously, blatantly illegal . . . and not a good idea for any club hoping not to be burned to the ground by the village elders. On the other hand you have human nature, exotic entertainers who are generally motivated and therefore willing to do a little bit more with their customers—in privacy!—to keep those $20 bills coming. The customers, of course, intoxicated by the allure of the entertainer, want more . . . contact . . . and with no one there to chaperone or, I daresay, police him . . . now we have quite a conundrum!

It is essential that the club maintain printed rules and regulations that strictly define the limits of conduct of their entertainers. It is in my best interests as an operator that I follow the rules, adhere to the letter of the law, and maintain a safe and exciting environment for customers and entertainers alike. I'd be happy to show you a copy of the handout that is posted in the dressing rooms of the dancers in my clubs, that is explained to every new dancer, which minces no words in telling it like it is. Dancers must not have contact with patrons, and if there is fleeting contact, the warm touch of a dancer's delicate hand on the suit-and-shirt-encased forearm of a gentleman, for example, it must be clearly nonsexual contact. Beyond that, we are all, as human beings, subject to that thing called human nature. Nobody is perfect. Imperfection inhabits the grey area. And life, and business, goes on as it has for thousands upon thousands of years.

Anyway, that's my story and I'm sticking to it. If you don't like topless clubs, stay the hell out of them. If you like them, visit one of mine. You're guaranteed the best experience available.

Carelessness Goeth Before a Fall

When you're on the ascent, it's easy to get sloppy—I've already alerted you about the big C of complacency as both a pitfall for the unwary and the cradle of opportunity for the competition. For two years, I had been kicking everybody's tail with Trumpps's and Tycoon's runaway success. Eight Mile wasn't the same anymore, and if you were any topless operator but me, your revenues were negatively impacted. That's competition. If someone else was eating my lunch because I hadn't mastered my game, shame on me. In business, winners and losers are defined by how much money you make and how successful you are at continuing to make it. Others don't necessarily feel that way—some among the second tier of operators in Detroit take it personally when I come out on top, and instead of ratcheting up their own performance, look for ways to try to hurt me.

The case of Ron Sweat, and his wife, Lilly, is a textbook example of what happens when ignorance, arrogance, and envy combine into a toxic form. Once pioneers in the business, opening and running a landmark of a bar called Virgo in the late 1960s and early 1970s (later becoming Bodyrock and then Cheetah's) just a mile east of Trumpps on Eight, Ron and Lilly reigned as king and queen in the topless universe. Over the course of three decades in the business, however, Ron seemed to be slipping. Some said that he was reputedly turning his brain to mush with his favorite drink, 1800 gold tequila, and I personally witnessed him drinking tequila all day long. I always knew him as a heavy drinker and recall conversations with him that bordered on the unintelligible. But hey, as long as you're taking care of business, it's your business, not mine. Around 1993, it began to get back to me via the grapevine that Ron was really out of it and that his wife Lilly was stepping in to run the bar day-to-day. Again, what did I care?

Then one day, I got a call from my attorney, Harold Fried.

"I have some news you need to hear, Alan," Harold began. "It's about Lilly Sweat."

"Yeah, what about her?"

"She's putting together a community group."

"So what?" I rejoined.

"Yeah, well, you're gonna love this. The purpose of the community group is to police the goings-on inside the gentleman's clubs."

"What the hell are you talking about? Are you serious?"

"I'm serious, Alan; she's already lined herself up with a church group, concerned citizens for morality and property values or somesuch, here on Eight Mile."

"What does she think she's going to accomplish?" I asked, incredulous.

"Apparently she's on a mission to clean up Eight Mile. Maybe she thinks she's holier than thou—out to grab some preemptive publicity as a classy operator—I'm guessing here, but that's what it looks like."

"She's nuts!" I shot back. "What should I care if she wants to talk to the media, let her take the heat. I mean, what can she do to us?"

"I hear she's put some spies out on the street with cameras to get shit on you. That's what."

I suddenly lost my voice. Man, I had to really give some thought to this one. Did Lilly Sweat have some dirt already that she was going to peddle . . . and to what end? If she had pictures from Trumpps or Tycoon's of some guy grabbing a dancer's breast, it might not look so good. But how likely, I thought, was it that she actually had some pictorial evidence? Maybe the best thing would be to just call her up on the phone. I have never been shy about talking to other operators about the business. Whether it's inquiring about another owner's property going up for sale or addressing common concerns, I have always figured that one should hold one's friends close, and one's enemies closer. Better to know what's going on and deal with it than be in the dark. A little information is often one's most powerful ally.

I picked up the phone and had Lilly on the line within five minutes.

"Lilly, it's Alan. What's going on?"

"Hi, Alan." She was nonchalant. "How you doin'?"

"Let me get right to the point, Lilly. I've been hearing some things that are a little, uh, disquieting, and I'd like to get it straight from you if there's anything to it."

"What's to what, Alan?" Jesus, I thought, she sounds like she's sopping it up like a sponge herself.

"I hear you're tight with some community activists or something, that you're forming some kind of community group to police our business."

"What . . . do you have something to worry about, Alan?" She sounded a little defensive, but she sounded a little offensive, too.

"No, I don't think I have anything to worry about," I replied. "I'm running first-class clubs in Detroit, I have a good relationship with the cops and the city. What I'm wondering about is where you're coming from here. You want to tell me what's going on or should I wait for a surprise?"

"There's no surprise, Alan. You're running a dirty business."

So she's out with it, I think. Is it jealousy, envy, or some half-cocked, booze-fueled delusion I'm addressing now?

"You mind your business, Lilly—I'll mind mine. You don't know what you're talking about!" I shot back at her. She had my hackles up. I tossed the phone back in its cradle and sunk down in my office chair. The fuck, I thought. But why worry? Business is rocking, and who the hell is going to listen to cries of immorality coming from the same stump she's selling her own lap dances from? Yeah, and *The National Enquirer* only runs stories it can verify and corroborate, just like the *New York Times*.

Busted Flat

The raid came like the Nazi blitzkrieg blasting its way into Poland, only instead of Wehrmacht shock troops and Polish regulars, it was the same Detroit cop squad that had saved my ass in the early days. But this time around, instead of targeting bikers, they'd set their sights on Trumpps when it was jam-packed with half-dressed strippers and suits and ties who were soon diving for cover. No, they didn't even knock. It was a month after my disturbing conversation with Lilly Sweat, and while the cops were wreaking havoc with the night's trade, I didn't even think to make a connection between the two.

It was peak trade, around 10:30 on a Friday night, when two dozen Detroit cops, dressed all in black with ski masks for good measure, came thundering simultaneously through the front and back doors flashing their badges with guns drawn—not just pistols, but assault rifles, too—screaming: STOP THE MUSIC!!! DETROIT POLICE!!! EVERYBODY STOP WHAT YOU'RE DOING . . . NOW!!! One of the heavily armed cops charged up into the music booth and leveled his weapon at my petrified DJ. He cut the music instantly, and the silence was deafening as the house lights were turned on—the only noise now being the barked orders from the darkly clad figures moving brusquely and deliberately throughout the club.

I emerged from my office to see what the commotion was and was almost knocked on my ass by a trio of officers shoving screaming dancers into the back of the club, into the kitchen. It was utter chaos . . . customers were trying to make their way out, but were blocked by police. I protested to the cops that I wanted to call my lawyer and I started back into my office, but I was roughly pushed into a chair and summarily told, "Shut up!"

While one contingent of cops menaced everyone into submission with Gestapo-like authority and forbidding firepower, another group was busy writing citations for lewd and lascivious conduct—apparently quite at random—to as many dancers as they could count.

I spoke up after getting over the initial shock. "What's the meaning of this?"

The nearest cop turned to look over his shoulder at me and barked, "You're closed for the night! And you're under arrest!" Turning to one of his compatriots, the cop added, "Get this fucker cuffed!" So much for professional conduct, I thought.

Meanwhile, some customers were being handcuffed—for what random reasons I couldn't fathom—while other customers were being let out of the club. Seven or eight dancers were also put into cuffs and, with the assistance of some of the departing crowd, were given jackets to cover up with as they were pushed out the front—only to discover they were being taped in the glare of videocam lights from the several news trucks out in force.

Who the hell had called the news media, I wondered. This was a real set-up, no matter how you cut it.

I was then loaded into one of two Detroit police paddy wagons, along with the dancers who had been arrested and the customers being hauled in. One of the cops was kind enough to inform me that we were being taken downtown to the Wayne County jail for booking. We were all in a state of shock and disbelief, as the entire operation had struck like a bomb going off, and in the space of less than thirty minutes we were on our way to being incarcerated.

I was speechless . . . until we got to the jail, that is, not far from the Detroit police headquarters on Beaubien street, a depressing hellhole of a joint, you may be sure. I wanted my phone call, I knew I was entitled to that, and as soon as I got to a phone I punched in the number for my man Harold Fried . . . hoping to hell he was at his home in Birmingham and would pick up.

After seven or eight rings, he answered. "Harold! Thank God, man—I'm down here in the freakin' Wayne County jail, they raided the club—you've got to get me out of here!"

"I've already heard all about it, it was just on the eleven o'clock news. There's nothing I can do about it till Monday morning. You'll just have to hold on till then and we'll get you bailed out first thing."

"Shit . . . " I sighed. "All right, Harold, first thing, man. Just get me out of here."

If you've ever been arrested for anything, and handcuffed, there's not a damned thing you can do about it. You feel impotence or you feel rage or you feel the burning pain of humiliation . . . or you feel them all. One thing's for sure, though. When you're locked up, you have plenty of time to think about what's happening to you, and all those horrible mixed emotions you'll have will surely fester. That, and you feel like you've been sleeping in a sewer by the time your lawyer gets you sprung. In my case, because I was taken in on a Friday evening (you don't suppose this was calculated, do you?) I was stuck in jail for close to forty-eight hours.

But I do have a funny story to tell. Like everyone else who got busted that night, I was put into an orange prison-style jumpsuit before being led to the cell that I'd been assigned. Along with my employees and entertainers, I was led down a long, dreary jail corridor . . . at least I'll have friendly company, I thought. But as we were herded into a cell, I was stopped at the door, the last to go in. The sheriff put his arm out in front of me and commanded, "You stop right here."

"What's this all about?" I asked.

With a real smirk, he replied, "We've got a cell just for you. Right this way."

With that, I was led a few doors down and pointed toward a slammer full of big, menacing-looking black dudes. Oh. Shit. I looked at the sheriff and he looked at me with an air of satisfaction.

"You'll be going in here," he said. "But there's a panic button there on the wall and just in case you get into any trouble . . . you can call us!"

"Thanks a lot," I mumbled. I thought to myself, unless I'm getting the shit kicked out of me or raped, I am not giving him the satisfaction of pushing that button.

I walked into the cell, and one of the black guys was eyeing me. Here it comes, I thought.

"Hey, man," he said, in a husky voice. "Don't I know you?"

"I don't know . . . where would you know me from?"

"Hey, I know you, man, you run the All Star, don't you?"

"Yeah . . . ," I said, hesitating.

"How 'bout that," he came back, breaking into a huge grin. "You know, my man James likes it over there, I had a couple beers myself and you got some fly lookin' ladies!"

"Hell yes," I said. "That we do."

"You play cards?" my new friend asked.

A couple of hours later, the same sheriff who had so sanctimoniously thrown me into what he figured would be my own personal purgatory came walking by. In the middle of a great hand of poker, I looked over my shoulder and waved at him. "Hey! How ya doin'?" I called out. "I guess I didn't need the panic button!" He didn't really look at me and kept on moving. The food sucked, but the company was fine and the cards were a real bonus.

More about the All Star later in the book, but suffice to say, opening this highly successful all-black bar on Eight Mile around the time I'd conceived Trumpps was one of the best moves I'd ever made. Especially when it came in handy as an ice breaker in the Wayne County jail!

Riding back up Woodward forty-eight hours later in Harold's Jag, I got the lowdown.

"You're being charged with running a lewd and lascivious business, Alan."

"Where the hell does that get its teeth in the law—public morals? What is this, the Puritan colony of Plymouth Rock, for Chrissake?"

"It's more than a ticket. They're going to try to prove you've violated the law not as an incidental thing, but as an ongoing enterprise . . . that you were aware and promoted . . . "

I interrupted Harold—"Promoted what? A lap dance that got a little out of hand?"

"Go home and get a shower, Alan. I need to read the charges and break it all down so we know what we're up against."

"What we're up against," I glowered, "is not gonna be good for business."

I didn't know how right I was. After I had a shower, I had to get down to Trumpps and do a damage assessment. See what could be done. I was afraid maybe they'd padlocked the place—thankfully, I was wrong—but even worse, the news trucks were still out in force, gearing up for the noon news. It was not yet eleven o'clock in the morning, barely two days after the blitzkrieg bust. I parked around back and let myself in the club. My manager, Brian Everidge, was in the office, on the phone, looking like someone just ran over his dog.

"Hey, man."

Brian hung up the phone. "Shit, Alan, I was trying to see how many dancers I could get lined up for the lunch business.

I couldn't even come up with two gals who'd commit to coming in."

"Maybe we can count on the day girls who haven't heard about the bust yet, they're on the schedule."

"Yeah, well, a few of them are up in the dressing room . . ."

"We're fucked, here, Brian, you know that?"

There wasn't anything to be done, except open up and see what would happen. So we did. We had a skeleton staff that day—doorman, bartender, a few waitresses—most of the others had been calling each other with the news, which had spread like wildfire, and were calling up to find out if we were even open. Brian had told the essential people to come in for the day shift and told everybody else we'd get back to them as soon as we had a handle on the situation.

Mostly, we had some hard-core trade, regulars who hadn't watched the news and started showing up for a lunchtime Bloody Mary and some sports TV. Monday day wasn't that busy until late afternoon, then evenings would usually cook. But with the news crews, and the noon news further freaking people out, I had little confidence that we'd be able to cruise through. I sat slumped in my leather chair, looked at Brian, looked at the floor, and said, "Do the best you can. I'm goin' home and crashing, gotta talk to Harold and get this thing sorted out." As I walked out the back door to my 'Vette, it started to rain. A pathetic, cold, March rain.

Back at my house in West Bloomfield, I watched the news in dismay. Reporters were standing in front of Trumpps and saying things that would definitely scare customers off . . . about how the Detroit cops had hauled away customers . . . now who would want to take a chance going anywhere near not only Trumpps, but also Tycoon's and BTs? It was so bad, I couldn't even leave my house for a week—that's how long the local television media milked the story. I hid out, calling in for reports from my staff. Compared to where we had been, my clubs were dead. With so much negative publicity, and so much heat, there was nothing that could be done. Nothing except to try to stay in business and find a way to hit back.

My only choice was either close my doors and call it a day or reach into my own pockets and keep paying everyone—from the parking valets up through my managers and everybody in between—bouncers, barmen and barmaids, hostess, shotgirls, coat-check girl, waitresses, insurance, utilities, food and liquor . . . thousands of bucks a week now in negative cash flow. Death becomes inevitable, and the only question is, how long will you bleed?

I had made up my mind. N.F.W. So into my pockets I went, and now I can tell you that the name of my club ultimately does not reflect an admiration for the Donald as much as it represents me playing my last card, my very own trump card: ultimately my absolute refusal to be buried by people who would like to have me out of the market so they could have what was left of it to themselves.

But if it was destruction that Lilly Sweat and her community activists wanted, it had come upon all of us now. In her greed and ignorance, Lilly had unleashed great forces beyond her and anyone else's control. All of Eight Mile was devastated, not just my clubs. When you set off a nuclear explosion, it does not discriminate. Anything in its radius will be turned to radioactive ash. And so it was. Except that in order to bring pressure to bear on the powers that be, in particular the activists activated by Sweat and company, I would seek to spread my own version of the old Cold War policy of MAD—Mutually Assured Destruction—as far and wide as I could. If we, the topless club owners, were all to suffer equally, then we would have the incentive to unite against a common enemy. Or to put it another way, if I were to be destroyed, I was going to take everyone else with me.

It turns out I didn't have to do anything except stand by and watch as the storm that the Sweats unleashed not only crushed everyone else's business on Eight Mile, but also led to their own destruction. Every club on Eight Mile was raided, including Lilly and Ron Sweat's. It's sometimes called blowback, or in street vernacular, pissing into the wind. Besides losing control of their own bar due to excessive boozing, both Ron and Lilly had been busy cooking the books, skimming cash that was never declared. On top of all that, employees and entertainers, who didn't have to be told that the owners weren't minding the store, pushed way beyond the limits of what can be gotten away with even in a topless bar. Some people evidently began selling and using drugs on the premises, and before long not only the police, but also the IRS and the DEA as well, were in on the action. Ron and Lilly were arrested and put on trial—meanwhile, their club was shut down and their cashflow reduced to nil. After running up undoubtedly huge legal bills, Ron was sentenced to eighteen months on federal charges and his wife had to wear an electronic tether. They had little choice but to unload the club at a bargain-basement price just to get out from under, and by the time the smoke cleared, the couple were too weakened to make any kind of comeback.

Ultimately, although it took the better part of two years, business slowly began to build again. Some of the "B" clubs on Eight held on because they had always eked out a living from the blue-collar trade, to which boobs are boobs and elegant surroundings an unnecessary luxury. My high-end clubs—Tycoon's, Trumpps, and BTs, had it tougher because it always costs more to provide the best surroundings, the best food, and the most beautiful dancers. Since Eight Mile took the majority of the heat and suffered the most lost business, I was lucky to have a position in Dearborn that still rocked. Even so, I was down to my last two hundred grand in savings—which doesn't sound like a bad position, but when you figure you're running overheads approaching fifty thousand a month or more just to keep your doors open, it's a very weak position to be in. No matter how successful a club may be, banks—especially twenty years ago—would not loan topless clubs any money, especially in an emergency!

It was just as business began picking up again that I began to seriously think about staking a new claim in another location—one far from Eight Mile and the misguided politics of the city of Detroit. Busting all the topless bars on Eight Mile might have scored some headlines, but it did nothing to remove the bars on the windows and doors of people living in the neighborhoods. Instead of addressing real crime in the city, the authorities did nothing but damage the livelihoods of those doing business in Detroit. I assure you, it is not the patrons of topless bars breaking into people's homes. It's hard-core criminals that take some real police work to capture. Topless bars are easy pickin's.

It was years later that my gamble on a yet another stretch of Michigan Avenue was to prove my smartest, most profitable move yet. However, there was another threat looming on the horizon . . . a deadly threat that would come from someone very, very close to me.

Other Voices: Brian Everidge, General Manager Flight Club

The first time I walked into Trumpps, I was in awe. Never really went to titty bars, maybe one or twice in Canada, where the legal drinking age is nineteen. But Trumpps, man, the place really screamed "New York!" at 140 decibels. It was 1990. I was twenty years old and had been working as a hi-lo driver in a local warehouse when budget cuts cost me my job.

But I was always pumping iron, working out, and I was good enough to get a spot with the Detroit Buccaneers playing semipro football. I was bulked up pretty good and still am. I had also bounced a little at a couple of regular bars in the Detroit suburbs. A friend from high school who was bouncing at Trumpps, which had been open just a few years at the time, told me he could probably get me in starting with one day a week. Which is how it all began.

The first time I showed up, the women were hanging from everywhere you looked, like ripe fruit waiting to be plucked from the trees. Or just fall in your lap! They were all perfect tens as far as the eye could see. And the place was jam-packed with businessmen, athletes, players. The sound system reverberated with one rockin' number to the next, deep bass subwoofers taking the sensations right down into your bones. Then you'd turn around and take a look at the stage and all of a sudden rising up out of nowhere is a clear, acrylic shower booth with a dancer inside spraying herself with a handheld shower massage and wow . . . you'd start sweating if you weren't already, in spite of the ice cold AC that kept the girls' nipples sticking out like 9mm slugs.

My first night bouncing was smooth sailing. The whole trick with being a bouncer is LOOKING like trouble, so most of the time you don't have to do much more than talk to a customer to get them to settle down and behave. But sometimes you have to ask someone to leave. Sometimes they do and sometimes they don't. And sometimes they leave and come back with a gun, which happened to me. More about that in a bit, because most of my stories at Trumpps reflect the hedonistic, heady times and wild nights that characterized the late 1980s and 1990s in the business. It was a nonstop party.

We had a lot of musicians coming through on a regular basis. Guns 'n' Roses graced us with their presence one night, arriving in a stretch limo. Slash came in first, I recall, and he was staggering . . . in fact, he walked right into me! I had to catch him and steady him on his feet.

"Dude . . . where's my paaarty?" he asked, or should I say, slurred. I pointed him in the direction of his table and he wobbled off to join his bandmates, hangers-on, and dancers who were flocking to get a piece of the exciting action.

Axl Rose was sitting outside in the limo, behind smoked glass, waiting to make his entrance. He finally did come into the club, in little better shape than Slash, and somehow managed to make his way to the secluded table in the back where we had seated the Guns 'n' Roses contingent. They were there for hours and didn't make any trouble for us, enjoying the scene and scenery like any other group of guys. Although the refrain we constantly heard from the girls was, "These fuckers are so damn cheap! They think we should be giving them private dances just because they're rock stars!"

Maybe the funniest story of this stripe occurred when The Black Crowes were in town to play a gig. The whole ragtag band showed up by limo, as usual, and when I first got a look at them by the coat check (before I knew who they were) my response was simply, "NO!" They were wearing jeans so ripped up they were on the verge of falling off, dirty tennis shoes, T-shirts that looked like they were dug out of a college dorm laundry bin . . . you get the picture. Their bodyguard asked to talk to me and insisted they were there to have a good time like anybody else, and hey, couldn't I be cool and set them up with a nice table so they could drop some bucks? OK, they were rock stars after all, and their money is green, so I finally gave them the nod and set them up in a primo spot.

The evening passed uneventfully, until the band was about to leave. Chris Robinson, their lead singer, was very upset.

"My lucky scarf!" he exclaimed, "One of your girls stole my lucky scarf! You gotta get it back, man! I can't leave without it!"

I trudged up to the dancers' dressing room and barged in. You can't be too subtle at one o'clock in the morning.

"All right!" I yelled. "Who's got the scarf that belongs to The Black Crowes? Did one of you girls take it as a souvenir?"

No, no, no, they all remonstrated. "We didn't take it!"

"Yeah, yeah, yeah," I replied as I began going through their dancer bags, trunks and suitcases. "If I find that scarf in one of these bags," I threatened, "I'm gonna be pissed!"

Sure enough, I found the scarf.

"All right Crystal, what's the story?" I interrogated.

"Those cheap fuckers wouldn't pay for a dance . . . so I took it as payment!"

"Yeah, well, that's beside the point," I said. "It's his scarf and you had no business taking it off him! Now get back out there and behave yourself!"

"Cheap fuckers!" she screamed as she stomped back out onto the floor in her four-inch platforms.

On the other hand, a tip of the hat to Bon Jovi and Ritchie Sambora, who came in one evening and really partied like royalty. I recall that they dropped $2,000 on a bottle of Louis XIV cognac and knocked back the whole thing in a sitting and they never got out of control.

One night, Gene Simmons and his tongue came in along with another guy. I always got off listening to KISS when I was a teenager cruising Telegraph and Woodward. I was looking forward to meeting him. His manager had called ahead to request a nice booth for him and we had one reserved, although the people who had been sitting there had to be asked to take another spot. Gene picked up on this while he was waiting to be seated and came striding up to me.

"Hey, why did you move those people out of there?" he demanded.

"We were just getting your booth ready for you, Mr. Simmons," I replied.

"Yeah, but those people had it first, didn't they?"

"That's right," I said. "But it's not a problem. We relocated them to a very nice table by the stage."

"Yeah," Simmons persisted, "but that's not really fair, is it? I'm not like that, you know, taking someone's booth away from them."

I was getting a little bit steamed, but I held steady to the diplomatic course, and tried one more time. "Please, why don't you sit down and relax and enjoy your stay with us," I offered, gesturing to the booth.

"You know . . ." Gene hesitated. "I really don't know if we want this booth." I was finally exasperated. "Look . . . do you want to sit here or not?" I just looked him straight in the eye.

"OK," the tongue replied. "That's fine."

Celebrities may be difficult, sometimes, but on balance, they have to be accorded good treatment, like all paying customers... and also, it's a fact that having celebs in attendance amps up the aura of your club and draws yet more clientele who are there to see as much as be seen.

The real problems, even at the finest of clubs, are the anonymous "little Napoleons," guys who have a built-in chip on their shoulder and are just looking for an excuse to go off. I had one go off on me one night in 1993. A big dude and a little dude came in together this night. The little guy was nondescript but just plain mean-looking or, rather, he looked perpetually pissed off. He had greasy hair and a pockmarked face and he bitched about EVERYTHING . . . he didn't like paying the valet, the coat check, the cover charge. He resented showing his ID, said the dress code was "fucked up," and didn't like the first two tables we showed him to.

In a matter of an hour after seating him and his buddy, we had two complaints from our staff. One was from a waitress who said he assaulted her sexually, grabbing her ass. Another came from a dancer who said he tried to stick his fingers in her crotch. Knowing that the best offense is a good defense, I gathered two of my fellow bouncers and we went to Little Napoleon's table. Standing over him, I said, "It's time to go." His friend stood up and looked to be ready to cooperate, but Little N wouldn't budge. "Sir, please stand up, you're going to have to leave the club," I told him.

Little Napoleon stood up all right, and as he did he brought his hands up under the plate of food he had been eating and flung it violently off the table, sending french fries flying everywhere. He appeared ready to start swinging, so I moved around behind him and grabbed him in a massive bear hug, pulling him down into his chair so that he couldn't swing at anybody. I then picked him up, chair and all, and walked the whole package outside and set him down on the ground. He knew he was licked at this point and wasn't fighting us, but he was screaming at the top of his lungs, "I'm coming back! I'm gonna shoot you, motherfucker! I'm gonna come back and kill your ass!" In the nightclub business, this stuff happens. You take it in stride and ninety-nine times out of a hundred, that's the end of it. If the security at a club is good, like it was at Trumpps, other patrons barely notice something's happening because we put the fire out fast, move the troublemaker off premises, and get back to business.

Three hours later, Little N becomes the one out of the hundred. My parking valet comes in and tells me he has been watching this guy circling around on Eight Mile, doing boulevard turns and cruising slowly past the club for the past fifteen minutes. I still don't figure it amounts to much, and besides, I've got a club full of customers to police.

Minutes later, when I'm told again by the valet that the same guy is still circling around past the club, I decide to deploy two bouncers—me and my buddy Bubba— outside the front doors to get a handle on things. This is where, looking back, the mind plays tricks in recollecting exactly what happened. Just as I opened the door from the vestibule to the parking lot, I saw a fuzzy image of a guy in front of me wearing one of those pith helmets that you see early African explorers wearing in the movies. I remember opening my mouth to say "Is that him?" to the valet, but before the words came out there were three very loud POPS . . . POP-POP-POP!

Bubba took one in the knee and went down screaming. He was hit first, we later figured, because I had turned away and therefore took the other two shots in my back. I ran back into the club pumped on adrenaline. "Everybody get down!" I yelled, thinking Little Napoleon was going to follow me in and keep blasting.

Suddenly I was struck by an intense burning sensation and started walking back toward the front door. The shooter had fled. I was starting to get weak in the knees and I was helped to lie down on the floor, where I lay under a blanket while waiting for 911 to arrive.

I was lucky, though. Somehow, the two slugs fired at close range from a .38 special had missed all organs and bones, even as one chunk of lead buried itself an inch from my spine. The other was removed that evening by trauma surgeons and I was discharged from the hospital within forty-eight hours. I was very fortunate and I was also blessed by being young—just twenty-three years old—so I recovered pretty fast. I took three months off from work and after the first month I partied like it was 1999 all summer long. Little Napoleon was picked up and convicted of attempted murder and given 15–25 years. As far as I know the little piece of shit is still cooling his heels inside.

Trumpps represented the first golden age of topless entertainment in Detroit, and in the country, for that matter.

ASSASSIN

Try this one on for size: It's 11:00 p.m. You walk into your girlfriend's apartment after a long, hard day (and night) at the office . . . maybe grab a cold one, flip on the tube, and kick back for the news. You're talking to your gal, not paying that much attention to the program, and, between the commercials for Wallside Windows and the hot new lease available on the latest Dodge or Ford, a teaser sticks in your mind . . . something about a murder plot and a local club owner . . . but no names . . . so stay tuned! Nothing but nothing can prepare you for what comes next.

The first words out of the news anchor's mouth were: "Today, two men, Alan Howard and Dino Tilotti, were arrested by the FBI for allegedly being part of a $12,000 murder-for-hire conspiracy to kill local topless bar owner Alan Markovitz."

"Whaaaaaat???" I said out loud. I was stunned, didn't think I'd heard right. But the anchor kept on talking, while the video clearly showed two guys I'd never heard of being hustled in handcuffs into the back of cop cars. It felt just like having a close call with an eighteen-wheeler on the freeway . . . not really hitting home until you park your car in the garage and a chill shoots up and down your spine as you realize you could've been road kill.

The phone rang and shook me out of my macabre reverie. It was my father.

"Alan, are you all right? What's going on? The man on TV just said two guys were hired to have you killed! You'd better call the police!"

"Yeah, Dad, I know—I can't believe it," I stammered. "I mean, for all I know there's someone out there waiting for me."

Now it really started sinking in. I didn't have all the facts. My mind was reeling, trying to get a handle on what was happening. I started freaking out as I flipped channels and realized that all three local stations were on the story. Should I call my lawyer first, get some advice? Stay home or go somewhere else, somewhere I don't usually go? Somewhere that someone who had been hired to kill me wouldn't know about?

Were there others out there the cops didn't know about? And how in hell did the FBI get involved in this, they're Feds! My head was spinning, trying to come to grips with what the few facts on television were telling me. None of it was making any sense . . . except that it was all too real, or perhaps surreal, to process.

What was ten times weirder was the soon-to-be-revealed truth that it was my own business partner at BTs who had set the whole thing up.

Hannah Arendt's 1963 book about the Nazi Adolf Eichmann, who was captured by the Mossad and put on trial in Jerusalem, brought the phrase "the banality of evil" into the popular lexicon. In the case of one Freddy Giordano, I would argue amending that to the "buffoon of evil," because this clown, fortunately for me, has a hard time getting anything right. It is an insult to both good Italians and to the Mob that Freddy was, and in my opinion remains, a wannabe gangster. Between his clumsy methods and the great work of the Detroit-based FBI, a possibly successful hit against yours truly was discovered and interrupted before I even had an inkling what was happening. Before Freddy knew what was happening, too!

Good police work—any law enforcement officer will tell you—involves a lot of watching, listening, and waiting around, drinking cold coffee while waiting for a hot lead. The lead that led to the arrest of Freddy Giordano came as a pure coincidence: The FBI was investigating other crimes relating to a couple of thugs named Dino Tilotti of Sterling Heights, Michigan, and Alan Howard, a drug dealer out of Massachusetts. The FBI was actively working a case involving Howard, whose phone they had tapped, and what do you suppose they picked up? Tilotti calling Howard about helping him do a job, to the tune of $12,000, to whack me. Tilotti had spent cell time in Boston with Howard and like thugs and murderers from time immemorial; one had sought out the other. Thick as thieves, right?

The one thing Tilotti didn't mention over the phone in the conversations the FBI had picked up was the name of the bag man, my partner, Freddy Giordano. But the hit was going to go down. Details were discussed on the phone across state lines between Tilotti and Howard, which automatically made it a federal rap. Then Howard made the trip to Detroit. After he arrived and met with Tilotti, the FBI began to follow them around the Detroit area, including a couple of trips to my house in West Bloomfield to case the place.

The plan was to either plant explosives in my car or to stage a robbery that would cover up my cold-blooded murder. And I knew absolutely none of this, until that night when the FBI decided they had the main part of their case neatly assembled and swooped down on the two hit men with a vengeance . . . just a week, by all reckoning, before the day they had selected for the actual hit to take place. It all played out in lurid color on the local news, and in real life, right before my eyes.

Heeding my father's advice, as well as my gut, I decided to get down to the police station in West Bloomfield, where I was living at the time. What else are you going to do? I showed up at the station around midnight and announced myself.

"How do you do, Mr. Markovitz," the desk sergeant intoned. "Can I help you?"

"Yeah, I hope so," I replied, a bit flapped by their cool professionalism. "I just heard on the television two guys were arrested today by the FBI for conspiracy to have me killed!"

"Ah, yes," the officer replied, "I believe we have heard something about that. Have a seat and someone will be with you shortly."

I figured no one was going to bust into a police station and gun me down in the next fifteen minutes, so I helped myself to a cup of cop coffee and sat down to ponder the bizarre turn of events. I couldn't figure for the life of me who could have ultimately been behind such a plot. You always hear on the crime shows it's someone close to you, someone with a motive. Who had a motive? My partner?!? Sure, Freddy could be a real jerk, but was he brazen enough, stupid enough, crazy enough to have me killed? For what?!? For my half of the business—the only motive I could come up with. But then again, Freddy did strike me as the jealous type. Jealous of my success? Jealous that I had a nicer smile than he does? My mind was racing, trying to make sense of the whole thing. I couldn't believe Freddy would actually be smart enough, or rather, stupid enough to think of something so brazen.

In a few minutes a detective came out and took me to a small, fluorescent-lit office and told me what the police knew.

"Local police assisted in their arrests, but the FBI was responsible for busting Tilotti and Howard, so they must feel they have enough on him to make federal charges stick. They'll be spending the night in downtown Detroit at the Wayne County jail pending a judge's decision on whether or not to set bail, determine if there is a flight risk or not."

"So what do you think I should do now?" I asked the detective.

"Look, Mr. Markovitz, we certainly appreciate that this is no joking matter. You do have the right to protect yourself, of course. It's up to you what precautions you choose to take, but it is probably not a bad idea for you to stay somewhere else tonight, or for the next few days, until you speak with someone at the FBI and get a better idea of what's going on."

"Sure, that makes sense. I can stay at my dad's tonight," I said.

"Give me a number where you can be reached, and I'll be sure to contact you in the event that we receive any more information, Mr. Markovitz."

I beat a hasty retreat out of the police station and slid exhausted into the seat of my Corvette. What a freaking day! I made my way to Telegraph Road, made a Michigan left, and made a beeline to my father's condo. Finally inside, kicking off my Ferragamos and treating myself to a glass of cabernet, I settled back into his plush sofa with *The Tonight Show* on the tube.

"Whaddaya think, Dad?" I said wearily. "You think I oughta go in to work tomorrow?"

"Well, the FBI got these guys, right? They're not going anywhere . . . and if there is anyone else involved, they'd be crazy to come out of the woodwork with all the cops on this thing."

"That's comforting," I said. "I suppose work might help me take my mind off this whole thing until I get it into perspective, get some more details. Maybe Freddy knows something." As bizarre as this logic chain sounds, it made a great deal of sense to me at the time. But I also took precautions. I called up my man Big Paul, who worked at BTs as a bouncer, whom I'd known for over ten years. He was a former Mister Michigan champion body builder and was built like a fire truck. He's also a real sweet guy, but in a clinch there's nobody better at your back. He'd stick with me in the coming days for backup. As my mind raced through disturbing images of someone sneaking up on me with a gun and blowing me away I got into the television show and soon the pictures in my head faded and I was coddled in dreamland. At least for a while.

The next morning over a steaming hot cup of coffee, before I could really grasp the idea of riding into BTs, even with Big Paul by my side, reality in the form of a phone call from the FBI changed my mind. A secretary from the FBI office in the downtown Detroit Federal Building was on the line. She wanted to know if I could meet a couple of federal agents in two hours at their office. I felt like I was walking into a reality TV show. I had had plenty of contact with cops, detectives, and other authority figures by this point in my topless career, and was comfortable around them. If you're running a high-profile business that serves liquor, all kinds of weird and scary characters come into the mix and you learn to deal with it a day at a time. But the FBI? Whoa. Now we're definitely kicking things up a few notches, I thought to myself.

It was at this time I met Detroit federal prosecutor Eric Straus and FBI agent Lou Fischetti. My second experience with the Feds. Lou Fischetti was the more gregarious of the two, very charismatic and with the natural ability to put you at ease as well as to draw you out. Eric Straus, on the other hand, was more reserved, more pragmatic. He was tall, trim, wore glasses and had a full head of hair, like a lawyer who could also be a soap opera star. They both made me feel that I could relax, that I could trust them, and that I was in good hands.

"Alan, we know these two guys were contracted to kill you," Straus began. "We have them both cold, on tape, a federal wire. Because your murder, as well as the $12,000 figure, was discussed across state lines, this is a federal criminal prosecution. But we need to find out who else is involved. It may be more than one person."

"Who else do you think it could be?" I asked.

"How about your business partner? It wouldn't be the first time."

"Don't you guys look for a motive?"

"Yeah," Straus said, "always. Except these two guys don't have a motive except the money. And some person, or persons, have to be behind that. Why don't we start with Freddy. There's the phone."

"So I should just call Freddy—and say what?"

"Hey, he's your partner. There's no reason you shouldn't be calling him. Let's just see what we come up with, Alan. I'll monitor the call with Lou, you'll do all the talking."

I took a deep breath and exhaled slowly. I hadn't seen Freddy for the past two or three days. It suddenly dawned on me that he had never called me, like so many other of my friends and business associates who had heard the news the night before.

The Genesis of a Plot

I have long reflected about how I came to be involved with Freddy in the first place. As you already know, my father's partnership in The Booby Trap evolved into his share of BTs. He had transcended being only my father. He was my most trusted partner and even though he was operating pretty much in the background, he definitely pulled his share of the load. He was tough, disciplined, and business-minded. Like me, he never failed to remember that for all the glitz attached to running a topless club it was serious business, "Not monkey business!" as he often put it when someone asked him about his line of work.

But the day came when my father got tired of working every day. He was sixty years old, after all, and he had worked hard his whole life, since he was a kid. Besides helping me out with my clubs, he was still hands-on a couple of days a week in his TV repair business. It was 1988. He wanted to move to a warmer climate—maybe California, maybe Florida—and I couldn't blame him. He knew I was capable and hard-nosed enough to take care of business on my own, which is always a compliment coming from one's dad. He also wanted to cash out his fair share! So, I was suddenly in the position of shopping for a new partner, someone who could pony up the six-figure cost of buying in.

When you're in topless world, it's an understatement to say you meet all kinds of people who would like to be in the business. Who doesn't want to live like a movie star, drive flashy cars, and be surrounded by throngs of admirers of the female persuasion? Yeah, yeah. It's not as easy as it looks, but maybe this far into the story you're getting the picture. The other incidental is being able to actually produce the cash and fork it over. Once you do that, you're going to be truly "bonded on," as electrical linemen say when they scale up on top of those 500,000-volt high-tension lines with the electricity still running through them. You've gotta find a partner with good judgment and good-sized cojones who you can trust at your back, not someone trying to put a bunch of slugs in your back.

Dearborn, Michigan, is a chummy little municipality in many ways. Once the powers that be know you, and you have shown that you can take care of your business without rocking the boat too much, doors begin to open. Names are dropped, friends are made, connections are established. It was in this manner that I met Freddy, who had first come into BTs like most people do. He was a customer. A regular, as a matter of fact. Once someone starts coming in often enough, and dropping money, you tend to pay a little more attention to him.

Freddy was always outgoing, even to the point of being a bit presumptuous. Let me explain. He liked to play the big shot. Looking back, he sometimes acted is if BTs was his own club, meeting and greeting other customers who were also regulars. If someone was a roller, Freddy might buy him a drink or two so he could cozy up and bask in the glow of being with a big roller. I'm not saying he wasn't likeable, because I ended up putting Freddy on staff as a fill-in floor manager, which is another word for host. You meet and greet customers, sometimes get them a better table, that kind of thing. It was good for business, and often a guy like Freddy paid off because he brought others into the club—friends, friends of friends, sort of a network approach. That's part of how the hospitality business works. But I learned the hard way that friendly does not always make a friend, and that it pays to beware of what your instincts may be trying to tell you . . . if only you listen to them.

After Freddy had been working at the club for a year or so, we had casually discussed the fact that I was looking for someone to buy out my father's share. It was common knowledge.

Freddy, always the player type who liked to impress, had told me that his aunt was an heiress to the Meisel half of what used to be the Meisel-Sysco food service company, which is now a multibillion-dollar corporation that's traded on the New York Stock Exchange. If you run one restaurant, or a thousand of them, chances are good you buy your little packets of ketchup, sweetener and sugar, napkins, cooking oil, frozen hash browns, barrels of pickles, you name it—from Sysco. There's a lot of money in that business.

Freddy told me that he could bring enough of that money to the table to make a deal happen, if the opportunity ever arose. This was the late 1980s. My dad's half share of the club came to, we figured, about $600,000. So, when Freddy told me he could get his hands on it, I was interested, as was my father. The truth is, although a topless club can be one of the most profitable businesses around, it's not that easy to find a buyer like you're selling a Chevrolet, because it's a tough business to run . . . a hands-on business. At first blush, it appeared that Freddy had both the hands-on ability as well as the cash. What he didn't know, he could learn from me. So it goes. The money came to the table, the deal was inked, and Freddy Giordano became my partner 50/50. The timing was perfect. My father was able to taste some of the fruits of his decades-long labor from the hell of Auschwitz to his retirement in Florida, the Sunshine State. May the sun always shine on you, Dad. Live and enjoy, as you richly deserve it.

It's one thing to acquire a new business partner, but how in hell do you end up with a business partner who wants to have you killed? Who is willing to pay twelve grand—is that all my life is worth?—to a couple of lowlifes who are only too happy to murder for the sticker price of a '97 Dodge Neon? It's like they say in the old war movies: you never hear (or see) the one that gets you. Except in my case the FBI got lucky—I got lucky—when they tripped on the scheme while running a wiretap on Howard and Tilotti.

The idea that your murderers are lurking nearby, hatching their nefarious plans while you go about your daily business, happily oblivious to the cancer growing near you, is perhaps more chilling than the actual violence of the act. One day you're here, the next, you're dust. A simple matter of 12K, from Freddy's standpoint, if he really were behind the hit, his payoff being half of a highly profitable topless bar. With me out of the way, Freddy would be king!

Baiting the Hook

With prosecutor Straus and agent Fischetti facing me across the Formica-topped conference table, I stared at the avocado green business telephone between us. It was the moment of truth.

"Remember, Alan," Straus reminded me. "We will be taping the conversation and hoping you can get Freddy to say something—anything—that might implicate him in the conspiracy to have you killed."

"What do you think the odds are that he's going to do that?" I asked.

"We don't know until we try. But it's happened before. Of course, he's going to deny he had anything to do with it. But you've got to play it like everything is normal. Ask him if he knows anything, has heard anything. In trying to deflect heat off himself, he may inadvertently give us something we can use."

"All right," I said. "So I just ask him if he knows who did it?"

"That's about it," Straus replied. "Are you ready?"

I picked up the phone and punched in the number of the club. The phone rang a few times and the hostess at BTs picked up. I recognized her, and said, "Hey, Debbie, it's Alan. Uh, did Freddy come in?"

"Yeah, Alan," she replied, like there was nothing at all unusual going on. "Do you want to talk to him?"

"Yeah." And just like that, Freddy was on the line.

"Hey, Alan, what's up?"

"Well, Freddy, you know . . . a lot has happened in last twenty-four hours. I'm kind of shaken . . . I mean, do you have any idea . . . do you know who did it?" This is too freaking bizarre, I thought. After a long pause, finally . . .

"No," Freddy said. "I have no idea."

I also took a long moment. "Yeah, well, I guess I'll be coming in to work later."

"Sure, I'll see you later."

"If you hear anything Freddy, you know . . . talk to anyone . . . obviously I want to know what's going on here, the cops will want to know anything I can tell them."

"Sure, Alan."

That was all he said. Our sub-sixty-second conversation was over.

As soon as I hung up the phone Lou Fischetti pumped his fist in the air and and blurted, "It's him! I know it!"

"How do you know?" I asked.

"Hell . . . I've been doing this a long time, Alan."

"That was great," Straus said. "You have to play it like every-thing is business as usual, while we make the rest of the case. Besides, we have some other information that we'd like to share with you. I think you'll soon see why we're sure we just caught a monkey by the toe."

When you catch criminals for a living, it's no lie that you develop a sixth sense about your work. Fischetti and Straus could read Freddy's manner over the phone like an open book and they knew they had a live one. They were about to reveal a lot more to me and then put together a bulletproof case against Freddy who was now my public enemy number one.

"Excuse me a moment," Straus said as he pushed away from the conference table and made for the door, "I'll be right back." I was left sitting there, somewhat stunned by the experience of talking to Freddy, with agent Fischetti.

"Alan," Fischetti said, "these guys almost always give them-selves away. This Freddy, he's no pro, he's just a player, a wan-nabe. They get their idea of being wise guys from television, while the real wise guys are playing for, well . . . for real. But guys like Freddy can even be more dangerous because they're reckless."

Straus walked back into the room and casually tossed a rum-pled piece of notebook paper on the table. "Take a look," he said. "Anything familiar there?"

I stared at the piece of paper. "Yeah, it looks like . . . a map . . . to my house!"

"Do you recognize the handwriting?

"Damn!" I exclaimed. "I'd swear . . . this looks just like Freddy's writing!"

I looked back up at Straus and he was smiling. "You think you can get us a few samples of Freddy's handwriting, Alan?"

"Would tomorrow be soon enough? I just need to get down to the club and see what's lying around . . . besides Freddy, that is."

Straus and Fischetti both laughed.

Face to Face with Evil

Going into work that afternoon ranks as one of the most twisted experiences I've ever had.

Driving down the Southfield Freeway my mind was reeling. It would be the first time I'd actually be meeting with Freddy face-to-face since I learned he had allegedly paid $12,000 to have me whacked. I have to say "allegedly." Yet here he was, free as a bird, and what—denying everything? Was there ever a clearer case of the emperor having no clothes, but having the gall to walk his bare ass down the street in front of everybody? Crime psychologists tell us that people who have committed horrendous crimes, people like O.J. Simpson, actually build up such a wall of denial in themselves that they can lie with a straight face to everyone around them . . . even though they know they are guilty.

I pushed the power window button on my 'Vette to let in some fresh air to wash the weirdness out of my thinking. Straight up, I knew it was true about Freddy, even though I didn't have a clue leading up to the arrests of Dino Tilotti and Alan Howard. Freddy was a dumb punk, in sum, and dumb punks undertake dumb schemes. Sometimes they even get away with them. But not this time. His life has been a classic case of reaping what you sow.

Now I was exiting the Southfield Freeway and heading west on Michigan Avenue, the Ford Motor Company World Head-quarters glass house on my right. Only a couple miles to BTs. I felt a light bead of sweat break out on my forehead and absent-mindedly wiped it off, fiddling with the radio to further distract myself.

Before I knew it I was pulling into the parking lot and hand-ing the keys to one of the valets.

"How you doing, Alan?" he asked.

"Fine. I'm still alive!" I chuckled.

"It's better that way, Alan," he replied.

Sure, I thought, you like working for me better than the ass-hole inside, whom I was about to face in a matter of moments. With that I ducked through the doors of the club, leaving the bright sunshine outside and entering the dim and seductive world of Dearborn's hottest topless bar.

Freddy was in the office sitting at his desk, facing my desk, reading a copy of *The Detroit News*, which ironically bore a front-page story about Howard's and Tilotti's arrests the day before. But his nose was buried in the sports section instead.

"Hey, Freddy," I said as nonchalantly as I could.

"Hey, Alan. What's up?"

The balls on this guy. But what are you going to do? What would you do? It's 50 percent my club and that means a lot of money that needs to be accounted for, and a thousand other details that need to be attended to in order to keep control. I was not about to let a third-class goombah like Freddy fuck it up because I was too afraid to walk in with my head held high and deal with the situation.

So we talked the same talk we always did. How's the lunch trade? How many girls have we got today? Did the liquor delivery show up yet? How about the proof for our newspaper ad? Business as usual.

You try acting normal to the guy who is trying to have you murdered and is still your business partner and see how comfortable you feel. Believe me, it's Welcome to Bizarro World, the full-length feature! In spite of the FBI telling me to play it cool, just like everything was normal, and wait to see if Freddy would spill, screw up, cop, whatever, I couldn't keep my mouth shut. I had to put it to him just to hear what he would say.

"So, Freddy, listen . . . I mean, I'm going to find out one way or another how this thing got put together. Did you have anything whatsoever to do with this fucking thing to have me whacked?"

What the hell did I expect him to say?

Freddy just looked at me with beady, lying eyes, ready to lay his Academy Award–winning performance on me.

"No fucking way, Alan. You're my partner. We've got a good thing going."

I just looked at him without saying a word. But I thought to myself: Way. Way, my man. I knew it in my bones. Freddy obviously did not know what I knew, all the inside info I'd gotten from the FBI. It gave me a perverse pleasure to listen to him lie while I continued to play the game.

Finally I said to Freddy, "Yeah, well, we've got a club to run." With that Freddy stuck his nose back in the sports section and I walked out on the floor to see how the afternoon was going with the business lunch crowd. I did my best to lose myself in the afternoon hubbub. If there is such a thing as the comfort of normalcy, for me it was being around shot girls, dancing girls, and lobster tail.

Half an hour later I bumped into Freddy as he was leaving the club, saying he had a few errands to run. I made a beeline for the office and started shuffling through the papers on Freddy's desk. It didn't take me long to come up with several documents that bore his handwriting. I quickly made photocopies, replaced the papers, and exited the club myself. Enough work for today, I thought.

King Fredo had fucked up. During separate and subsequent interviews with Tilotti and Howard, the FBI learned that Freddy had initially contacted Tilotti, who had roots in the Detroit area and was a night manager at a topless bar called Edjo's, on Seven Mile and Woodward, back in the 1980s. Tilotti then made the call to his old Boston cellmate, Howard, to bring him in on the hit. The map to my house that the FBI had obtained was just the icing on the cake needed for the Feds to convene a grand jury in order to put the facts together on the conspiracy. Many people don't know that a grand jury is essentially a fact-finding body and that testimony given before such a jury is not admissible at trial, though such facts and testimony can be used in constructing a case.

When Tilotti was put in front of the grand jury, he did testify that it was one Frederick Giordano who approached him and offered $12,000 for my murder. It was Tilotti who provided the map that Freddy made. And it was Tilotti who, because he was sitting in federal prison in Milan, Michigan, and unable to post bond, agreed to testify in federal court that Freddy hired him and Howard to kill me. Yessiree, Freddy was screwed. In the next several days, FBI handwriting experts would confirm that Freddy's writing samples and the map were both made by his hand, and they would add their testimony to the grand jury . . . assuring that there would be a federal trial that would nail Freddy's ass to the wall. For Tilotti's future testimony, he would be given a big break on the conspiracy charges he was facing as well as other charges pending against him. Instead of serving 12–14 years, he was looking at the possibility of daylight in four years, with time already served to be applied.

Gonzo journalist Hunter S. Thompson has been famously quoted on his rewrite of the Marine Corp slogan: He turned "When the going gets tough, the tough get going" into "When the going gets weird, the weird get going." Nothing truer could apply just before and in the immediate aftermath of Freddy's soon-to-come bust by the FBI. A couple months had passed by the time the grand jury had been convened and Tilotti had testified. The hit had been decided on. Depending on last-minute circumstances and my movements, it was to be either a bomb wired under the hood of my car or a robbery, in which I would be tied up to a chair, my home ransacked, and myself shot in the back of the head. With all this fresh information, federal charges were being drafted, along with the best part of all—the arrest of Freddy Giordano.

In the meantime, my life was a surreal smear of one day into the next, seeing Freddy every day and choking on the idea that I still had a business partner who had tried to have me killed and for all I knew may still have been trying to have me killed . . . even with federal charges about to come down on his head! Maybe his fear of being charged would drive him to it; there was no way of knowing. All I could do was assume he wouldn't try anything at the club—I didn't think he had the balls for that—and keep Big Paul close by my side. I ended up staying at my father's house for six months while everything played out. As the Feds pointed out, there could have been other players we didn't know about, so it was best to stay as under wraps as possible when not at work.

Finally, close to three months from the date of Tilotti's and Howard's busts, the FBI called me back in. The anonymous secretary only said "We have some more information for you." It was another late morning meeting at the downtown Detroit Federal Building. Again, it was with prosecutor Straus and agent Fischetti. I was warmly greeted but not told in any detail what was taking so long. When your head is on the chopping block, every day feels like a month. I was anxious as hell to find out what was happening.

"We're now certain there are no other players in this thing, Alan," Fischetti began. "It's Giordano, Tilotti, and Howard . . . and Howard is dead."

"Dead!?!" I exclaimed. "I can't say I'm too upset to hear that, but what happened?"

"Drug overdose. Looks like after he made bail he got his hands on some high-quality heroin. He was found face down in a motel on Woodward." I just shook my head in amazement.

"As far as you're concerned, Alan," Straus added, "we think it will be safe for you to return to your home at this time."

"Right, I understand. But what about Freddy?"

"We think you're going to like this next part," Straus said. "We have an arrest warrant ready to go on one Freddy Giordano."

Man, I was grinning from ear to ear. I felt like I had just won the lottery and a ten-ton weight was being lifted off my chest after being there for what seemed like years.

"So, is there anything else you need from me?"

"We need you to get on the phone and make sure Freddy is at the club, that he's going to be there long enough for us to roll on him."

"Like, right now?" I asked, almost aghast at how fast things were suddenly moving.

"We like right now just fine," Fischetti remarked in his jocular style.

With that, I found myself back on the FBI telephone once again, punching up BTs. By lucky coincidence, I had recently ordered new carpeting for the club and it was supposed to be delivered this very day. I had my words already in mind. The phone began to ring. This time, Freddy himself answered in our office.

"BTs, world's finest."

"Freddy, my man," I said sweet as pie.

"Yo, Alan!" What, was he playing hip-hop goombah today, I wondered'? He sounded like he was in a good mood. I really believe that, by this point, he believed that he was untouchable, or somehow wasn't going to get sucked in.

"Freddy, listen, we're supposed to get the new carpeting delivered today, remember?"

"Yeah, I remember. They called, said they would be bringing it after two."

"Good, good," I said. "Hey, I'm not going to be there till later, are you going to hang around and make sure they send the right stuff and get it squared away?"

"I'll be here, yeah."

"All right, great, I'll see you later." I hung up the phone and looked at Fischetti and Straus.

Straus was already picking up the phone and punching up another number. Someone answered on the other end and he only said, "It's Straus. We roll at noon." Freddy was going down.

Going Down in Dearborn

"You can go now, Alan," Fischetti informed me. "We'll take it from here. Our only recommendation is that you stay away from the club until we pick Freddy up. It'll keep things neater this way, do you understand?"

"Makes perfect sense," I replied. "What's after this?"

"We'll be in touch, don't worry. Go home and take the rest of the day off!"

"Hey, I work for a living, you know," I said with a smile. If I wore a hat I would have tipped it to these wonderful Feds as I walked out of the conference room on a cloud. I got in my car and took a nice, slow drive out of downtown all the way up Woodward to the Avenue Diner at Fourteen Mile Road, in Birmingham, a mod, fancy restaurant project I was developing. It would do me good to keep my mind off Freddy and BTs for a few hours while things, shall we say, developed. One minute I felt like a kid on Christmas morning who couldn't wait to open his presents and the next I felt like I was waiting for a bomb to go off.

About two hours later, my cell phone chirped. It was Mike, the daytime floor manager at BTs.

"Alan! You won't believe it! There's cops and news trucks all over the place—the FBI just arrested Freddy! They took him out of here in handcuffs with about a hundred cameras on him, it's like a bomb went off down here!"

"Oh, yeah?" I said, trying my best to be nonchalant. "Like a bomb went off, you said? Is it all over now?"

"Yeah, it all happened in about ten minutes, just like in the movies! They hustled Freddy out of here so fast it made my head spin!"

"Son. Of. A. Bitch," I muttered. "I guess maybe I'd better come down there."

"All right, Alan, the news guys are asking about you, I think they wanna talk to you."

"I'm sure they do, Mike, I'm sure they do," I added.

As I drove back down to pick up the Southfield Freeway for Michigan Avenue, I felt immense relief. The prospect of talking to the TV crews didn't bother me one bit, nor did the fact that it would still be weeks, or months, before Freddy went to trial. The slimeball was in custody. It was a sunny day, and I felt pretty damned fine about the abrupt acceleration of events. As I drove I called my own lawyer, Harold Fried, who had been advising me every step of the way since I began working with him at BTs.

"Harold! Guess what???" I whooped when he answered.

"Alan! What is it—what's happened?"

"The FBI just took Freddy down at the club. He's busted, man."

"That's good news. Where are you now?"

"I'm on my way to the club. There's tons of news media there, Harold."

"All right, Alan, that's fine—but don't say much, speak in generalities. Don't give anything away, got that? We want to see how this shakes out."

"I got you, Harold, don't worry. I know exactly what to say . . . or rather, what not to say."

"Good, Alan. I'll be watching the news then. I'll be available if you need me for anything, just call me on my cell."

Harold Fried, rhymes with tweed . . . a very intelligent and learned lawyer in the classic and traditional sense. When you're in my business you want someone solid who really knows how the law works, not in theory, but in actual practice. Whole lot of difference between the two, that I can guarantee you. Harold has advised me in many of the aspects of criminal as well as business law, and when tough issues are on the table he knows what to do, or whom to call in as a specialist, depending on the matter at hand. They say don't trust a lawyer, instead trust the man to do what the man has indicated he will do from past experience. Harold has proved to be a man who is a lawyer that I can trust. I intended to follow his advice to the letter.

When I hit Michigan Avenue from the Southfield Freeway and turned west toward BTs, I have to admit I had a few butterflies. But I was pumped. To me, it was like Terminix had just eliminated a rat problem and I was going to do the final inspection. When I rolled up to the club, the entrance to the parking lot was jammed with satellite vans from the three major TV news channels in Detroit—2, 4, and 7. There were also newspaper reporters and sound and camera guys milling around and as soon as I pulled in by the front doors they were all jockeying for position.

I left my car with the valet and walked quickly inside to talk to my manager, Mike. I wanted to know if there were any cops or FBI who needed to see me first, and after I determined that that wasn't the case, I had Mike go outside to inform the media I would be willing to come back outside in five to talk. It turns out there wasn't that much to say. Besides, the real story and the footage that was going to be looped over and over the rest of the news cycle was Freddy getting led out of the club in handcuffs by federal agents in their trademark nylon jackets, with "FBI" in foot-tall letters on the back. Gee, I wonder who called the news media and gave them enough time to get there just before the Feds swooped in? As opposed to the horror of getting raided by the cops and having the media gang up on me, this was one time I was glad to see them!

They shoved their mikes at me and asked the typical questions: Did you and your partner Freddy Giordano have an ongoing feud or dispute that led to his arrest? No, I replied, it had been business as usual. Did you know there was a contract out on your life? It's news to me! I don't have all the facts yet, I told them. I don't know any more than you guys know. Did you hear the FBI read their charges against Freddy? Listen, I just got here . . . and I have a lot of questions myself, let me tell you! As a matter of fact, that is pretty much all of what I said. When I spoke with my attorney later, he said I had spoken well, just like a lawyer.

As expected, the media glommed onto the most obvious and sensational headline—that Freddy was arrested for conspiracy in hiring a couple of hit men to kill me. The facts are a bit more convoluted. The FBI had enough evidence to arrest Freddy for the conspiracy, but the details weren't all that clear to anyone outside the case. Now, the FBI needed to get all the fine points ironed out, question Freddy, find out exactly the sequence of the conspiracy, track the money, and get all their ducks in a row. In short, they needed the rest of the details to make their case. With Tilotti on ice, it was time to start squeezing Freddy. The case had to be consolidated, solidified.

Back to the banality of evil. These kinds of cases have to be played out a day at a time, and even with a seeming lock on Freddy with Tilotti's promised testimony, it ain't over till the fat lady sings. A couple of days after his arrest, Freddy got himself a slick high-profile lawyer by the name of William E. Bufalino II. He made $200,000 bail and was, of all places, not only back on the street but back in the very same office we shared as partners at BTs.

This Bufalino, I have to say, was good. Freddy could afford him, after all, because he was making a lot of money at BTs. Now his money was going to work for him. I, on the other hand, had the resources of the United States Government and the federal prosecutor on my side of the aisle. But Bufalino, he comes from a highly adapted gene pool. His old man used to lawyer for Jimmy Hoffa. Another family member, Russell Bufalino (not a lawyer) took over the northeast Pennsylvania mob from one Joe Barbaro, who was a Philly boss from 1940 to 1959. It was at his home in 1956 that the most famous mob convention of modern times took place . . . and was raided by the very same FBI that was now helping me. Among those who hoofed it out when the G-men knocked were the likes of Carlo Gambino, Paul Castellano, Joe Columbo, Vito Genovese, Sam Giancana . . . you get the idea. All guys that Freddy idolized, I am sure, but never quite lived up to. I mean, hey, he couldn't even get a hit on his own business partner right, could he?

Jump ahead another week. Freddy posts 200K and walks out, awaiting trial. Where else does he go, besides the club? Just like an alcoholic uncle who is hiding bottles of booze all over the house and is obviously smashed by noon, you ask him, "Unc, are you drunk?"

He says: "Drunk? Oh, nooo—hic—I'm not drunk! What ever gave you that idea?"

Then he falls on his face and you begin to wonder if you are losing your own mind. By keeping Unc around the house, that is. But your uncle owns half your home, in this case, so it's not so easy as all that.

I'm now back at the club again (someone has to run the place, right?). A few days later, after Freddy has been formally charged with murder for hire, in walks the lying conspirator himself. I am seething. I know that I have been told by my lawyer, by the FBI, by my father, my girlfriend, and my own common sense to simply play it straight and let the wheels of justice slowly grind Freddy into a lifeless pulp. But I can't. I can't do it.

I was sitting at the desk doing some paperwork when Freddy came strolling in looking like the cat who ate the canary. The prick was actually smiling. I'd smile too if I had just gotten bailed out of the Wayne County jail a few days earlier—sunshine is ten times brighter when it has been denied you for even a brief period. He stopped a few feet away from me at the corner of my desk and just looked at me.

"Fuck you!" I spat the words at him. I would have liked to spit right in his face at that moment. Freddy appeared a bit dumbstruck, just stared at me for a long couple of seconds.

"It wasn't me!" Freddy exclaimed.

"Yeah . . . right," I mumbled as I turned my attention back to my paperwork.

Like a Shakespearean tragic comedy (not one of William's best, I might add), so began a long, strange détente where one party knew he was the lying scumbag he really is and the other party knew he was the lying scumbag he really is and both parties were forced to pretend everything was hunky-dory and business-as-usual because in the United States of America we are all innocent until proven guilty in a court of law. Which normally is a wonderful thing, unless you're me. Or you're a defense attorney, let's say, whose client has raped a 12-year-old girl or something equally heinous, and you happen to know he did it but you choose to defend him anyway.

In my case, I was determined to defend my half of BTs, as well as myself, from Freddy and his greaseball ambitions to remove me by violent proxy. If it meant living in some kind of loopy real-life David Lynch movie, so be it. Running a topless club acclimates one to the mundane, the ugly, and the bizarre rituals and characters that inhabit the world behind the glitzy stage curtain.

Weeks flew by. I heard nothing from the FBI, or from anyone else, and working with Freddy became almost normal, if you consider living in Bizarro World normal, that is. Neither one of us mentioned a thing while we waited for the other shoe to inevitably drop. What was there to say, really? It was a standoff, the business had to be run, and we were both more consumed than ever with keeping BTs humming. All the publicity that had come out following the arrests of Howard, Tilotti, and Freddy had actually caused a spike in business. We were getting slammed both night and day. I think that, in addition to being the hottest topless club on Michigan Avenue, we had the added distinction of being the newest tourist attraction! All the regulars at the club had some juicy tabloid-style gossip to share, and I was greeted warmly by one and all as the cat with nine lives.

Freddy, on the other hand, seemed to truly revel in his newfound notoriety. I believe that he fancied himself as some sort of untouchable, a Detroit knockoff version of New York mob boss John Gotti, who was nicknamed the "Teflon Don." As co-owner of BTs, Freddy played his role as the cock o' the walk to the hilt. It seemed the longer we both maintained the fiction of normalcy around the club, the more he seemed to believe himself to be totally innocent of the charges that were filed against him by the Feds.

Throughout all this, however, I still had my other clubs to run. You'll recall from the previous chapter that my latest endeavor at empire expansion, Trumpps, was up and running and setting new revenue records from the git. Freddy had it

burned into his bent head that because we were equal partners in BTs, he should have automatically received the same
arrangement when I decided Trumpps was a go. But the fact
is, partnership in one club or project does not imply assumed
partnership in another. Yet even with a murder-for-hire rap
hanging on him, Freddy persisted in pestering me for his share
of Trumpps, which I obviously had no intention of giving up
to him. Maybe, in his contorted thinking, to continue to pester
me for a slice of my action somehow proved that the FBI case
against him was, in fact, fiction! In reality, Freddy hadn't liked
being rebuffed from a partnership at Trumpps. He felt I owed
it to him.

The funny thing is, until the murder plot came to light, I had
been prepared to cut Freddy in at a compromise of 20 percent
of Trumpps under the theory that I would rather compromise
than fight. In Sun Tzu's *The Art of War*, the best way to win the
war is not to go to war at all. That was my philosophy. Freddy
could have been sitting real pretty, but he blew it when it was in
his very hands.

Now, all bets were off. At long last I got another call from
federal prosecutor, Eric Straus. We finally had a trial date. It
was time to put the cockroach, Freddy, squarely under the spot-
light and convict him for conspiring and funding my murder by
Dino Tilotti and Alan Howard.

In the meantime, of course, it was business as "delusional."
The only parallel I can offer up is the O.J. Simpson reality warp:
Can anyone in their right mind possibly believe he didn't murder Nicole Brown Simpson and Ron Goldman in cold freaking
blood? Especially now that the world has been given the Rupert
Murdoch–financed story *If I Did It?* If you saw the proposed
cover design for that book, you will note that the word *If* is a

different color from the words *I Did It*, so at a glance all you really see is *I Did It*. Brilliant marketing.

On days when I felt I could get away with it, I stayed out of BTs and let my other managers run the place. But bottom line, it was my club after all, and I was not abdicating just because Freddy owned half the loaf. I was ready to stand on my head, if necessary, until justice was served. It would be almost six whole months until the trial date rolled around. Behind the scenes, however, Freddy's lawyer William Bufalino was keeping busy.

With Alan Howard dead of a drug overdose, the FBI's case hinged on their wiretap transcripts between Tilotti and Howard, physical evidence in the form of the map Freddy drew to my house (which was obtained from Tilotti), and most importantly, Tilotti's testimony itself. But Tilotti had visitors in the federal pen in Milan. Bufalino, I later learned, was one of them. Acting on Freddy's behalf, he apparently had a very interesting conversation with Dino Tilotti. On top of that, something juicy had to have been put on the table by Bufalino, because it's the only possible explanation for what happened next.

Crime & No Punishment

Federal Court, Detroit, Michigan. The payoff. It's time to nail Freddy. Eric Straus is there, along with FBI agent Fischetti. I'm sitting behind them on the right side of the courtroom. On the other side sits Freddy with his attorney, William E. Bufalino II. The jury of twelve has been seated. There is a constant, low murmur in the court. Straus has assured me that Freddy is as good as in the bag, as Dino Tilotti is present and willing to to sing, to testify, to elocute that, in point of fact, one Freddy Giordano ("That's him sitting right there, your honor!") agreed to pay $12,000 to secure my murder. Conspiracy to commit murder. It's practically just a formality! "Let's get on with it," I think as I nervously hunch over and tap my foot. My father has come to the proceedings with me to see these worms put on the hook. The Feds will methodically make their case over the course of the next three days. Deliberately, forcefully, finally . . . Freddy will be convicted. I have no doubt of the outcome.

The bailiff walks past the bench and calls the court to order. A few whacks of the gavel just like on TV.

"The court is now in session . . . all present will now stand!"

In comes the judge, an imposing, somber and dignified figure in his sweeping black judicial robe, ascending to the bench.

"All please be seated," he says. The bailiff hands the gavel over to him and, not unlike a schoolteacher, the judge begins by asking if all parties pursuant to the case are present and prepared to begin.

After a few "yes your honors" the judge looks toward the prosecution and simply adds, "Present your case."

Eric Straus, who is prosecuting, stands.

"Your honor, may it please the court," Straus began. "The prosecution is prepared to present evidence, and testimony, that will prove beyond any reasonable doubt that Frederick Giordano, now seated in this courtroom, engaged in conspiracy to commit murder and offered the sum of $12,000 to the party named by this prosecution to secure this murder, who will testify to the very same."

As Straus calmly and slowly paced in front of the jury box, he continued. "Because, as the wiretap evidence we will present will show, this conspiracy to commit murder was conducted across state lines . . . it is a federal offense, with federal penalties attending to your conviction, based on the sum of the facts and evidence in this trial."

No doubt about it, Straus was laying out the case like a pro. I was impressed. We had the goods and it was only a matter of presenting the facts clearly to the jury. They would have to convict!

It was Bufalino's turn to make his opening statement. "Ladies and gentleman of the jury," he started. "I intend to prove to you that my client, Frederick Giordano, who is the partner of Alan Markovitz in one of Michigan's most successful adult entertainment venues, to wit, BTs located in Dearborn, Michigan, had neither the incentive nor the motive to enter into a contractual agreement to have Mr. Markovitz murdered!"

It's what I had expected to hear; Straus and Fischetti had prepared me for this type of defense. It was Bufalino's job to take whatever he could, any scrap of plausible belief, and turn it into as much reasonable doubt as he could get away with.

"Furthermore," he continued, "I will show you that the prosecution is lacking, in plain fact, the testimony as well as the evidence they need in this case. Therefore, I will prove to you beyond a shadow of a doubt that the prosecution has no case . . . and you will have no other choice but to acquit Mr. Giordano of all charges against him!"

Bufalino was good, I had to hand it to him. I am sure Freddy was paying no less than fifty or a hundred grand for this defense. What I didn't know, and nobody knew at the time, was that Bufalino had a big ace up his sleeve. And that when he played it, we would all be sitting with our jaws on the floor.

The rest of the afternoon that first day consisted of the rather formal presentation of the wiretap transcripts and testimony as to the authentication of the tapes of Howard's and

Tilotti's conversations. All the procedural stuff takes a lot longer than you would believe from watching *Law and Order*, let me tell you. Same thing with the introduction of the hand-drawn map that Freddy had provided Tilotti and Howard. You have to get your handwriting expert qualified, put that across to the jury, get it all down in the transcripts, cross every "t" and dot every "i" to minimize the possibility that a crafty defense will get an appeal based on some arcane procedural error.

It was all tedious but necessary. I knew from experience that if you want to make something really fly, you have to build it right. From where I was seated, behind and to the right of Freddy, I noted that slimeballs don't like looking over their shoulders at their business partners whom they have hired someone to whack . . . especially when the whack doesn't go down and all the parties end up in the principal's office. Despite being impressed with Bufalino's opening, I remained confident of the final results of the trial.

It was four o'clock in the afternoon. As my mind drifted on the problems and daydreams of everyday life, I heard a voice cut through the stuffy atmosphere of the court room. It was the judge.

"We will adjourn until tomorrow morning, nine o'clock." Just like that.

Filing out of the room, Straus clapped his arm across my shoulders and reassured me. "We're right on track, Alan. Tomorrow we'll finish up the rest of the procedural stuff and begin calling witnesses, starting with our wiretap evidence with Lou. Then, we'll get Freddy up on the stand so we can grill him over the map. After that, we'll go to the main act, Dino Tilotti."

"And put the last nail in Freddy's coffin."

"That's the general idea," Straus replied.

Day two went pretty much how it was supposed to. Things were becoming a lot more interesting, too. By early afternoon, the evidentiary phase was in the rear view and it was time to put the pedal to the metal. I was even allowing myself to get excited. I wanted to get a taste of some blood, Freddy's blood, by proxy of the federal prosecution. They wanted it as badly as I did. There is a great truth in the dedication of the guys in the white hats; they do want justice to be served. It is what they live for. They see better than the rest of us just how much the criminals and sickos of the world get away with, and it makes them that much more determined to strike a blow for all of us on the right side of the law.

At last, it was time to call Freddy to the witness stand. But not for the grand finale, by any means. That was what Tilotti was for; the Feds were saving the best for last. The idea now was to begin to tack Freddy's hide down inch by inch.

"The prosecution now calls Frederick Giordano."

I watched as Freddy slowly, and with visible discomfort, rose and shuffled to the witness chair. He's not a big man, and with his pronounced brow and dark, dense curly hair, I could not help but picture him as a Neanderthal in a cheap suit. Not that his suit was cheap. It was the incongruity of seeing Freddy attempting to look presentable that amused me and disgusted me simultaneously.

Straus now introduced the map into evidence, holding it high above his head in a dramatic fashion as he strode forward to address the witness. "I now present to you, Mr. Giordano, a hand-drawn map that was obtained from one Dino Tilotti, who has testified that this is the very same map that you personally handed to him shortly after his arrival in Detroit. Do you recognize this map?"

Freddy was stuck between perjuring himself by lying about the map . . . or admitting that it was made by him. Of course, making a map to your business partner's house doesn't prove anything by itself, that is. A point that Bufalino would hammer home forcefully to the jury. Perhaps Bufalino had instructed Freddy to admit it was his . . . what good defense attorney wouldn't?

"Yeah, I drew it," Freddy admitted.

"Did you draw it with a specific purpose in mind?" Straus riposted.

"Yeah. To show how you get to Alan's house."

"And for what reason would you draw a map showing directions to the home of Alan Markovitz?"

Freddy was squirming.

"To show someone how to get there!"

"Did you draw this map for someone named Dino Tilotti?" Straus shot back.

"I don't remember," Freddy replied.

"That will be all, your honor."

That's how Freddy finished up with Straus. The classic "I don't remember" is foolproof, on one hand. It has been used successfully by many other witnesses in countless trials where there was sufficient obscurity of general evidence to permit them to slide. But in cases where there is enough supplementary evidence or conflicting testimony, "I don't remember" looks like what it really is: a dodge, a flat-out gambit to evade justice while generally looking guiltier than ever. But where the burden of reasonable doubt exists, it is often enough of a play to succeed.

Yet another day had passed. The judge had adjourned with the conclusion of Bufalino's cross of Freddy, which as we had expected had been perfunctory. The only point Bufalino had to make was that nothing is proved by the existence of a map that could have been drawn days, weeks, months, or even years earlier. That Tilotti had the map was significant only insofar as it could be proved that Freddy hired him to kill me. What the prosecution did not have was a tape of Freddy making an offer, or even having a conversation of any kind with Tilotti. Someone else could have given that map to Tilotti. Maybe someone who wanted to rub Freddy's face in the shit, for all anyone knew, which Bufalino made sure to impress upon the jury. Everything was now hanging on Tilotti's testimony the next day.

Bada bing, bada boom. It was supposed to be an easy one, right? A slam dunk. I mean, a blind man could stuff this one through and still have time to eat a grilled cheese sandwich before the buzzer! But Freddy was neither blind, nor without the means to hire an excellent defense attorney. And everything in life has a strange way of taking a tortured turn when you least expect it.

It was the big day, day three, time for Tilotti to talk. There was a palpable sense of drama in the courtroom. The federal prosecution was moving in for the kill. Freddy looked to be stranded by his own stupidity, as well as ignored by even his own family. Throughout the trial no one, except his brother who came for just one day, showed. I was about to savor the trump card of justice served . . . and so was the FBI.

At last, the moment came. Eric Straus announced, "The prosecution now calls Dino Tilotti to the stand." I note that Tilotti seems to have just a bit of a swagger to his walk as he approaches the bench and takes his seat. Once seated, he lifts his chin and seems to look down his nose at Straus and the bailiff, as he is sworn in.

"Place your left hand on the book and raise your right hand," the bailiff says. "Do you swear to tell the truth, the whole truth, and nothing but the truth, so help you God?"

"Yeah," Tilotti says. "I do."

Straus moves in close. He is facing Tilotti. The courtroom is dead quiet.

"Mr. Tilotti, you have heard the recorded evidence of your conversations with Alan Howard regarding your intention to murder Alan Markovitz for the sum of $12,000, have you not?"

"Yeah."

"And, you freely admit now, to this court of law, that it is, in fact, your voice on those tapes discussing this murder-for-hire, do you not?"

"Yeah, I do." The moment of truth.

"Now, Mr. Tilotti," Straus says very slowly and carefully, while turning to point directly at Freddy Giordano, "is that the man . . . Frederick Giordano . . . to whom I am now pointing, who hired you to murder Alan Markovitz?"

Tilotti looks at Straus, then he looks at Freddy. Then, he seems only to look vacantly out onto the gallery of the court room. And then, nothing . . . Tilotti says nothing. Three seconds, five seconds, ten seconds tick by like an eternity. The judge turns to Tilotti.

"Mr. Tilotti!" the judge demands, "you are to answer the question!"

But Tilotti is mute. He is not talking. He not going to talk. We all watch in horror as Tilotti, in his stone silence, destroys everything the Feds have put together. Just by closing his yap.

The court bursts into a din. Straus whirls around to look at Bufalino, who is sitting at the defense table grinning. The judge grabs his gavel and smacks it repeatedly on the bench. He knows it's all out of his control, anyone's control at this point, except Tilotti's. The hubbub in the court continues, with the judge whacking his gavel ever more loudly. "Order in the court! Order in the court!" the judge commands, fruitlessly. There is nothing more to be done. Tilotti is sitting there like a brass monkey, dumb as a fence post.

"Court will be adjourned until further notice!" And with a final strike with his gavel, the judge gets up and quickly withdraws to his chambers. Straus is now turning to face me, walking in my direction.

"What happens now?" I ask. "What just happened?"

"You know what happened, Tilotti went mute, that's it! We're probably looking at a mistrial. Without Tilotti we're sunk. I'm sorry Alan, no one anticipated this."

I slumped back into the polished wood bench, blown away by what had been a slam dunk, now turned to shit in a matter of moments. Bufalino had already exited the court room with Freddy. I turned to my left just in time to see Tilotti being led from the stand. As he passed me I got a good look at the scumbag. He turned his head toward me. He had a big, fat smirk on his face.

JUSTICE REDUX/HIT 'EM IN THE WALLET

Straus and Fischetti were sympathetic . . . and pissed. They had egg all over their faces. A case they had worked many long months to put together was now in tatters. Worst of all, Freddy, the piece of garbage who had orchestrated everything, had walked out of the court, still presumed innocent under the law! As we stood in the hallway outside the courtroom, we discussed what came next.

"The only thing we can hope for is to try to flip Tilotti a second time," Straus explained. "But that doesn't look good. Someone must have gotten to him and put something pretty sweet on the table for him to dummy up like that."

"Yeah," Fischetti chimed in. "And we have a pretty good idea who. We think Bufalino put the fix in. There's nobody else who was in the position to be a go-between for Giordano and Tilotti, plus Bufalino's got client confidentiality."

"You mean he could've passed an offer from Freddy to Tilotti while he was sitting in Milan?"

"It's entirely plausible," Straus said. "We'd have to look at visitor records."

"So where do we go from here?" I asked.

"Go home, Alan. We'll let you know what the next step is. All I can tell you is, we're not giving up on either flipping Tilotti for real or making him pay for pulling this cute little stunt. There are other federal penalties we can hit him with, and we'll use whatever we can until we either nail him . . . "

"Or hell freezes over," I chipped in.

"Either way, he's ours. They're both ours. It's just a matter of time."

I wished I had shared the pragmatic optimism of the FBI. But one thing was for sure—when you fuck with the Feds, they don't forget about it and they do not get over it. Neither would I. In a daze, I left the court that day with only two certainties. One was that somehow or other I was going to legally rid myself of the large vermin in my own establishment. Two, was that I was going to have to deal with the vermin face-to-face until I could achieve my primary objective.

Twenty-four hours later I was back at BTs. Freddy was sitting at his desk with his nose back in the papers, like usual. As I walked into the office, I was unable to contain my fury. The instant he looked up, I erupted. "Fuck you!!!" I spat.

"It wasn't me!" Freddy retorted.

"Fuck you anyway, whaddaya mean it wasn't you?!? Who the fuck was it then???"

Freddy rose up from his chair and slapped the newspaper onto his desk. "Maybe those guys wanted to get rid of you so they could buy your share of the bar! Maybe they thought I'd make a great partner with you out of the way!" Creeps and criminals invariably seem to have a highly distorted way of seeing the world in order to justify their own evil or megalomaniacal tendencies. Freddy was, and is, no exception.

"Yeah, well, I know one thing, Freddy," I shot back. "I know I'd make a great partner for BTs with you out of the way!"

"What the hell are you saying, Alan?"

"Find a fucking buyer for your share, that's what! I want you gone, I don't care what it takes."

I had never meant anything more in my life, and when I set my mind to something, I can and will move heaven and earth until I achieve my objective. Burning, fervent desire and commitment to a specific course of action and a well-defined objective are what the positive thinking crowd have been writing about for years. There is great truth to it, and I can tell you without reservation, it works. If you learn any single thing from this book, aside from the fact that real life is vastly stranger than fiction, let it be that determination plus a plan of action will make you rich, famous, lucky in love, whatever your heart desires. At that moment, my heart desired nothing more than the removal of Freddy Giordano from my life, from my business, and from my sight. In the meantime, it would be both my purpose and my pleasure to make Freddy's life as difficult as I possibly could.

A week later I got a phone call from the FBI. The bad news was that they had met with Tilotti and he wasn't talking jack about anything. He was still sitting in Milan, however, for contempt of court and other charges pending against him. It was matter of record that he had admitted his participation in a contract murder for money—so he was basically toast. On top of this, the prosecutor, Straus, was about to add new charges of perjury to Tilotti's bag of woes. Anything and everything but the kitchen sink.

Freddy was free. Without Tilotti the FBI had no choice but to drop all charges against him. He was the big cheese but he had managed to walk on the rap, albeit with a wallet maybe $100,000 lighter. But far better than fifteen to twenty years in jail. And to think that if the Feds hadn't wired Alan Howard for other crimes, Freddy might have gotten away with having me killed for a relative pittance.

Weeks rolled by. Back to business as usual, as if working with a guy who had skated on conspiracy to murder his partner could be considered usual. And business was good, even great. All the publicity surrounding the trial had accomplished that. Both Freddy and I were making out like crazy; it was, in fact, a perfect time to sell the club for a juicy price. But now, of course, Freddy being Freddy, he didn't want to sell. Why should he? He's making plenty of money, he's just gotten away with conspiracy to murder, and he has no shame.

I retaliated by trying to jam Freddy any way I could. One day, for example, a manager whom Freddy had hired and whom I didn't particularly like, was coming in to open the club up for the day. I had my own managers, kind of like a little fiefdom, who were loyal to me. You need more than a few managers—day, night, weekend, etc.—so each partner has discretionary power, so to speak, to hire whom they want. But I didn't like this one guy, and I loathed Freddy, so knowing the manager had keys only to the front entrance of the club and not the back, I parked my car a half an inch from the front doors and locked it there. When Freddy's boy showed up to open, he couldn't get in.

Naturally, the manager calls Freddy on his cell to report that he can't open the club! Freddy is irritated, demands to know whose car is blocking the entrance. Manager tells him he thinks it looks like my car. Freddy asks the manager, so where in hell is Alan? Manager tells Freddy he doesn't know . . . he's looking around . . . where's Alan? Where's Alan? I am laughing my ass off in the valet booth twenty feet away. I come out, and the manager, who has to be respectful of me because he knows I own half the joint, asks me if I will move my car.

"Shit, man," I reply. "I just walked over to the post office there, you know, and now I can't find my keys!"

"Uh—what should I do?" the guy begs.

"I don't know—I don't know where my spares are—and I'm late for an appointment in Birmingham. I'm going to have to get a ride. Call Freddy and ask him what to do!"

I left the poor SOB standing there with a stymied look on his face, knowing he was going to have to call Freddy and get bitched out for not taking care of the situation himself. Then I had the valet give me a ride uptown to get some lunch, on me, while I let the situation ripen for a little while. After a nice, leisurely lunch, we drove back and found Freddy there fuming, his manager looking pretty freaking sheepish and a flatbed tow driver trying to figure out how to winch a rear-wheel-drive Ferrari without damaging something.

"Hey, I found my keys!" I said as I hopped out of the valet's ride. "Let me move that, I didn't do a very good job parking, did I?"

I know Freddy would like to have shot me himself, and that it was a terrifically juvenile stunt for a grown man to pull, but it made me feel good for the rest of the day knowing I had dragged Freddy off the golf course. Sucker's a poor excuse for a duffer anyway.

It went on like this for weeks. Welcome to life with the Bickersons, right? But the fact is, I was getting nowhere with Freddy. He didn't want to sell the club and I didn't want to give up control over the process. In discussions with my business attorney, Harold Fried, the only solution appeared to be to force the sale of the club by suing Freddy for dissolution of our partnership due to "irreconcilable differences." A short way around the logjam would have been to find a buyer for Freddy's share, which at the right price he would sell and I would be done with him. So I tried that.

But, after another many months had gone by, there had been no reasonable offers for the club. Based on an appraised value of the real estate, fixtures, improvements, and liquor and cabaret licenses as well as cash flow, fair market value for BTs should have been somewhere around two and three-quarters to three million dollars. Naturally, there's no law that says you can't lower your price to guarantee a sale, but getting the true value of a thing depends upon another party's being willing and able to pay it. In the case of the latter, the sky is the limit . . . but you might be waiting a long time before that magic buyer makes an appearance.

Finally, lack of progress in finding a buyer at a price acceptable to both Freddy and me forced the court to order a private auction. Now, Freddy's true nature would be revealed, at long last. He wanted BTs for himself and agreed to the private auction (the mechanism of which I will describe shortly) because he had guys with money behind him who were willing to let the asshole bid against me to buy the club. Freddy's backers were some pretty sharp cookies, among them Ned Homfeld, the founder of Spirit Airlines, but they weren't experienced with running gentleman's clubs. They had more cash than they had street smarts about the business, but they wanted it badly enough and trusted Freddy enough to let him do the bidding for them.

A private auction is as fascinating as it is simple. The way it works is, a floor price is agreed to, from where the bidding begins. In the case of BTs, the floor was set at one million dollars. Each bidder is allowed to have a second, or counsel, for advice and support. There are no special qualifications, except that your advisor should be someone who is experienced in business and can offer good advice in a clinch so that you don't get excited and overbid. Or your counsel can also help to determine by his experience where he thinks your counterpart is, just like in a poker game. Could they go any higher? Should you keep bidding, or is it time to fold and take what's on the table at the moment of truth?

As the bidding begins, it is a fluid psychological game that depends on who most wants to own the business, and how much they can afford to bid. Each bidder must first show good faith by showing up with a cashier's check—earnest money. (For this auction we both came with checks for $500,000.) As each bid is made, the other bidder has the option of either accepting the bid or rejecting the bid and making a counteroffer. You are bidding for the total sale price of the club, but on accepting a bid, you actually pay 50 percent of the final figure to the other bidder for their half interest. Remember, Freddy and I were straight 50/50 share owners of BTs.

Freddy opened with an initial bid of one million. If I accepted his bid, that would mean that I would be obligated to pay Freddy that $500,000 within a period of thirty days or the private auction would be invalidated and we'd have to start from scratch. But of course, I knew and he knew that BTs was worth a lot more. I also knew that he had backing, or else he would not be sitting at the table because he didn't have the ability to come up with anything like half the real value of the club by himself. I could have ponied up immediately and gotten Freddy out of my life forever. But I couldn't stomach the idea of paying him even a plugged nickel after what he tried to do to me, and I smelled blood in the water. As the old saying goes, "Living well is the best revenge." And getting top dollar, especially well above market valuation, is definitely living well.

My second was an older gentleman by the name of Irv Strickstein, sort of a mentor to me as well as a friend. Irv had made a huge fortune over the years in the wholesale lumber business. He would buy it directly from the producers, companies like Weyerhaeuser, who owned hundreds of thousands of acres of trees that they processed into millions of boardfeet of lumber which he would then sell by the carloads to builders and lumber yards. He had plenty of experience with large financial transactions, private auctions, public auctions, and buying and selling businesses. He was an expert at the process, a guy I privately called my "ringer." Irv had told me, "Alan, I'll just sit there with you. When things get really interesting I'll give you a nudge and we'll step outside into the hallway to discuss the next move."

Freddy, on the other hand, was flying solo. He had a second "standing by" via cell phone, who turned out to be Gary Kotlarz, the schmuck who you'll recall forced himself on me as a partner at Tycoon's because he owned the building, formerly a restaurant called Biff's, a few years earlier. I knew that Freddy wouldn't even be sitting at the table unless he had some deep-pocket investors who wanted to be in the topless game even more than he did—Ned Homfeld (founder of Spirit Airlines) and Bruce Bryan, another businessman who worked for Homfeld. Kotlarz wasn't as savvy about big-bucks transactions as Irv Strickland, plus he was at a disadvantage over the phone because he couldn't read the subtle signals and body language going down.

We were sitting in the richly paneled conference room of the law offices of the court-appointed arbitrator. I was feeling confident. I countered Freddy's opening bid of $1.05 million with an offer of $1.4 million, a jump of $375,000. He could have grabbed my offer and walked away from the table with a tidy $700,000. But this sum did not even begin to wet his whistle. Freddy was in for the whole tamale . . . he wanted the club because he wanted to be Mr. Big. His investors would be bowing to his phenomenal expertise as the main man, the wizard running the show! Plus, they were ready with their checkbooks, waiting for Freddy to bring home the prize. Freddy didn't flinch and he didn't hesitate. He countered at once with a bid of $1.8 million.

But I was loaded for bear myself. In for a penny, in for two rocks and change: $2.2 million.

If he bit, Freddy would have made himself an instant millionaire, but never underestimate the underpinnings of raw, unadulterated greed. The bidding took off like a Roman candle from there. We bid $400,000 or $500,000 at a pop, and at that rate we were up to $4.1 million before you could say Jack Robinson, with Freddy being the last to bid. Time to catch my breath. I looked at Irv and he looked at me. With a nod of his head, I knew it was time to retrench a little before making my

198 | Alan Markovitz

next move. We stepped into the hallway outside the conference room and spoke in low, conspiratorial tones.

"What do you think, Irv? Should I try to ratchet it up another couple hundred thou?"

"Nah—I think he's tapped. I can feel it, I've been here before. You try to bid it up and he's gonna think twice and blink, and maybe bite."

"So . . . that's it then. It's time to go for the kill."

"I know what I'd do, Alan, but it's your call."

In business, you can afford to be a little bit early in striking a deal, but you can't be a second too late. Better to leave something on the table than to lose the whole tamale through greed.

We calmly walked back into the conference room and took our places across the table from Freddy as I did my best to keep a poker face on. I took my seat and placed both my hands palm down on the shiny burl surface of the gigantic meeting table between us and looked Freddy right in the eye. Then, I turned to look at Irv, seated immediately to my right. He seemed to give me an almost imperceptible nod, as if to say, "OK, Alan. Make your move."

I looked back at Freddy, smiled, thrust my open right hand across the table, and declared, "It's yours!"

Freddy reflexively extended his own hand to shake on the deal, and with a slightly dazed, deer-in-the-headlights look on his face, broke into a vaguely queasy smile as I pumped his hand a couple of times for emphasis. The deal was done! Sold for $4.1 million! Under the terms of the sale, I got to walk with the $500,000 earnest money Freddy had brought to the table with the expectation of $1.55 million within the next 30 days. A total buyout of $2,050,000; not bad for less than an hour's work. Considering that I had invested $360,000 in BTs thirteen years earlier, it was a pretty sweet payoff in the end. By that time, I had already put my plans for The Flight Club into motion, and the only additional term of the sale was a non-compete covenant that prohibited me from owning or investing in another topless club in Dearborn for five years from the date of the sale. No problemo, Freddy. I'll just move my ass down the road a few more miles and set up shop in Inkster. No worries, mate!

Funny, though, how Freddy seems to alienate whoever he ends up in business with. Along with general ineptitude, the guy seems to always promise more than he's capable of delivering. He only got the money to buy BTs because the two guys with the real bread figured he could run the show while they enjoyed the dividends, the prestige, and the thrills where they now had access. Eight years later, in 2003, Freddy's partners forced the sale of the club because of some bonehead moves Freddy had made that cost them a bundle.

Remember that BTs had been designed and built in 1985 and not structurally improved since, due to a simple lack of space. Nonetheless, Freddy became enamored of upgrading BTs with the addition of a super luxe VIP area (like The Flight Club, which opened in late 1996, incorporating an upper level, or mezzanine, with a VIP area into its plans from the beginning). A secluded, plush VIP room where patrons of a club can enjoy a more private "couch" or "lap" dance is a big draw. It keeps your customers happy, keeps the girls happy because they have a special place where they can maximize their earnings, and keeps folks in the club spending money on drinks, food, and cigars a lot longer per visit.

What Freddy did was absolutely beautiful for its sheer stupidity. Despite zoning covenants that restricted the cabaret D license to the existing square footage of the club, Freddy had the idea to purchase the building next door, which had formerly been a medical office. The two buildings shared a common concrete block wall. Since Freddy was running the show, and Homfeld and Kotlarz thought he knew what he was doing, they green-lighted his plan to buy the derelict structure for $275,000. The idea was to attach it to BTs even though legally it was a separate entity, with its own address, and could not be combined with BTs unless the city approved it—a highly unlikely prospect. Of course, Freddy didn't bother going through Dearborn's zoning board, or even applying for so much as a construction or demolition permit.

In the dead of night, Freddy hired a crew and jackhammered straight through the common wall and opened up what was to be a gigantic new VIP room. In a matter of days, they had gutted the new space and had begun remodeling. It should come as no surprise that Freddy has enemies, or at the very least, folks who know him and just don't like him at all levels of local government due to his arrogance and penchant for bonehead moves. It didn't take long for the unauthorized construction to come to the attention of city inspectors, and they soon began writing citations and levying fines for the new construction. Of course, Freddy had no permits! The police got in the act, too, writing tickets to BTs for noise, creating a public nuisance, general health and safety violations, and so forth. Finally, the Dearborn city lawyers intervened and BTs received a court order to cease and desist business operations.

BTs was then forced to rebuild the common wall between the two buildings and restore the premises to exactly its previous state, no more and no less. The cost of acquiring the adjacent building, the demolition and reconstruction and various legal fees added up to a loss of over $350,000. Freddy's partners were pissed with a capital "P." I later learned that when loss of business was factored in, the total cost of the bath BTs took was somewhere in the neighborhood of eight hundred grand!

By 2003, Freddy's partners had finally had enough. My new club on Michigan Avenue in Inkster was hammering them by then, too, and they wanted out. Freddy was again subject of a forced sale, but this time, the best they could do was $3.3 million . . . a far cry from the $4.1 million agreed to in the private auction following Freddy's foiled attempt to have me killed. The new buyer was a businessman by the name of Nick Faranso, to whom I had sold Tycoon's to a few years earlier.

THE GIRLS

Whatever you want to call them—dancers, strippers, exotic entertainers, chicks, babes, broads, women, wimmen, grrrls—it's all the same to me. Yet each and every one is strikingly different from the next and shares a singleness of purpose that is the sisterhood of stripperdom's creed: The fulfillment of man's fantasies is equal to the fulfillment of their purses. In exchange for every drop of erotic soul that these ladies can and do wring from themselves while teetering on seven-inch platforms, in return for radiating those intoxicating rays of femininity, promise, and allure, their patrons will leave the club feeling that they were and are men among men, masters of the universe, who have tasted these exotic fruits and been transported to other worlds for the relatively inexpensive price of admission. It may amount to a few hours, pay for some, or a couple of car payments for others, but the fact that most of these men will yearn to return is the sterling proof that the brand of entertainment

I package and meter is the best brand available under the sun or moon.

That being said, I can hear you raising the question: but what are they really like, these dancers? How do I get inside their heads, their souls . . . and let's be honest, their pants? The answer, grasshopper, is the sound of one hand clapping. Let me explain. The psychologists tell us that we instinctively want all the more what we cannot have. They also tell us that when we do get it, it ain't what it seems and we may well not be able to handle it or know what to do with it! This, in my humble opinion, is what makes strippers so damned fascinating. It's what makes them, and their successful nurturing and management, critical to the success of my business. It is also the reason that you are advised to enjoy these salacious seductresses in the safety and sumptuousness of one of my clubs. Like I laid it out in the beginning of the book, the operation of jet aircraft and strippers is not unalike. If you don't know what you are doing you can get out of control in a heartbeat and auger in with your tail shot clean off. Better live to tell the tale of the tail that got away, and hunt another day.

So, who are these girls, these women who make your heart and head throb with pleasure and promise? They are women who you may very well see passing you by in the other direction at the supermarket, or in the bank. They may be students of journalism or medicine or law, or perhaps studying to be real estate agents or cosmetologists in their free time. They may be blessed with the dew of youth, or maybe they are seasoned sirens who have seen it all and yet return night after night, day after day to the land of the bump, the grind, and the slither. They love the challenge, they love the action, they love you.

And what is it, really, that you, the patron of The Flight Club, do? Why, it couldn't be simpler. You make it all possible. You attract the women who find you irresistibly charming, engaging . . . and financially able. You come to blow off steam, celebrate or consummate a business deal, to be pampered and understood and given the tender and undivided attention of the most delectable women on earth . . . in exchange for what? Will that be paper or plastic? Credit or debit? How about another dance, my man? Wade on in, the water is fine! Perfect weather for a little trophy fishing.

Perfect weather for Chloe. She loves fishing, in fact, off the Florida Keys. She's pretty good at it. She's also got a decent handicap on the greens. Plays two difficult musical instruments and is a fan of classical music. She believes in community service. And she is somewhere north of forty. Yet she looks well south, toward the low thirties. Beyond all that, however, Chloe, a platinum blonde, is a stunning five-foot-six pour of fine Champagne . . . from her gorgeously turned ankles (one festooned with a four-carat-total-weight diamond ankle bracelet) up to her long, taut and sinewy thighs that make you think of the raw energy stored in the haunches of a female cheetah. Her hips remind one of the swaying, sauntering Marilyn Monroe on the day she gave that breathy little happy birthday song to President Kennedy. Now we're up to Chloe's chest, a lyric of luscious C-cups with a beckoning crevasse of cleavage that would make Pamela Anderson fluorescent green with envy. Chloe is the personification of the word *titillation*. Yet she exudes class, whipped up in a cocktail shaker with a dash or two of sass and, believe it or not, no bitters and no bitterness. Everything Chloe says and does is shot through with a frankness and honesty that men for whom she entertains should note and study for future reference. Maybe that's why she has lasted the better part of a decade and a half on the strobe-lit stage, keeping both her sanity and her sultriness intact. It's not easy, what Chloe does day after day, night upon night. But it allows her to shuck off the remains of the day and slip into her favorite sweatpants with a clean conscience.

Chloe first came to dance for me when I was a younger man and she was a younger woman. We have both learned a lot since the day she auditioned and was hired on the spot. Staying power, as I have suggested, is paramount in the club business. Chloe would probably just call it survival. But listen: I've already told you she puts her heart and soul into everything she does. You'll come into the club sometime, blinking as you reorient yourself from the jarring light of day, adjusting to the dark and the mesmerizing mixture of cigar and cigaret smoke and fine perfume on pheromonally charged females . . . and Chloe will be there waiting for you.

Our brunette bombshell of a hostess, Heidi, who could be running hospitality for the Hilton chain but fortunately works for me, will swiftly guide you through the pleasing din and tempest to your own table, swung out to accommodate your seating on our plush leather upholstery. In you will slide, like a visiting head of state, and the drink of your choice will be whisked before you in a matter of moments. Inevitably, a smile will form upon your face as you look around you and find that wherever you cast your gaze, there is a sizzling hot strumpet cavorting to the sweet sounds being pumped out of the $100,000 sound system.

Then Chloe will appear. It will seem as if you had just rubbed the side of a mythical silver lamp and in a sudden POOF of smoke and flash of light, she is in front of you, smiling . . . smiling . . . and sliding her warm body onto the leather next to you. Her thigh will contact yours for a brief moment and the transfer of heat energy will make a Lennox industrial furnace pale in comparison.

"Hi, how are you?" she will ask, simply and directly, falling upon you as the summer sun setting on a perfect summer's day.

"I'm Chloe. What's your name?" If you're anything like most men, and I don't care if you're a mechanic, an office worker, or a CEO, you'll manage to choke out an answer.

"Alan," I would say, because I've been here before.

Then, Chloe would gently relax her hand upon your forearm. If you weren't wearing a suit jacket, she would feel the little hairs on your arm all stand on end, and she would say something like, "Ooh, it's kind of cold in here. You're not cold, too, are you, Alan?"

Chloe would be telling the truth, because in the summer, I like to make sure the air is cranked up enough to give you that I'm-chillin'-and-I'm-willin' kinda feeling and to assist the ladies in maintaining what is known in the trade as a "perky" appearance. I think it is fair to say that this look is not going out of style anytime soon. They refrigerate fresh flowers, too, so don't start getting all PC on me now, hear?

Back at the table, to quote Elvis Presley, "I'm in love, I'm all shook up!" But wait, it gets better. Because Chloe has been around the block before, she brings the rare amalgam of experience and exuberance to bear . . . this is a gorgeous woman who can actually engage in conversation, easy banter, or, if you're up to it, a bit of friendly debate and discourse on issues of the day. Just nothing about sex or politics, right? Well, maybe not politics. And Chloe oozes sex, so why put words in the way of simply enjoying the experience of being near her? A young dude should be so lucky as to sit next to Chloe and maybe learn something from her, and leave the club with a sense of enlightenment. Along, of course, with a healthy level of stimulation. Just being with Chloe is like having tantric sex. The kind that goes on for hours and hours on end. If you think I'm engaging in mere exaggeration or hyperbole, consider this—how does a beautiful, live woman differ from art? I would argue that she's far better than any art, than anything carved into marble by a Michaelangelo or Rodin, in that she's a living, breathing expression of feminine perfection . . . just by being herself. You have only to observe the phenomenon that I am party to every day. Each customer of my clubs invariably finds one or two dancers that, to him, embody some particular quality—perhaps a certain turn of ankle or proportion of legs to torso that drives him crazy with desire. For this customer, the simple act of beholding his ideal on stage is akin to dying and going to heaven. Add the additional dimensions of personality, grace, or humor and you have the magic recipe that makes a woman like Chloe not just a topless dancer, but a star of stage or theatre. If that appeals to you, then you need to come see for yourself.

In the meantime, a simple Thank you, Chloe, will do. Wonderful, therapeutic Chloe.

Let me tell you, there are still 299 more girls to go. I kid you not. More delicious dancers than you could pack onto a 747 jumbo jet. You would have to leave a couple of dozen in the boarding area, clutching their clutches and pouting over being left behind. You will have to send the plane back to pick them up, bub. But I've done all the work for you. This rotating roster of rambunctious and ravishing redheads, blisteringly beautiful brunettes, and blatantly sexual blondes is being maintained at my expense so that whenever you are ready, at your very whim, you can access them, enjoy them, and deploy them to do deeds of pleasure solely at your behest!

But seriously. These are real women. You don't spend thousands of hours around women without learning a thing or two about the feminine mystique. Multiply those thousands of hours times the hundreds and, yes, thousands of women whom I've had the experience of working with, witnessing, trouble-shooting—hell, I've practically performed brain surgery on them—and you'll realize that I have paid the dues and ferreted out all the clues. And I am here to tell you that women, these delicate little flowers, are some of the toughest creatures walking the planet Earth. They have been baptized by fire. They have come from a wide variety of backgrounds, but they share the blunt-force honesty bred of the working class and the shrinking middle class of the United States of America.

It's fitting that The Flight Club exists under the approach pattern for the big jets that land at Detroit Metropolitan Airport. That's because, similar to the pecking order and hierarchy of seasoned captains who don't automatically accept the new first officers coming on board until they've proved their cockpit mettle over time, dancers also enforce a social code and hierarchy. If you are a new girl coming on board, you may turn for comfort or advice to the "house mom" employed by the club inside the dressing room. You may even find that one or two of the veteran dancers are altruistic enough to extend a somewhat warm welcome to you as a newcomer. But for the most part, you are untested and untried. You are raw and subject to being mauled and ravaged if you do not quickly catch on to the way things work in a topless establishment. While it is all sweetness and light out on the floor and on stage, it is safe to assume that until you have proved yourself as reliable in combat, you will not be wholly accepted into the sisterhood of stripperdom.

If it were easy, any girl could do it. But stripping separates the women from the girls. You do not become one of the "girls" until you graduate, which could take as long as six months to a year to prove to the other veterans that you have what it takes to stick it out day after day, night after night, without quitting or breaking down on the job. It really is the same for pilots. Ask a pilot sometime, "What was it like when you were just learning how to fly?" If you were in their shoes, you would quickly discover that those around you who were already pilots, whether in the military or at a civilian flight school, might talk to you but would eye you with just a hint of suspicion. You haven't proved jack, you haven't soloed yet, hey! You might just get fed up and quit because you can't seem to land the damned plane without bouncing down the runway like a ruptured duck. If you're a dancer, it's the same thing: You fall off those seven-inch platforms and bust your butt, you do the crybaby thing when a customer says something rude, and you want to pack up your dancer bag and drag ass home. But if you've got grit, you say fuck it! Nobody is going to keep me from raking in some of that long green and calling my own shots and whoever doesn't like it can go screw themselves!

So the pilots learn to fly on their instruments, descending down through rain and fog, greasing one in. And the dancers learn to fly on their instincts, on their observations of the other dancers, and on their sheer determination . . . or they don't. Until that magic moment when you know that everyone else you dance with knows that you know what you're doing and you ain't a-quittin' . . . that is what it takes to be accepted and then the other girls (or the other pilots) will begin to talk to you like you are one of them. Because you are. You have made it, and now you can sit on the sidelines watching some new girl perform up on stage for the very first or second or third time and say to your fellow dancer-in-arms, "If that isn't about the dumbest bitch I've ever seen, look, she's got her G-string on backwards!" And your gal pal will laugh and maybe you'll do shots together and remember the first day you fell flat on your ass and lived to dance another day.

Fore Play

Golf and strippers. Strippers and golf. On paper, it looks like gin and tonic, or strawberries and shortcake, or perhaps white on rice. A marriage made in heaven, so to speak. It was a combination I was hell-bent on perfecting, because so many of my customers love to golf, and they love to come in after a hot day on the links and quench their thirst with beer and babes, one after the other. So why not, I thought, package up the whole shebang by putting some nudity on the green? How could I lose?

There is but one way to make a fortune (lots of hard work) and a thousand ways to blow it, many possible pitfalls being invisible to the naked eye and subject to greet one with all the pleasantness of stepping on broken glass in the dark. I won't say the golf/stripper equation didn't work beautifully, for a while, but I will say that I'm not taking topless entertainers anywhere near the tee-off zone again anytime soon.

The whole concept was stone simple. Find a nice out-of-the-way golf course somewhere that's amenable to importing some bulk business; that is, book the place for an entire day and sign up a few dozen golfers at a couple hundred bucks a head for a combo greens fee, topless female caddies, and beverages, and transport back to the club for dinner, drinks, and private dances. Finding the golfers was little effort. Some table toppers and word of mouth quickly filled a sign-up sheet and we booked a weekday at a local course that wasn't too busy. They were thrilled to get a lump sum without any hassle and excited about the profitable prospect of booking many such golf outings featuring our beautiful dancers.

The first time putting this concept to the test, everybody had a ball. While it's fair to say a lot of normally good golfers couldn't hit the ball straight that day and bogied the bejesus out of most holes due to bobbling boobies everywhere they looked, no one gave a hoot. The girls delighted in spreading their legs on the holes being putt (yes, they were wearing G-strings), and probably some of the guys actually putted better that way. Laughter and love of the game permeated the day, and by the time everybody shuttled back to the bar, the course owner was satisfied, I was satisfied, and everybody else was three sheets.

"Hot damn," I said to my manager Brian, "We've got to do this again! Book the course for next month and let's make this tits 'n' tees a regular gig, no?" Off to the races and all that, guv'ner! Not. Quite.

Yeah, the next month went off—gangbusters, as a matter of fact. We had more dancers, more duffers, and more fun than a barrel of monkeys. We also had an annoying TV reporter and tattle tale from a local news station, hiding in the bushes with a camera crew taping the topless frolics for the eleven o'clock come-on . . . you know, "See the shocking sexual antics performed in public on a golf course by dancers from a prominent local strip club, in full view of impressionable young children only yards away!" The closest homes, in a subdivision, were something like four hundred yards—a quarter of a mile away!—on the other side of a line of trees and hedges that shielded the golf course from the road and the homes on the other side of them. But ratings are ratings, and the news busted out some fat numbers that night, I am sure, as my phone rang off the freaking hook for the next few days between other media outlets seeking comment and puritanical bluenoses lambasting me for my lewd and lascivious conduct . . . and the rest wanting to know when the next outing was so they could book it.

I have only one other thing to say about women and golf. Chloe, whom you read about earlier, sometimes plays with men, as she doesn't know many other women who like to golf. Asked how she likes competing against men on the links, Chloe had only this comment: "Every man I have ever played golf with has cheated." I am sure that none of you guys reading this would ever even think about cheating in golf while playing against a lady, right? As they say in Scotland, "No man with real balls ever dared play funny with golf balls." I'm leaving it right there, just as you should play her as she lays, fellas.

Advice from the Pros

As Chloe so rightly puts it, when asked what is the best advice she would give to a young girl thinking about breaking into the topless dance game, "It's a big-girl decision." If you're not ready to make that kind of a decision, you don't belong in the club. And although girls generally grow up a helluva lot faster than boys—they have to—it bears remembering that the women you'll be dancing with are not, as Chloe says, "guidance counselors." If you need one of those, stay in high school or get a technical degree.

Her youth (she doesn't look a day over eighteen) and relatively rich recency of experience are what make a dancer like Hanna so intriguing. Hanna is cute as a button, a petite five-foot-one blonde with killer curves and a scant forty-two months—little more than an average car lease—under her belt, shaking her beautiful booty from the all-nude Déjà Vu

214 | Alan Markovitz

and Hustler clubs in New York, Baltimore, California, and Las Vegas to New Orleans and back. Back to Detroit, that is, where her flourishing career began when she went to see about waitressing in another local club and was persuaded to join in a game of "naked Twister" happening on stage.

"Growing up, I absolutely loved Twister," Hanna chirps, "and it wasn't any big deal taking my clothes off! All the other girls were up there naked, so why not? I had a blast." Included was an immediate job offer, which Hanna promptly accepted. Now she dances steadily at The Flight Club and says "It feels like family here." What more could you possibly want? She possesses a certain maturity that is often hard to find in women twice her age, along with a bubbliness, a joie de vivre, an irrepressible sexuality that will make you long for Hanna's company once you've had it for the first time.

It all goes back to the psychological conditioning a topless dancer undergoes, and is transformed by, forged by her need to relate to and communicate with every type of man to tumble down the pike and end up in a booth or behind a drink at the bar.

If there's a problem for a girl like Hanna, it lies in the indisputable fact that she has become far more mature and worldwise than the majority of "men" in her own age bracket. Add to that the fact that she earns, working perhaps four to five days a week, something like four times what the thirty-odd-grand young guys pull down in a year.

At the same time, Hanna undoubtedly can better understand and relate to men in their forties and even fifties, whose incomes, self-esteem, and experience more closely match hers, even though she's come by her stripes in a few scant years. If universities handed out degrees for experience in male psychology, Hanna would surely qualify for a PhD. So what does Hanna do with her preternatural maturity? For now, she banks her dough and goes home to play with her cat, visit her family, and watch TV. When her young friends call her up for a night of clubbing, Hanna often must suppress a yawn, because that's too much like work. Which isn't to say that Hanna doesn't like to get a little crazy once in a while, but when you work with crazies all day, sometimes all you want is a down comforter, some Ben & Jerry's Cherry Garcia, and a few hundred cable channels to flick through on your 52-inch plasma.

Hanna has so far avoided the trap of what is known as the "bottomless boyfriend," that is, a good-looking but jobless guitar player, for example, who needs as much care and feeding as a freaking pound puppy. And a car, and money for weed, and strings for his bass guitar, and by the way they just came out with the new 500 gig iPod, um, hey, I'm going to the party store to get some beer for band practice can ya help me out here with a spare fifty? But other girls who are not as mature, or without as much common sense, as Hanna do often go in for a little leech . . . they must think it complements their pierced tongues, navels, labia, and what-have-you like Paris Hilton's Chihuahua in a bag. Not to mention the subject of ink. You know, body art? But at The Flight Club, I don't even like to see so much as a tattoo. Maybe I'm old school, but I am of the firm opinion that that sort of thing only degrades female beauty. If a girl has a tattoo but is otherwise of the high caliber I demand, I may let her cover it up with a layer of good foundation. Quality control. On with the show.

You really ought to see Hanna. She used to drive a big-ass yellow Hummer and it never failed to amuse me to see her cute little figure climbing in and out of that thing. I think she's downsized, now, but the point is, youth is not always wasted on the young. Hanna has a better picture of who she is, what she wants, and where she is going than 90 percent of people her age, regardless of gender. Furthermore, I am of the conviction that if more people had the opportunity to face up to the real world and start making some real choices and goals for themselves, we'd all be a lot better off. America has become a country that is all about immediate gratification, the short-term payoff, and the go-into-debt-to-buy-it-now mentality that has fueled the explosive growth of the Chinese economy while gutting the heart and soul of our own country. I know that this is a stretch and a whistle beyond the topic of "girls" that this chapter purports to be about. Who we are and what we do are more rigorously and clearly defined by the experience of working the stage and floor in a topless club than in a law firm, stock brokerage, or any other place of business, bar none. I will stake my name and reputation on that statement and debate in any forum public or private; just you name the time and place.

Another dancer who works for me (as an independent contractor, by the way, just like all dancers in every club that I own or have an interest in) is June. June has been working her money-maker and her sparkling, wholesome girl-next-door personality for thirteen years now, since she was about twenty years old. You do the math. June is married, happily I may add, to a man who trusts and understands her and who understands that topless entertainment is a business. June knows that she cannot and does not want to be on stage forever. Thus, she is actively pursuing a medical education that will prepare her to become certified as a nurse anesthesiologist capable of pulling down $150–$200K per year. Way to go, June. You kick ass, girl.

Yet some people have the unmitigated gall to call some of these hard-working women "stupid," "sluts," or "prostitutes"? If more people minded their own damned business and kept their noses pointed straight ahead, we would all be a lot better off: the fact remains that topless entertainment has probably funded more higher educations and furthered more careers than grants and scholarships ever have . . . especially when one considers that dancing has historically opened doors to more women of working-class and blue-collar backgrounds, who would otherwise not have the opportunities, or the second chances, required to get a leg up the career ladder.

If you will also stop to think again for a moment about the determination and willpower necessary to function productively and sanely in the field of topless entertainment, you will gain another level of respect for the women who do it. June came out of the rough-and-tumble, grit and grime of economically depressed Flint, Michigan. You remember the Michael Moore movie, *Roger and Me*? It painted a vivid and horrific picture of the catastrophic effect of General Motors shutting down their production facilities there. To fight your way out of Flint, and do it 100 percent on your own, is a feat unto itself. Then, to literally dance your way to a high-flying job in the medical field? If that's not a movie of the week, or grounds for a medal and commendation, I don't know what is.

"I was getting really jaded," June told me recently, "based on my observations of the ugly underbelly of humanity that I sometimes get a revolting glimpse of. It's not the club, though once in a while you do get a real asshole. It's the world. If anything, being able to handle working in the club has given me the gumption to focus that much more intently on my goals."

June is a tall, curvaceous redhead who is as American as apple pie. It's not hard to envision her in a white lab coat, making notes on a clipboard and assisting in ascertaining the correct dosage and application of anesthetic for a surgical case, and then attending an operation with both focus and compassion. It's also not hard to actually see her in a brief, bejeweled G-string and tasseled top, or maybe without the top, inducing an erotic coma in whomever she may be performing for. But she is working her way toward that degree, so if you want to see her, talk to her, and enjoy her personal attention, you'd better get to one of my clubs. These are the sort of girls that characterize the talent at any of the clubs in my domain. Catch them while you can!

On the entrepreneurial side of the scale, take Celeste, a very exotic five-foot-ten vixen with cascading curls of nearly black locks reminiscent of Scheherazade, straight out of the *1,001 Tales of Arabian Nights*, except that she's French, Irish, English, Polish, and maybe a shot of Cherokee. She has pale skin that is set off by her dark hair and between the glittery eye shadow she favors and her heaving D-cup breasts, you are likely to be bowled over by her.

Celeste, interestingly, did not begin dancing till only two years ago, when she was thirty-five. An unpleasant divorce and two children demand that Celeste bring home the bacon, and being naturally restless, she had tired of the medical billing job she'd held since shortly after high school, working her way up from entry level to a supervisory position over 120 other employees. All this without a college degree, mind you. But, like any true entrepreneur-at-heart, she was prepared to seize a new opportunity when one presented itself. Her brother's girlfriend, who was making a fine enough living in topless to drive a BMW

330i, persuaded the naturally adventurous Celeste to audition at The Flight Club.

"I was always comfortable with my own body, and nudity," Celeste explains. "Maybe I'm part Swedish, who knows, but my whole family was just very laid-back about it, and as a little kid it seems like I was running around bare-ass naked most of the time, so why not?" Indeed, Celeste gave it a shot and took to it like a duck to water, though her beauty compares much more favorably to a well-endowed swan. Three weeks later, Celeste quit her old job and has never looked back.

Like most of the girls who dance, particularly those who are a little older and more mature, Celeste is actively investing in her future. She has already managed to buy two residential income properties along with the house she already owns and has some rather brash entrepreneurial concepts for new businesses that she hopes to work out down the road. Financial planning is something I strongly advise any of the dancers who ply their trade in my clubs to think about, and more importantly, act upon. It's way too easy for any of us to think that once the cash starts flowing it's never going to stop. It's also easy to blow it, evidence of the old "easy come, easy go" axiom.

A perfect example of this is another dancer I will call Crystal, a composite of many girls I've seen come and go over the years. The faces change but the grim reality remains the same: Drugs make you stupid and broke faster than a Ferrari Testarossa goes from zero to sixty.

Crystal is typical, statistically, somewhere around nineteen to twenty-five years old, though age is no exemption from cooking your grey matter beyond the point of no return. However, I must stress that clichés such as "slut" and "drug addict" are no more appropriate to exotic dancers than they are to any other individual in a particular age bracket. That being said, younger people are statistically more likely to experiment with drugs than older folks who don't have a history of drug or alcohol dependency. Put these young people, young women in this case, in an atmosphere where alcohol is being served and where some of their coworkers and friends outside work may be using—anything from coke, crack, or crystal meth to pot, ecstasy, painkillers, or whatever—and you have a far more volatile recipe for a long, ugly slide into a very toxic swamp. The stress of working the floor at a topless club, coupled with the natural tendency of some personalities (and those with certain biochemical predilections) will then turn into a nasty habit. Usually an expensive and nasty habit. Crystal still has the dew of youth going for her but doesn't yet realize that the years will fly by like the falling leaves of a wall calendar from an old-time movie. While I am not a counselor, I do my best to talk to girls like her, to encourage them to clean up and keep focused on taking care of business. But, as the old saying goes, youth is often wasted on the young.

From a business perspective, it's also worth noting that I do my best to weed out those entertainers, and other employees, who use drugs. It's simply bad for business. Just as some of the most successful rock 'n' roll bands have learned the hard way—that touring and tooting up or shooting up a storm are intrinsically incompatible—so have I come to appreciate the enhanced productivity of a drug-free work environment. All right, I can hear you shouting—alcohol is a drug! That it is, and it is central to my business, but society is merely the place where I live, not where I legislate the rules. War is hell, too, but it must sometimes be waged. That's why armies demand discipline and regulation and it's truer in topless clubs than it is in most places.

On the whole, the women who dance in my clubs know the score and are pragmatic about the experience. They are there to sell the ultimate legal and personal fantasy of their nearly naked company, whether at your table or in a titillating VIP dance. They are, by and large, consummate professionals. Why don't you come in and see for yourself? And remember that old saw from the Bible—judge not lest ye yourself be judged.

Other Voices: Rick Kempkens, DJ

You wanna hear about dancers? Man, I could write the book. I've been in this business for over twenty years and I've worked for Alan for fifteen of them. These girls are something else, they're like a whole other species. Sort of like that movie with Natasha Henstridge, you know, where's she's this drop-dead gorgeous woman whose body has been taken over by a wacked out alien? That pretty much sums it up.

Don't get me wrong, I love my dancers. They're fabulously entertaining. But my job description? Wrangling is the right word. Or better yet, call it choreography. I've got to keep 'em rotating off and on the main stage on a very rigorous schedule, two girls, two songs at a time, one wearing her top for the first song and taking it off for the second number as she's followed by a fresh dancer with her top still on. At the same time, I've got to cue up several songs ahead so I'm not scrambling at the last second . . . fortunately, I no longer have to juggle CDs; everything goes on the hard drive and I punch buttons and use a mouse.

Then, there are a couple of dancers on both of the side stages that front a dais with booths on either side of the club, running parallel to the main stage. You've gotta make sure you get them up there on time too, and often I have to take a break between songs to shout out some dancer calls because someone might be in the john or doing a couch dance. But I blend it in with the rest of my DJ speed-rap patter and the customers don't even notice, but the girls hear through the noise and they know they'll get fined if they don't hop to.

That's right, I control all the tip-out—or dance fees—that the girls have to pay to dance. I get a cut of it, too. So I'm part disciplinarian, part Swiss banker, and part entertainer, spinning the songs that keep the mood swinging, the energy level up, and everybody enjoying themselves and spending money. I play a little bit of everything: techno, modern rock, Rihanna and Madonna and Shakira, some soul, some R&B, but not much rap. You've got to find a happy medium where the dancers dig it and you please the customers at the same time. But generally, as long as the girls are happy with it, the mood is infectious.

But you want the stories, I know. Like the one about two sisters who used to dance for me, a couple of crazy blondes. One night they were having an argument. I think it stemmed from one of them taking the other's favorite outfit and tearing it, or God knows what. But they were dancing on stage together and they were throwing insults at each other. At first, I didn't notice it because of the volume of the music, but pretty soon they started yelling at each other and I could hear them over the tunes. What do you do when that happens? I pretty much just sat there watching, my jaw hitting the floor, because I'd never seen anything like it on stage before.

Next thing I knew, one grabbed the other's hair in her fist and gave her such a jerk she spun around on her heels, and as she came around she took a swing at her sister that connected. Then it was on! They went nuts on each other, and between slaps, kicks, and those nails they wear, it was a catfight you don't want to get anywhere near. It took two of our biggest bouncers to finally pull them apart. I wish I had that one on video!

Other times, dancers want to be your friend and sometimes they are. And sometimes they take "friendly" a step too far. One night I was asked by a dancer named Tricia for a ride home. She'd been drinking—is that a surprise?—and wanted to keep drinking, but it was after 2:00 a.m. and all the bars were closed. She insisted that I take her somewhere to buy alcohol, and even though I patiently explained that I didn't know of any after-hours joints and I didn't have any booze at my apartment, she began to get agitated.

"Find me some alcohol, damn it, or else!" she protested.

"Or else what?" I laughed, somewhat incredulously.

"Or else I'm gonna take off all my goddamn clothes and throw them out the window!"

"No, you're not—I'm taking you straight home!"

Despite the fact that we were cruising at seventy miles per hour down Detroit's I-94 freeway at three o'clock in the morning, Tricia very deliberately and with an attitude of disgust began pulling all her clothes off, every single stitch, including her socks and panties, and with a final flourish lowered the power window and flung them all out. I watched in the rearview mirror as her duds danced in our slipstream and quickly vanished into the distance.

I looked over at this admittedly gorgeous, naked dancer who was just glaring at me with her arms crossed over her perfect breasts and I began laughing like a hyena.

"I'm still taking you home," I said, nonchalantly. And I did.

Bottom line is this: if you don't lay down the rules with dancers, I guarantee they will walk all over you. Give 'em an inch and they'll take ten miles. I'm a professional and I operate in an estrogen-soaked work zone, but let me tell you, these ladies also have some testosterone coursing through their systems and it will come out and remove a chunk of your ass if you don't watch your step. With that being said, I've got to admit that I've got a dream job here. I love what I do.

Other Voices: Kaci, Dancer

I'll tell you what. There are two kinds of guys: cheapskates and guys who know how to treat a lady. OK, maybe there's a middle category too, the guys I like to call my bread-and-butter guys. They come in once, maybe twice a week and they don't dump their whole bank account in your lap, but they like to have a good time and enjoy themselves and keep it under control enough so they can come back. I mean, I'm in the club to make a living, so I like it when a guy gets that and treats me like a professional. Look, I am female and despite a lot of men being jerks I still love men and am susceptible to being attracted to certain guys. If I'm single, you know, there's always a chance! But only if a guy doesn't come onto me with all kinds of bullshit. Get real, be real—that's the best advice I can give a guy coming into the club to see me.

I've been dancing for almost five years, so I'd say that pretty much makes me a veteran in this business. I dance four to five days a week, sometimes six. I drive a BMW 5-series, I have a couple of Prada bags, and I take vacations in places like Cabo and South Beach. I also have a portfolio going. But then I'm twenty-seven years old. A far cry from twenty-one, but there are a few smart cookies who are young.

You're probably wondering if I get turned on dancing. That's one of the questions I get a lot. Let me put it this way: You're only young once. I like looking at my gorgeous body in the mirrors that line the walls in the club. I turn myself on and that obviously gets my customers more excited. Isn't that the whole idea? After all, I'm not going on Dr. Phil and exploring my sick inner need for attention based on my low self-esteem or whatever. I've got plenty of fucking esteem. That's why I dance.

747 ENGINE FAILURE ON TAKEOFF

The .40 caliber round from the cop's Glock hit me like a baseball bat to the face. I had no idea I was even shot, at first. Like I said, it was the evening of January 9, 1997, around closing time at 2 a.m.

Earlier in the evening the off-duty Inkster cop and his buddy (another off-duty cop) had come into 747, my latest and greatest incarnation of what premium topless entertainment should be. We'd been open only about one month on Michigan Avenue just west of Middlebelt, under the landing pattern for Detroit Metropolitan Airport, in Inkster. The building used to be a decrepit old former country bar called the Mustang that my partners and I had poured a couple million into making the slickest, swankiest gentleman's club in Michigan.

Cops generally like topless clubs, even though the police are usually the mere tools of politicians. The politicians use the cops to bust topless clubs in order to create the favorable impression that the candidate for higher office or office-holder is being tough on crime and protecting the community by busting these easy targets. But cops are guys. Guys are guys. What makes you think the boys in blue are all that different from you and me? And, what makes you think a cop is necessarily good? There are bad cops, just like there are bad guys in any segment of the general population. But they can and do get away with murder. In my case, they came damned close.

The facts: The cop who shot me did it with his own gun, a .40 caliber Glock that he personally registered with the Inkster police as his service weapon. He was in the club the night of the shooting with his partner—both of them off duty, both of them drinking. He was married. Nothing that unusual. He is white and his partner is black. No laws broken so far. Have a few drinks, enjoy a few lap dances, drive home, no problem. At the very least, a cop is unlikely to get busted for drunk driving by another cop, so a happy end to a happy evening. But the cop in question, a guy by the name of Lessner, must have had some problems that didn't show up in his aptitude test for becoming a police officer. Like insanity, rage, and senseless acts of random violence. The simple explanation that everyone in the club that night agrees on is that the cop who was the shooter did not want to leave the club. He had been arguing about something with one of my entertainers, a dancer by the name of Rose, who he maybe did or did not have a "thing" for. Finally, he was persuaded by staff to call it a night and, not appearing to be visibly intoxicated, was given back his weapon from the office safe. He and his partner exited the club. And, for a few precious minutes, that seemed to be the end of the story.

Except: A few minutes later one of the parking valets was inside the club, telling me and my night manager and partner

Ron Szolack that the cops were making trouble, bypassing the valet to retrieve their own vehicle, yelling and cursing. It was at this very second that I made the momentous, and unconscious, decision to go out front myself to see what was happening. As I stepped outside the main entrance to the club, I heard multiple gunshots. I suddenly felt an intense stinging, or burning in my face and neck. I really didn't put two and two together to understand that one of the bullets flying at thousands of feet per second had slammed into me. When I characterize taking the bullet with getting hit in the head with a baseball bat, it's because I was stunned and in shock from the sudden impact. It didn't quite register when my parking valet said that my face looked like hamburger, either. "I think you've been shot," he'd said. Shot? What?

Me?

I walked back into the club, aware that I wanted to get away from the situation outside, thinking it was dangerous. But of course it was too late. The pain began to kick in, and I found myself thinking I really had been whacked by a Louisville Slugger. I unconsciously stroked the side of my head and blood appeared on my hand. I remember Ronnie, my manager, running up to me and saying, "Jesus, Alan, you don't look so good—you'd better lie down!"

Lie down I did, or maybe "crumple" is a better word, right there on the floor inside the club. People were gathering around me, but their faces were getting dim as I began to drift in and out of consciousness. I knew I didn't want to fade to black. I was afraid that if I did, I would die. I fought to remain aware. Someone called EMS and told me an ambulance was on the way. It would be ten minutes, but it felt like an hour. Lying there with my head on a stack of linen table napkins, the real nice, heavy kind—with my blood seeping into them, turning them into a warm, sodden heap of crimson cloth—I waited . . .

The next thing I knew, I was in the ambulance, listening to the scream and whoop of the siren as if it were somewhere in the distance. The voices of the paramedics murmuring with seriousness—calling the emergency room at Annapolis Hospital, just a few minutes away, to give them my vitals and a basic description of their latest gunshot victim—white male, late thirties, apparently shot in the head, heavy bleeding, stand by for blood type . . .

But, once we got to the Annapolis ER, my plight became worse, and a bit more absurd. With doctors crowding around above me, I listened in disbelief to the ensuing debate.

"Do we know how many bullets he took?"

"We have on the report multiple gunshots, we don't have a count."

"What about entry and exit wounds?"

"It's hard to tell, he's really torn up."

"Yeah, we need to get an X-ray. How much blood has he lost?"

"It doesn't look like he's losing a lot right now . . . "

I remember a light being pointed into my eyes, waved back and forth. "Alan, can you hear us? Can you blink your eyes for me?"

"Yeah," I moaned through broken bone and torn flesh, with already drying, coagulated blood from my broken jaw hampering my effort to speak. "I can hear you."

To me, my words sounded slurred, muffled—I was in their hands now, nothing else to do. When you're the victim of a violent crime, you are compromised in your ability to even communicate, but in your head, your thoughts are still going a million miles an hour. "Pain, pain . . . " I slurred. They haven't given me anything for the pain, so this is fucking beginning to hurt like hell. That means I'm alive, that's good, but I'm in excruciating pain!

"We don't know where the bullet or bullets have gone, whether they're still in you, Alan."

Yeah, I thought, well, get 'em out! What the hell, is this a hospital or a debate society meeting?!? I felt like I was going to go delirious when I heard a voice say I was going to get a shot for the pain, to hold on, I was about to be transferred by a maize and blue University of Michigan medevac chopper to Ann Arbor where they had an ace trauma team who were gearing up for my arrival. Another ten, twenty minutes and I'd be in the renowned U of M system, where if the fine surgeons couldn't save my life and put me back together, nobody could.

My thoughts kept coming to me randomly: what a night, shit, I wonder how we did tonight . . . gotta call my dad, where's my cell phone . . . where's my wallet . . . who cares . . . sort it out tomorrow, tomorrow'll be better, gotta get back to the club . . . this is really gonna screw things up. The pain, is it gone now? I'm not feeling the pain, yeah, that's good, I think. I hope that's good.

I also recall being told a guy who was stabbed was going into surgery before me . . . what—stabbing is better than being shot? I wasn't thinking too coherently. And that's the last I remember of anything till I woke up from my first surgery, to see my doctor, Dr. Buchman, standing by my hospital bed. "Alan, how do you feel?"

I tried what I thought might pass for speech, but it probably came out as a guttural moan.

"That's all right, Alan. I'm here to tell you that you're a very lucky man. You were struck by one bullet that tore up your cheek pretty good on its way through. You lost several teeth, but don't worry, we wired them back in. Your jaw was broken from the impact and your upper palate was damaged as well. The bullet came to rest between your carotid artery and your jugular vein. A few millimeters further and you likely would have bled to death before the ambulance even got you to the hospital."

"Shit. What's next?" I mumbled. "Uh—this really hurts . . ."

"That's a morphine pump we've got you attached to. Take this, and when the pain becomes more than you're comfortable with, push the button. We'll want to wean you off this in the next few days, however."

As I lay there listening to what Dr. Buchman said next, I thought I was going to faint. Sometimes, the detailed description is more excruciating than the actual injury.

"You see, Alan, in addition to the six fractures, the impact from the bullet caused an extensive network of hairline cracks. It's sort of like what happens if you pour boiling water over ice, it happens instantly as the bone absorbs the incredible amount of energy from the bullet and has to dissipate that energy in a millisecond. Since you're jaw is wired up very carefully, those breaks and hairline cracks will heal, but it's going to take time and further surgeries. You won't be able to talk very well, if at all."

To cut to the chase, I was wired up tight for four long months, and lost 35 pounds in the process. My initial stint in the hospital was nine days, and when I got out I was shattered in more than the physical sense. I had six more surgeries over the next few years to look forward to, half by Dr. Buchman, who specializes in maxillofacial reconstruction, and half by other surgeons who took care of dental and facial work to restore me as closely as possible to my former self. The cop who shot me, all he did afterwards was get into his car and drive off.

So, what do you think would happen to you or me if we started blasting caps into a building and shot somebody in the head . . . and then left the scene of the crime? How about this— you have to resign from your job, but you've got a great union and they'll go to bat for you to force your employer to give your job back. The gun you used in the crime? Your boss lets you keep it, and the only way the county prosecutor gets hold of the evidence is by getting the Michigan state police to investigate the crime because he doesn't trust the local Inkster PD to do the job. In fact, the state police had to get a search warrant to search the cop's premises for his weapon because he wasn't giving up that gun voluntarily. In fact, it took three days before the cop could be persuaded to voluntarily turn himself in.

But wait, it gets even better. The criminal trial is a joke, because the cop, despite numerous eyewitnesses and forensic evidence that proved that he shot me with his own gun, a mandatory two-year felony, he cops a deal and pleads out to probation. He lied on the stand and said that it was an accident—that he just dropped his gun and it went off. The judge, Kay Terzak, was assigned the penalty phase of the trial after the jury determined the shooter was in fact at fault. But Terzak was very pro cop. Hey, it's your first random, accidental drunken shooting . . . no problem . . . we'll spot you one, but pleeease, do try to be a bit more careful next time you're at the strip club, won't you? He also lost his job with Inkster, but not to worry, there's another police department out there that doesn't have a problem with cops who are criminals. Plus, and forgive me if I'm a tad paranoid, I'm just a lowly strip club owner, the world would be better off without my type. Except it's funny how many cops, attorneys, politicians, little league coaches, and sundry other pillars of society love to spend a few days a month at the gentleman's club, enjoying the scenery and tipping a few.

Finally, the only way to redress the pain and suffering I went through, as well as the $200,000 Blue Cross Blue–Shield bill, was a civil suit which resulted in a jury trial, where the burden of proof for the cop's culpability is lower than in a criminal proceeding. Should be a slam dunk. And it was, thankfully. The city of Inkster was the party with the money and had a $1 million insurance policy in place for situations like the cop's, but the lawyers for the insurer argued that the club bore a certain percentage of responsibility for the shooting. Go figure that one, will you? I'm sure your insurance agent would be able to explain it in 25,000 words or less.

The civil trial to assign responsibility and determine damages was a joke of its own sort. I felt that I was treated by the judge as less than an equal member of society, because every time I, or my lawyer, tried to argue for a greater remedy for pain and suffering, we were squelched. That is, basically, told to stuff it. But they couldn't stifle my right to read my own victim impact statement . . . although the judge rebuked me for glancing at the in-court camera as I was reading it, by saying, "Mr. Markovitz, you are not to look at the camera, you are to look at me!" Still, we ended up with a close to $300,000 settlement, so I guess you could call it a wash. Except for the six or seven months that I had to spend at home recovering from the incident, the years of additional surgeries, and the profound depression I fought. Fortunately, my father and step-mom came to my assistance throughout this bleak period, and my very capable partners and managers kept 747 humming while I was gone. I was forced to rethink everything—chiefly, could I even go back to the business, the very place where I so nearly had my head blown off? Thinking back to my first shooting, in my twenties, when I was younger, stronger . . . seemed like a few lifetimes ago. You get shot this badly when you're in late thirties, a lot of people in my spot never snap back. And to add insult to injury, my fiancée, Terri, bailed on me in the middle of the whole mess. If that doesn't give you a death-warmed-over-black-hole depression to be proud of, you are made of some rare alloy from another planet in a parallel universe, my friend. Unless you're superhuman, you become a mere shell of your former self. A hollow shell. Which is exactly how I felt.

My fiancée Terri? Now there's a story for you. We had met almost four years earlier, in 1993. I was doing my banking at the time at a private institution up Telegraph Road in Bloomfield Hills, Telegraph and Long Lake to be exact. I was in one day taking care of some business with the assistant manager when I glanced over at the teller windows and felt like I took a fist to the gut—she was a knockout! I couldn't help but stare. I said to the manager, "Who is that teller over there—she's gorgeous!"

Without missing a beat, the manager dead-panned back, "She's a bitch."

I didn't care. I was hooked from the instant I locked eyes on her. She was a tall, sultry brunette who was a dead ringer for my favorite actress, Lauren Bacall, in her salad days, and just my type. She really got me going and I knew instantly that I had to meet her, whatever it took. I'm the same way with anything that I'm passionate about, business or pleasure. Maybe that's the secret of my success, that when I see something that fills me with a burning desire, I will do anything it takes to achieve my desire.

Even though I already had a business account at the bank, I decided on the spot that I would open a personal checking account, so that I had an excuse to go to her window, and I did, in the next twenty minutes. And I chatted her up, using her name—hey, it's right there on the little nameplate thing—and dragging out the process of opening the account as long as possible. I thanked her politely for her help and left, returning the following day to make a deposit and try to get her phone number. I simply asked for it, telling her straight up that I liked her and would like to ask her out sometime.

Terri was definitely very cool at first, formal, a little uptight.

"I don't normally make a practice of going out with customers," she told me. But she did give up her number. Wasting no time, I called her that night, asking her out to dinner Saturday, end of the week. Her answer was swift and directly to the point. "I don't think so." Damn! Shot down just like that. Ah, well, I've learned to be philosophical about these things. Maybe I could try talking to her in another week, slow it down a little, keep it casual and see what happens. But thirty minutes later, out of the blue, Terri called me on my cell—she had the number from my account record at the bank.

"I'm sorry I was so blunt with you before. I'll go out with you, but it can't be this weekend and next week isn't so good either."

It took me three weeks out to find a date she was able to make, but at last we had a meeting of the minds. We were on, and as cool as she was playing it, I had the sense she was really into the idea, that she was intrigued and perhaps flattered. I was going to pull out all the stops with this one, flat out do everything possible to impress her.

In the early 1990s, I had my own look, to put it mildly. I call it the basic Mr. T starter kit, after the iconic pimp daddy of the same name from the old A Team television show . . . you remember him, black dude with a Mohawk, multiple heavy gold rope chains? I trimmed out the attitude with a three-quarter-length coyote coat, massive filigreed box-frame glasses, and ostrich skin cowboy boots. And then there was my ride: A mint-condition bloodred 1985 Ferrari Testarossa. OK, I know, it all sounds a bit over the top, and it was. It's fun going over the top.

Saturday night I drove to Terri's place in Waterford, just south of Pontiac in a region of Detroit's suburbs known for its generous scattering of lakes, expecting to find a big, fancy house where this Lauren Bacall type would surely live. Instead I found a modest, well-kept ranch where Terri still lived, at twenty-five, with her parents, attending nearby Oakland University in her off hours.

Terri greeted me at the front door in a tasteful but curve-hugging little black dress, an off-the-shoulder number with long fitted sleeves that accentuated her lithe, beautifully turned arms and plunged to frame the kind of cleavage that Michelangelo would have loved to have carved for the ages. Man, she was gorgeous! And she carried herself like a movie star, with a killer combination of dignity and smoldering sexuality that had me getting . . . you get the idea.

I had picked a fine little Italian restaurant way down the Detroit River in Wyandotte, charming, dark, romantic . . . and leaving plenty of time on the drive to chat and get to know one another better. I was a real gentleman, very polite with her, and we had great chemistry. As we sat across from one another over large tulip glasses of Cabernet Sauvignon, I thought to myself, this is more like it . . . I've just got to wean myself off these dancers. I need a nice, sweet regular girl without all the complications. Yeah, well. Maybe with fewer complications. Nothing in life is perfect, nothing is ideal. As gorgeous as some topless entertainers indeed are, when you take them out of the club, put 'em in sweatpants, and add twenty pounds, you'll see how human they really are.

But I was focused on my dynamite date, Terri, not the club girls who had been yanking my chain lately. She would become the first girl outside the business that I had dated since college and become serious about. I felt like I was getting my act together for a change, and I actually began thinking what it would be like to settle down with one woman. Terri had it all: looks, personality . . . and as I was to find out on our third date, she was totally crazy in bed. For all her well-groomed wholesomeness, Terri was practically insatiable in the sack. What more could any guy want? Sweet, smart, beautiful, and totally capable of turning your libido inside out. And remember, I'd sown my oats with some of the best, from the early days of The Booby Trap when half the dancers were years older than I was! Having been there and done that, I finally felt ready to take myself off the market with one special lady.

Unfortunately, the idyll of the following four years with Terri as my one and only came to a crushing end, culminating with being shot in the head. I think that between the demands of my business—and the type of business I'm in—coupled with the total chaos and extreme violence that she lived through with me in the aftermath of the shooting was just all too much for her.

I came back home in the wee hours after work, after I had returned to work, seven months into the year 1997, and found the note. It read:

I'm sorry Alan, I can't live like this anymore. No hard feelings, I love you, Terri.

She had moved all her things out. That was that. Exhausted, devastated, I dropped onto my unmade king-size bed and fell into a troubled sleep.

Moving On

Check one: ____I get restless, ____I get bored, ____I get pissed. So I open a new topless club.

Maybe check all three. Now you understand my psychology, though it's not quite as simple as it appears. Opening and operating topless clubs is what I do. And I have going on three decades' experience doing it, which is why I am formidable competition. Gaining experience and knowledge makes it easier for me to open and operate topless clubs. But it does not guarantee successful results—that still requires hard work, no matter how many years you have behind you.

About the time that everything came to a head with Freddy, things started falling into place for my next venture. I have learned that in my line of work, with long lead times from identifying and acquiring a property to getting through all the zoning, site planning, permits, and construction blueprints, you must think and act two or more years ahead. If you don't, you're forever behind the eight ball and you'll never grow. Just as they teach at the top business schools, if your business isn't growing, it's dying.

Furthermore, I had a great impetus to get as far away from Eight Mile as I could. My experience with almost going belly up at Trumpps when the heat came down from the police and the "community activists" had taught me a big lesson. I intended to never again find myself in such a vulnerable position. In the past, under Detroit Mayor Coleman Young, a live-and-let-live attitude prevailed between the city and topless entertainment. Young and his administration were pragmatists. They knew that the convention business—which Detroit sorely needed more of—thrives on out-of-towners being able to indulge their appetites with a broad range of adult entertainment, particularly gentleman's clubs. Young knew this was a mutually beneficial, symbiotic relationship, and he was content to leave club owners alone as long as they stayed more or less in line.

The one thing I will always remember about him is that there was no bullshit in him. If he didn't like something he would tell you flat out where you stood with him. By the same token, he understood the legal and legitimate status of the gentleman's clubs in the city and didn't aim to make any political points by coming down on us. To Coleman Young, crime was crime—black or white—and he owed it to the residents of Detroit to know which kind of crimes needed priority. Violent crimes and property crimes, in that order. After that, his job was all about attracting business, jobs, and investment to the city. His was an uphill battle, perhaps, but he sure didn't waste any time sticking his nose in other people's business. Coleman Young was a good man.

With the advent of the Archer administration, it suddenly became more politic to come down on high-profile clubs in order to reinforce the image of "cleaning up Detroit" and making the city more respectable and family-oriented, so to speak. But Archer talked out of both sides of his mouth—he'd glad-hand you if you were contributing money to his PAC, but when it came to being seen at a public fund-raiser with one of his donors, he'd give you the cold shoulder. I know. I had both experiences with him. Of course, I still had my interests on Eight Mile, in the form of buyout agreements under "management" rules, under which buyers of a topless club can run the place as if it is their own while they make payments, like a land contract, toward 100 percent ownership. But I had decided it was too risky to keep all my eggs in that particular basket.

While Michigan Avenue was an unknown entity, it looked to be wide open. That could cut two ways. The topless clubs already operating on Michigan from Leggs on the West Side near Ypsilanti, all the way to Bogarts and Henry the VIII near the location I had my eye on—Michigan just west of Middlebelt—were very profitable but host to a rough crowd. This was not the clientele I wanted to cultivate, and I was not sure if I could draw upscale patrons to an out-of-the-way location. But Michigan Avenue was a diamond in the rough, perhaps the only place in all of metro Detroit that had the potential I was looking for, and a suitable property was available.

The Mustang was a dive of a country bar, on eastbound Michigan Avenue just west of Middlebelt Road, bracketed by a Detroit Edison electric substation on one side and a discount furniture dealer on the other. It wasn't much to look at—painted concrete block and a gravel parking lot. But it did come with something that is now virtually impossible to obtain: a grandfathered cabaret license permitting topless entertainment, approved years before at the same time that the two nearby topless bars, Henry the VIII and Bogarts, were licensed. But the Mustang wasn't utilizing its license; it had been inactive for several years.

Inkster history and the story of Michigan Avenue bear some attention. Michigan Avenue runs west from downtown Detroit proper all the way to Chicago. The stretch of Michigan where The Flight Club is located lies between Dearborn (and Ford Motor Company World Headquarters) and the far west side where the Detroit suburbs fan out into Wayne, Ypsilanti, Ann Arbor, and beyond. It isn't the prettiest stretch of highway you've ever seen, by any means, but it is as heavily trafficked as Eight Mile. With the airport and I-94 just to the south, also running east/west from Detroit to Chicago, I-96 to the north running from Detroit and northwest to Grand Rapids, and the north/south I-275 just to the west reaching up into the beginnings of the Detroit area's monied suburbs, The Flight Club is an easily accessible location.

Interestingly enough, Inkster was founded in the 1860s by a Scotsman named Robert Inkster, who operated a steampowered sawmill near the intersection of Michigan Avenue and Inkster Road. Flash forward: By the 1930s, in the midst of the Depression, when Henry Ford's automotive empire was the envy of the industrialized world—and Inkster was a largely black community—old Henry spent upwards of half a million dollars (more than $10 million today) to create and rehabilitate housing there, to the benefit and appreciation of Ford's many black employees, both blue- and white-collar. Ford hired many other minorities, as well, long before other white businessmen. Perhaps that's why some people have said Ford was as much a "social engineer" as a mechanical one.

Also, in the 1950s, black leader Malcolm X lived in Inkster. Later, the core of the Motown music group The Marvelettes (Gladys Horton and Georgia Dobbius) were residents when they wrote the chart-topping hit "Hello Mr. Postman."

Frank Vitale, the owner of the property, thought something could be worked out with the city of Inkster. A dormant license seemed to be just a formality, he said. Of course, he's going to be optimistic—he wants to sell the property! Who could blame him? But remember—caveat emptor—Latin for "Let the buyer beware." Everybody in this world of ours is trying to sell you something . . . it's up to the buyer to know what he's getting himself into. If more people stopped for just a minute or two and applied this logic to decisions that we are all confronted with every day, there would be a lot less fraud and a lot more happy people in the world.

I told Frank, "OK, we'll put $50,000 down against a purchase price of $500,000 . . . but only if we get the cabaret license and can actually use it. If it's a no-go we get our deposit back.

"What about the legal bills?" Frank wanted to know.

"I'll pay all the legal bills until we get this sorted out—that's on my end."

The Mustang was open and operating as a country bar at this time and, as the owner, Frank was also running it. But he'd never even considered utilizing the cabaret license, so it was time to test the water. How? You make a phone call or you visit the city, Inkster, and tell 'em what you want to do. Unfortunately, the answer was a blunt, bureaucratic "No!" The license hadn't been used for years and the city's opinion was that the license had "expired." They just didn't want another topless club to deal with, like most municipalities.

The next step: My lawyer made some phone calls on the state level, to discover Michigan's position on the issue. Not surprisingly, Michigan simply deferred to Inkster's stance on the license and basically punted it out of their jurisdiction.

As unusual, in America, you need a good lawyer . . . a really good lawyer. These are not easy to find, but fortunately for me, my personal and business attorney, Harold Fried, had a referral for me. We needed a guy who could understand and argue at the highest levels and who understood constitutional law. The guy Harold came up with was a professor of constitutional law at Wayne State University, Professor Sadler, a PhD who was highly respected, had done work with the ACLU, and only took cases that were interesting and challenging to him.

My dad ran point on this one for me. "From a Jewish survivor, to a successful Jewish lawyer, we'll have a lot to talk about,

Alan." he told me. "Let me set up a first meeting with him at Trumpps . . . he'll get a good look at what we do, and I'm sure I'll be able to impress upon him that we're serious business-men."

"OK, Dad, it's all yours," I said. I was both very comfort-able and confident leaving the matter in my father's hands.

The meeting took place the following week. Professor Sadler was normally not a patron of gentleman's clubs, but he was entertained and intrigued by the business. He and my father had a good chemistry from the moment they shook hands, and they spent a good two hours sharing stories and talking about the way the topless business operates. My father carefully laid out the situation with the Mustang, and Professor Sadler lis-tened intently.

"He's hooked, Alan," my father reported. "He's going to take it to the federal level; we'll file suit and get a ruling."

"You think he's the guy who can go the distance, Dad?"

"If he can't do it, nobody can."

It took us many months to get on the calendar, but nothing good comes without a fight.

On our first foray into federal court in Detroit, we drew a judge who was an older, black woman with a well-known con-servative bent. Now, you can say what you will about judges being impartial and all that, that's what they're supposed to do, but it seems to me that "interpretation" of the law leaves a helluva lot of room for judges to make decisions that they are politically motivated to make. I had a bad feeling about this one—and I was right. She pretty much took one look at the case and when she saw the word "topless" she figuratively blew her top and ruled against us so fast you'd swear there was a revolving door on the courthouse.

After that fiasco, Professor Sadler assured me, "We're not licked. It's just getting interesting. I can appeal the case to the Federal Appellate Court in Cincinatti. I've been there before—it's a three-judge panel, a good bunch. They will listen seriously to our argument from a strictly constitutional perspective."

Finally, after a few more months, we had a date on the docket and off to Cincinatti we went. Without going into the excruciating details of the case, the appellate court more or less said that since the city had originally granted a cabaret license for that location, it was grandfathered in. The city of Inkster had not seen fit to attempt to revoke the license, and since precedent states that the license stays with the physical location that it was granted to, the city had no choice but to let us operate as a topless club. The judges even said that the decision of the Detroit federal judge was "an attempt to legislate from the bench," a big no-no. Courts are supposed to interpret laws and uphold them, not make them. The appeals court even granted us damages! We would be able to go after Inkster for whatever money we could justifiably have made had we been allowed to operate—from the time we were denied the license to the date of the ruling.

I was ecstatic. Professor Sadler told us that unless Inkster took the case to the Supreme Court, we were good as gold; that even if that happened, decisions by the Federal Court of Appeals are very rarely overruled. Now, we could move forward and see if the city was still willing to mess with us. I called up Vitale and told him "Let's rip!" I plowed another $20,000 into the project with the idea that we'd build up a simple stage and put some girls in, topless of course, under the Mustang name for a couple months, 6:00 p.m. till 2:00 a.m., and see what happened. When that went without a hitch—the Inkster cops even stopped in to say hello!—we knew we were probably solid and continued to gear up for the big time.

Now we could really start to think seriously about the damages the Cincinatti judges had awarded us. After careful deliberation between me and the accountants, it was calculated that from the time we had first put money down on the bar and tried to activate the license to the time of the appeals ruling, we had lost out on a gross figure of $2 million. But we didn't want the money. Instead, we would drop all the damages against the city of Inkster—and believe me, $2 million is a lot to a cash-strapped municipality—if we were instead allowed to build what we wanted on the site, without restriction. Of course, we had plans all drawn up, and we would be tearing the old building down and building something beautiful and totally high-end to replace it. It was a great deal for Inkster in light of their resounding defeat in court, and they took it.

We were off and running. It would take another two million dollars before we had it where we wanted it, and we still needed a name. But we were miles away from Eight Mile! Either the new club would draw high-end clientele to a part of Michigan Avenue that had never had a club of this caliber before . . . or it wouldn't. But I was betting two mill that it would work; it truly was the time to pull out all the stops. But the name, the name! What to call it? Being near the airport, maybe something that tied in with aviation would be good. There was already a club in nearby Romulus, to the west of Detroit Metropolitan, that had an airport-themed name—The Landing Strip. But man, I dug those jet planes. I always liked to fly, and I had dreamed for years of one day having my own personal jet, a dream that would indeed come true. All right—what was the biggest, baddest jet—everybody knows the answer to that one! The Boeing 747! Sweet. Short. Powerful and to the point. Everybody I bounced the idea off of liked it. It just had that ring to it . . . and I liked the idea of having a club that had a number for a name. I got hold of one of the graphic artists that I'd used before, designing signage and logos for my other clubs, and described my vision: I wanted a gorgeous pair of female legs, kind of like the nose art that was made famous on B-24 bombers during World War II, designed around the numbers, with wings. The final design bears a distinct resemblance to the metal "wings" pins that are awarded to pilots in the Air Force when they graduate, or the wings airline captains wear. With the design finalized and colorized, I had a gonzo neon sign built that would be affixed high up on the top of the club's 25-foot façade. I had a real good feeling about this one.

It takes time to build a club at a new location. As I have said repeatedly, you've got to build the best, offer the best service, and above all attract and keep the hottest dancers . . . once the word starts getting out, customers will follow. It's a simple formula, but many, many operators just can't seem to get it right or are content to run "B" clubs and take home less than the lion's share of the market. To get the lion's share, you've simply got to think—and act—like a lion! Hence the name 747, which quickly became the buzz in the Detroit adult club market. Despite getting shot, and having to stay away from the club to convalesce, the biz was on a screaming vertical climb. Hell, inside of the first six months we were clocking some $20,000 days. And that's seven days a week. Till you're totally rocking out at max gross, you plow as much of that profit as possible back into improving every single detail of the club . . . relentlessly and continually.

So, with the shooting behind me, having overcome fits of anger and depression, having lost my fiancée Terri because she couldn't or wouldn't take the heat any longer, 747 became my refuge and my reason for being. Besides, I still had my interests in my other clubs—All Star and Trumpps. Tycoon's, which I had sold, provided the rainy day fund I'm so fond of now, knowing how quickly business conditions can turn on you. My father was terrific in keeping an eye on my business while I healed, and my very capable manager and partner, Brian Everidge and Ron Szolack, were running the ship. That's why taking percentage partners pays off—it's their business too and vested partners are true partners.

It was not long after I started to get back into the club a couple or three times a week that I got a feeling something hinky was going on. Granted, in a dimly lit topless club, there's always something "hinky" you need to keep your eye on. Dancers getting a little too friendly with customers, employees who might be skimming, customers who may be engaged in illegal activities, you name it. But the trouble I smelled came in the form of a couple of out-of-town suits. They were well-dressed, but not too well-dressed. Kind of a cross between accountants and lawyers. But they looked a little bit too straight, if you know what I mean, maybe a tad bit boy scouty. One of my people saw one of them snapping a picture of the 747 logo sign. On its own, not that unusual. Out-of-towners, especially European tourists, often take souvenir photos. But these guys were also surreptitiously picking up business cards, table toppers, even a club menu. What the hell did they want all this stuff for? They even bought a half dozen assorted 747 logo wearables from the club boutique—T-shirts, caps, golf shirts, that sort of thing.

I forgot all about the funny fellows who seemed to love anything and everything 747 till about a month later when I received a registered letter from a law firm in Seattle with about six names on the letterhead—you know: Jack, Lipschitz, Biggs, Billings and Scrodd—that kind of name. Who the hell do I know in Seattle, I wondered, as I ripped the envelope open and unfolded the heavy, legal letter inside. Ahhhh . . . on behalf of our client, Boeing . . . hey, Boeing makes the 747 . . . we hereby demand that you cease and desist using the Boeing trademark "747" as the apparent name of the club . . . yeah, yeah, remove it from physical plant as well as all marketing and promotional materials . . . blah blah blah. What the hell! Maybe there was a Boeing 747, but it's just a freaking number after all! They oughta have been flattered I'm out there promoting the legend of such a fantastic airplane, but it's just a number, after all.

Let me tell you, that stupid figure ended up costing me about six figures. As you may have already deduced, I am persistent, tenacious, even stubborn. Those are among my best qualities. But they can work against you sometimes. I picked up the phone and called Harold Fried and told him about the letter. He chuckled, said something about not being too surprised. His advice was that it was probably not a bad idea to give in and change the name of the club. Boeing had some very deep pockets, Harold reminded me. It was unlikely they would be inclined to just roll over or forget about the issue. Or be intimidated. Yeah, maybe so, I replied, but I had a lot of dough invested in that number, and my logo, and that was all wrapped up in the success of the club. I wasn't about to screw with success. What chance did we have, I argued, of challenging Boeing on the trademark? Bless him, Harold's a sporting chap and relishes a good fight. It was his opinion, after studying the matter for a few days, that our use of the numbers 747—and they are just numbers after all—was a usage that was nonconflicting with Boeing's. Something along the lines of: You can't make a pair of shoes and call them Hush Puppies because there is a trademarked brand out there actively selling shoes under that name . . . but you can probably open a restaurant called Hush Puppies, especially if you serve hush puppies—those little breaded potato balls popular in the American south.

Well, we weren't selling airplanes, after all . . . we were selling topless entertainment! So what if our logo gave the impression of flying and airplanes; that was an association, not an outright attempt to confuse or defraud the public. Harold figured we'd write a firm letter to Boeing's lawyers telling them of our position in legal detail. He'd seen a vigorous response make similar lawsuits go away before. It was worth a try. How much could Boeing really care about one lone gentleman's club in—of all places, Inkster, Michigan—using numbers that by themselves did nothing but coincidentally recall their flagship airliner?

Come to find out Boeing's pretty damned tenacious for an upstart multibillion-dollar corporation! The fight was on. Harold pulled a trademark lawyer in on our side and he sent off a great letter, but, instead of getting a nice letter back saying "Sorry to bother you," we got a real lawsuit. Boeing's philosophy is to aggressively pursue any and all cases of perceived trademark infringement with great abandon, that is, with as much money as it takes to vanquish their foes. What followed was many months of depositions, questionnaires to patrons of 747 to determine the commonality of the perception of those numbers as representative of a plane versus a gentleman's club; conferences upon conferences, and many, many billable hours to the lawyers. I was pushing well past the $50,000 mark and getting little or no traction. At a certain point, you either win, lose, or get tired and tapped . . . whichever comes first.

After consuming most of the year 1999, the suit was looking more and more like a futile, wasteful exercise. I was at the point where I saw that I could easily blow another fifty grand . . . and still lose. Boeing was not going away peacefully. So I capitulated. In straight parlance, I said, "Fuck it. It's not worth it." The sooner you recognize that, you call it quits—but you don't really quit—you merely have to change direction. Suddenly change doesn't look so bad. Boeing wasn't looking for damages, they just wanted me to cut it out. That was their bottom line. In the end, it was a simple, billable phone call to the Boeing lawyers to say "OK, you win," to which they very politely replied "Thank you very much. Good day!" So the folks who really scored were, naturally, the lawyers.

In the end, I still loved the association with aviation that the 747 moniker had provided. I didn't want to give that up. As for the logo, that was mine . . . the legs and the wings I owned. After thinking about the logo for a while, I realized I needed something totally generic but at the same time very specific. Somehow my mind drifted to those VIP airline lounges that frequent fliers or first-class ticket holders get to enjoy; they were kind of like private clubs, I thought. So, a flight lounge . . . or a flight club? Not a flight club; The Flight Club! The Flight Club. Eureka! That's it!

My graphic artist did a dandy job shoehorning the new words into the legs 'n' wings logo, and in a matter of weeks we had a new neon sign built to hang upside the building. Then, of course, we had to scrub "747" from every matchbook, biz card, menu, and promotional material we had as well as destroying all the 747 wearable merchandise still in stock. Our phone book listing, website, everything had to be changed. I'm sure we ended up spending at least another $50,000 or more putting the name change into effect, pushing the total cost of the battle over those three little numbers into the low six figures.

Flight Club Air

When you're flying high, the temptation is to fly even higher . . . or further afield. After changing over to our new name, The Flight Club, business just kept getting better and better. I was vindicated in my decision to risk an unproved location for an ultra-upscale club, vindicated in my decision to move away from Eight Mile, and totally vindicated in spending over two million dollars to build The Flight Club into the hottest club—not only in Michigan, but nationwide, as rated by real customers who have visited The Flight Club as well as other top clubs across the U.S. and voted on them (along with posting commentary) on TUSCL.com, a website devoted to rating the best clubs in every market. As this book was being written The Flight Club was number one among all gentleman's clubs coast to coast, a ranking that I will spend any amount necessary and do anything to defend.

That doesn't mean, however, that everything I do works out perfectly. Even when you're on top in my business, you have to innovate. Along the lines of "flying high," I soon hatched a new idea for setting The Flight Club apart from the competition in a totally on-theme way. I started my own charter airline, Flight Club Air, with direct topless service between Detroit and Las Vegas. The idea was a no-brainer. Everybody loves Vegas, especially folks in the Detroit area, who are known to overwhelmingly fly to Sin City rather than Atlantic City for their gambling and entertainment.

In addition to making money off the all-first-class, all-inclusive food and drink flights, I would be fairly certain of garnering tons of publicity for the club. We would start by offering weekly flights, departing on Fridays and returning on Mondays, so that everyone (including the girls) could have a full-blown blast and get back to work bright-eyed and bushy-tailed the first of the week.

Shopping around, I discovered that with not one but two world-class major airports sitting right next to one another—Detroit Metro and Detroit Willow Run—there was a whole lot more charter service available than meets the eye. A lot of people don't know that in addition to being one of the busiest cargo airports in the country, Willow Run is an amazingly easy-in, easy-out center for private jets, everything from corporate-owned planes to the personal aircraft of some real high rollers, like GM's Bob Lutz, who keeps a couple of his own planes hangared there, including a Czech-made fighter that he flies himself.

I soon had a deal arranged for a Boeing 727 that would give me fifty first-class seats at $1,995 a pop, all you can drink, and service by six to eight entertainers who upon reaching 40,000 feet would lose their tops. With the bubbly and booze flowing, they stood to do very well indeed giving private (or maybe not-so-private) lap dances for the well-heeled passengers, in addition to a guarantee of $500 each for the weekend, plus accommodations. The very first flight, which was scheduled in April 2003, was sold out, due in large part to the splashy full-page ads I'd taken out in the sports section of *The Detroit News*. The phone was ringing off the freaking hook.

At just under $100,000 gross per flight, I figured the cost of the plane and crew, at $90,000 for two days, would give a reasonable profit margin of $10,000, less of course three or four grand for the girls and a thousand or two for the alcohol, finger food, and laundry. Got to provide those nice linen napkins on a first-class titty bar flight, you know. I also had to amortize some kind of ongoing advertising campaign until word of mouth kicked in and people started booking flights in advance. We took all the bookings at the club, simply taking credit cards and giving verbal confirmation and departure instructions to the customers.

This simple system worked very well, but I soon found out that human nature—read: a bunch of strippers—turned loose on a plane and then in Las Vegas for two days in the proximity of a bunch of horny, well-heeled men was a perfect recipe for chaotic, unpredictable behavior. The very first time we did the run things began to go awry. Luggage got lost. Strippers got lost. Strippers got drunk and argued with passengers over whether they got three versus six private dances on the plane. Passengers complained. And, as you might surmise, costs did not stay fixed. There's an old, old joke familiar to folks involved in any kind of aviation enterprise. It goes like this: How do you make a million in aviation? Easy—start with a ten million! The price of jet fuel is only one intangible factor that fluctuates—usually upward—beyond one's control. At over $4 a gallon, a jet like the one we used to fly to Vegas easily runs up to $4,000 an hour (close to 1,000 gallons per hour) just to stay airborne. At three to four hours' travel time, the fuel bill for each trip could push to nearly $40,000 alone. The costs go up, particularly if there's a weather delay, gate delay, or strong headwinds that grossly increase the amount of fuel burned, and time that it's being burned, between point A and point B.

After we had run a half dozen flights, we were definitely getting the bugs worked out. The numbers, however, were a different story. Two grand was about the most that even rich dudes were willing to pop for the experience. You and I know that it's not a problem to get a seat to Vegas for a few hundred, round trip, if you shop it even the slightest bit. Granted, naked ladies who were each selected to be as close to being a "10" as possible were a draw, but you can see them just about everywhere you look in Las Vegas or by simply coming to The Flight Club any old day. When I sat down with my accountant to see the actual bottom line, I was floored.

"Alan," he told me, with the same serious, sober face used by Alan Greenspan to announce adverse economic news, "you're spending, on average, $95,000 every time you fly the plane round trip."

"Yeah . . . so I'm only making . . . " I knew what was coming.

"That's right. You're making sometimes about $5,000 a flight, but if fuel goes up even fifteen or twenty cents a gallon you could be making as little as $800 or $900 per charter."

"That ain't so hot, is it?"

"That ain't so hot."

The writing was on the airplane lavatory wall. There are a lot better ways to deploy ninety grand a month than rolling the dice on a profit that could be under a thousand. Or maybe zip. Between the bleak numbers and trying to manage exotic dancers by remote control nearly 2,000 miles away, it just wasn't worth it. If I had to spend more money to put chaperones on board, I'd definitely be gushing red ink. Flight Club Air, in retrospect, was probably worth a lot more in terms of the free publicity that we got as a result of running the experiment. Jay Leno riffed on us in his monologue and *Saturday Night Live* did a takeoff during their "fake news" portion of the show that was later rerun over and over again. Business in the club just kept getting better and better . . . those numbers have been on a steady uptick ever since we opened. As a result, I decided to keep my eggs in the basket that I knew best, running and perhaps opening additional topless clubs in major markets, where the upside was and is humongous.

I have since learned that I was actually doing better than some of the major airlines. Because of intense competition, having to maintain large numbers of feeder routes and being unable to summarily cancel flights that aren't fully booked, a big carrier like Delta, American, or Northwest can routinely do a coast-to-coast flight of a 757 with over two hundred people aboard and make as little as $200 for the entire run. And if just one less first-class passenger were to book that flight, the airline could easily lose $200 or more . . . all for a flight that burned $20,000 or more in jet fuel alone! No, thank you.

Keeping the Flight Club Flying

With 60-plus regular employees and a roster of three hundred dancers, believe me when I tell you, running The Flight Club is a high-stress, high-workload environment. You're sitting back in the office trying to eat your tuna and cottage cheese (don't let anyone tell you that a successful CEO can really get away with three-martini lunches and cheeseburgers three times a day) and every five minutes, no—every three minutes—there's a knock on the door and it's either a dancer or a manager, or another employee with a problem. Although, to be fair, it's usually one of the dancers. If you are a dancer and you are reading this, I have some advice for you, and it's the same advice I give face-to-face in the club: show up on time, do your job, police yourself, behave like a professional, and then take your profits and go home. I am not running dancer day care. I am not your daddy. I am not your priest or your rabbi or your confidante. I am a businessman who is in business to provide the best of topless entertainment to the most demanding of clientele, and in order to do so I have created the most exciting, dazzling, sumptuous atmosphere possible in which you and your talents are showcased. Against this mind-blowing backdrop, I provide jumbo shrimp the size of viable fetuses, prime beef designed to dissolve on your palate, drinks distilled by the gods, and cigars that Zeus himself wouldn't mind blowing all night long—all at a fair and reasonable profit for the purveyance thereof. I like to think of my clubs as adult Disneylands. You want a business plan? That's it in two words.

My only point is, it's an over-the-top business that has to be run to a fine point, or it flies apart from its own centrifugal force. A lot of people think I'm living a fantasy life, but the reality of having been shot twice and having had a murder contract taken out on my head underscores the daily meat grinder of running a club. It truly is a case of "don't try this at home." When I was younger, and more impressionable, I knew that I had to draw a line in the sand—drugs and alcohol were off limits—the women and the money, a little more difficult to counterbalance. But somehow, just like a pilot who knows that no matter how dense the soup is on an instrument flight plan, he's got to trust his instruments and land the damned thing so that he can fly again tomorrow, I always managed to keep my head screwed on enough so that a few turns wouldn't unscrew it totally. Yeah, some days I felt like Linda Blair in *The Exorcist*, head spinning like a merry-go-round.

For example, I had a young manager, Bruce, at one of my other clubs in the late 1980s. He started as a clean-cut, hard-working kid, parking cars. He was honest, sincere, dependable. He worked himself up to assistant manager, and then a fulltime manager. He was married, but he always loved the ladies, loved being around them, but never let them or the life suck him in. One of my current managers, and partner, trained him and trained him right, taking the older-brother approach. I had confidence that this guy was in it for the long haul, that if anyone would become seasoned enough to end up on top, maybe even partner material, it was him. But after I sold the club, something happened. I didn't see Bruce for a couple of years, but I started hearing stories about him.

Seems Bruce got into coke. Started spending like a high roller. Bought a Corvette and then a couple of Harleys. And a houseboat. Then, he apparently got a girlfriend, one of the dancers who worked for him, and that led to him setting up a little love nest for the two of them—an apartment on the side. His girlfriend started milking him for money, too, and then he was suddenly juggling a double life, doing tons of blow, drinking . . . you can see where this is going. Not unlike working in asbestos removal, or coal mining, there are definite occupational hazards to working in a topless environment. After his marriage failed, Bruce had to get out of town; he was deeply in debt. He had to look for a new line of work, one without the temptations to which he had fallen prey.

It's not just the employees. Customers who grow too fond of the life can and do get in over their heads, too. More than one patron of my clubs has told me, "I don't golf, or sail, or keep a box at the stadium. This is my country club." It's not unusual to see food and drink tabs at The Flight Club of $500 or $1,000. Sometimes, you'll see a guy come out of nowhere, start spending four or five days a week at the club, dropping $2,000 to $3,000 a week or more, and he'll suddenly disappear, never to be seen again. I think about the largest one-time tab I've ever seen was something above $20,000—over the course of a single afternoon and evening! Now, how do you spend that much money at a topless bar? Easy. You buy bottle after bottle of Dom or Cristal at $350 a bottle. You buy drinks and food—lobster, shrimp, steaks—for your friends, the shot girls, the dancers. You get a fifth of fifty-year-old Hennessy for a couple grand. And then you have endless lap dances in the VIP lounge at the rate of $25 for three or four minutes. That's good for $400 or $500 an hour. Plus, you tip everybody with hundred-dollar bills, from the bathroom valet to the hostess to the bouncers. I seem to recall that particular customer cleaned the club out of every single bottle of bubbly, and when his ATM card stopped working, one of the employees had to drive him home because he was totally tapped.

Naturally, for customers such as these, the club will go out of its way to make them happy. Just as in Vegas with its high rollers, all you need to do is tell us what your favorite drink is and we'll have it Fedexed from France if we have to. Your favorite meal? Hey, you like Kobe beef? We'll get you the whole cow. Cigars? If you can handle the freight, we'll bring a guy up from the Dominican Republic to hand-roll yours. But, ultimately, since you're an adult, it's up to you to know what your limits are. It's up to you to indulge responsibly. It's up to you to refrain from spending your next mortgage payment on lap dances . . . but, if you insist, we are here to accommodate and we will gladly take your money in exchange for providing a few more minutes, or hours, of your favorite fantasy. You are king of the world and all the beautiful women in it exist solely to throw themselves at your feet at your slightest whim or desire.

Did I say "king" of the world? Maybe I should have said "queen," because this business runs off something more powerful than anything else I've run into in my nearly half century on the planet: female power. There's a somewhat more coarse, and, some might argue, more accurate phrase . . . five letters, beginning with the letter "p" followed by power. I do not use the phrase lightly, or in a derogatory sense. If it weren't for the dancing girls, the beer, wine, liquor, and lobster would all lose 50 to 70 percent of their retail value, because it is only the lure of real-life pinup girls that makes The Flight Club a magical destination. That's why I am fond of saying, economically speaking, the topless bar biz is like the Energizer Bunny of businesses—it just keeps on going and going and going and . . . going.

But the women of this business, they are neither the "exploited" nor "the sweet little blushing flowers" that they have been characterized to be. Women can be lustier, hungrier, crazier, more determined, and more devious than men have any idea. They have been taught by men and by the realities of gender bias favoring men that they have to work twice as hard, be twice as cunning, and at times twice as ruthless as any man. Particularly for a woman who does not have a fancy sheepskin, topless dancing may be the only instant route to a six-figure income, the only way out of a blue-collar environment. This explains why there is more in common between strippers and women real estate agents than first meets the eye—they are both professions (if you don't think being a topless dancer is a profession, try it, amateur—see how long you last!) that have relatively low barriers to entry. To dance, you have to be tough, gutsy, and mentally tough as well as having the ability to hustle. Looking good sure helps. To sell real estate you have to get through a two-week course, pass a written test, and be ready to hustle. And looking good helps. The upside earning potential is great in both cases, and you get to meet a lot of people with money, connections, and power that can help you on your way up—if you have something to offer.

On the other side of the coin, as consumers of topless entertainment, more and more women are showing up at the club. Topless clubs have been encouraging "couples" for a long time as a way to expand the customer base, but I think it has been perceived by many of us inside the business as a gimmick—until the last five or six years, that is. Before the last couple of years, I had never seen so many women coming in, not just with their husbands or boyfriends, but even to have bachelorette parties! I see it as further indication of the mainstreaming of my industry and the acceptance of alternative lifestyles that accept homosexuality, bisexuality, and experimentation in general. Twenty-five years ago it was also very unusual for a woman to go shopping for sexual aids, toys, vibrators, and the like. To do so would have necessitated a trip to an "adult book store" or other unsavory establishment where grizzled old guys in black trench coats could be found drooling over the magazines or watching 8mm loops in dank, sticky closets. Today, a short trip to the strip mall (how appropriate, no?) yields the opportunity to buy all manner of outrageous sexual apparatus: dancer-type clothing and lingerie from the clichéd crotchless panty to the five-inch patent-leather dancer platforms that are au courant at the club. All in a clean, safe, brightly lit atmosphere with enthusiastic and knowledgeable sales help. For that matter, you can also find adult merchandise on QVC these days.

Usually, when a woman comes to the club with a boyfriend or a husband, it's partly out of curiosity as to what really goes on inside and partly to share the erotic experience with him. The general idea is that the experience is a turn-on for both parties and the sex later on at home will be smoking hot as a result. Seeing your guy get a highly erotic lap dance from a beautiful woman can be a real enhancement to a couple's sex life, as opposed to worrying about what's going on when you're not there. It's also a perfect opportunity for a woman to get a little taste of something deliciously taboo by getting a lap dance of her own from the dancer of her choice. In fact, many women are the instigators, making reservations in advance for their significant others! And here's a little secret exposed: I've witnessed many men have their minds blown when they see how overtly sexual, wild, and outrageous their gal can be, especially when she's got a few drinks in her! More than once I have seen women become intoxicated and take their clothes off inside the club and even climb up on stage to take a few swings around the old pole before we can get things under control. On other occasions, a woman has gotten so turned on watching her boyfriend get a lap dance that she pushed the dancer away and became the dancer herself, climbing right on top of her "lucky" guy. Unfortunately, it was necessary to spoil their fun, turn on the water hose, and otherwise encourage the couple to take it home.

FRIENDS, SCOUNDRELS, & CHEATS

You have no doubt heard the old saying, "Keep your friends close, and your enemies closer." Except that sometimes, someone you think is a friend is really the enemy in disguise. And some people, ironically, who are out to get you actually end up doing you a terrific favor. And along the way, without question, you meet a wild variety of endlessly complicated and fascinating people with whom you have the pleasure of doing business while engaging in the business of providing pleasure.

One of the most imperious characters I have ever met is a guy who is in the same business as mine, a Jewish guy like me, by the way, who my dad has remarked is "the kind of Jew who would sell you out in the camps for an extra ration of bread." Maybe that's unfair—maybe he would hold out for two rations. Rob Katzman owns a couple of all-nude clubs across the Detroit River in Windsor, Ontario, and a "B" bar in Detroit called The Toy Chest. You could say Rob is sort of an absentee owner who puts minimal effort and imagination into his establishments. Since I am always on the lookout for opportunities to acquire new properties, when I heard back in 2004 that he was thinking of selling The Toy Chest, I called him. Knowing I had the wherewithal to do a deal, we talked turkey: How much? I asked. He had a figure in mind—$3.3 million for the whole shebang—the business, property, fixtures, everything. After taking a close look at the numbers, I decided it was a good deal and called Rob back to inform him that with clear title I would come up with the money. As always, we call in the lawyers.

Looking back with razor-sharp hindsight, what happened next should have set off major alarm bells for me, but it didn't. I received a call from Rob Katzman's attorney, a cat by the name of Alan Rubin, who cheerily tells me that since Rob and I have already agreed on a purchase price, he can represent both me and Rob Katzman, thus saving time and money as the deal sailed through. This is perfectly legal, by the way, even if it seems a little odd, suggesting a conflict of interest. But I wanted the club, wanted to do the deal in a hurry, and felt that we'd have some good camaraderie working together on what would be a mutually profitable piece of business.

Since we had settled on $3.3 million as the sales price, Rubin told me he needed a $1 million deposit to lock everything down while he drew up the final papers. I duly instructed my bank to put the million into the trust account that had been set up by Rubin. Now, here is where things suddenly started sliding sideways like you won't believe. In a matter of days, I had the final contract in my hands, all right, but I was blown away by the terms that had been inserted. Normally it takes up to a year after the sale of a topless club before the liquor and cabaret licenses are transferred, during which time the new owner operates the club as his own under a "management agreement" clause. Whatever profit I make from the day I sign the papers is mine, and upon delivering clear title to me and receiving the balance of the sales price, the bar is then mine for all intents and purposes.

But here's the kicker. Katzman's lawyer has put in the contract that if, during the time that I operate the club under the management agreement—prior to successful license transfer— I receive two violations (or tickets) from the state Liquor Control Commission, he gets the bar back and gets to keep my million dollars. Whoa!!! But it gets even crazier. The contract goes on to stipulate what amounts to not one but two free bites out of my apple. If, after paying over the balance of the $3.3 million, my first application to transfer license is denied and I have to reapply with a new partner or representative and get a second strike against me, he gets to keep both the bar and my $3.3 million! I was beyond flabbergasted.

I called Katzman and dressed him down point-blank, "Look, you're out of your mind, you're just trying to poison the deal and all the while you're sitting on my million dollar deposit!" I swear I heard him smirking on the other end of the line. Katzman tells me he or Rubin will get back to me—the same Rubin who is supposed to be representing both of us, except he doesn't seem to be holding up my end too well. A few days later, I hear from Rubin, who tells me that Katzman has pulled a $450,000 mortgage on the bar that has to be paid off—and suddenly the sales price goes up to $3.75 million! So, when was this note pulled? Hello? But even so, I want the property badly enough that I am willing to play along and somehow work everything out.

I tell Katzman and Rubin that I'll skip the management agreement, he keeps the club in his name and takes home the profits while the licenses transfer and he gets the balance of the sales price, including the surprise $450,000, at closing. I was sure that, as ridiculous as things seemed to be, we could hammer out the problems at the negotiating table. But my lawyers were all telling me, "Alan, don't sign this, don't sign this!" But I never believed we'd actually close with the terms about Katzman getting the bar back and keeping my money remaining in the contract.

About this time, I get a call from Rubin with more good news. "Alan," he says, "I'm sorry but Rob Katzman has fired me—I'm not responsible for this deal anymore. You need to get your own lawyer." Wham-bam-thank-you-ma'm and that's that, right? Nooo, I find out a couple of days later that Rubin has transferred my million dollars into the escrow account of Rob Katzman's new lawyer. But I'm still thinking, that as surreal as this transaction has become, everything can be worked out, it's still a good deal.

Finally, after all this, we had agreed on a closing date and it's looking like I'm going to get traction. Showing up at the law offices of Katzman's new lawyers, Jaffe and Associates, at the appointed hour, everyone sits down and—yet again—there is a surprise on the table. Katzman's new legal beagle announces that Katzman has $100,000 of personal debt "related to the club" that he wants tacked on the total. I am beside myself, as I lean over the table and lock into Katzman's eyes. "You are out of your mind and you are trying to kill this deal so you can keep my million dollars." Katzman just stares back at me for a few seconds and breaks gaze, deferring to counsel. His lawyer looks at me and says, "It's all on the table. Are you going to sign or not?"

"No!" I declare, pushing back from the table and getting to my feet. "I'm not signing what amounts to extortion! I'm outta here!"

Three days later I receive a letter from Katzman's lawyer informing me that I had "violated the terms of the closing" by not closing on the "agreed upon date" and that Katzman was keeping my million dollars, it's his! I later learned that my money was yet again transferred into Katzman's personal, interest-bearing account. If that's not a slick way to steal a million dollars of someone else's money, I don't know what is. It reminds me of how the Nazis used to manipulate the law in Germany to steal assets from Jewish businessmen—except most modern Nazis are not Jewish! Send me your size, Rob, and I'll have a nice SS uniform located for you.

Two years later, after initiating a lawsuit against Katzman and going through arbitration with the expectation that I would finally get my money back, I learned yet another bitter lesson in business—it's legally possible to steal a million dollars. So, beware of highwaymen who wear suits and ties. I simply had to take my licking and move on, taking the kind of hit that would totally devastate most businessmen. I had really wanted that club, especially because it is located just a few miles north of Ford Motor Company World Headquarters and would have given me a really nice geographical distribution of properties in the metro Detroit area. But, had the deal not gone sour, I wouldn't have had the opportunity to forge ahead with a far more lucrative venture—the creation of my new Penthouse club, born out of an encounter with one of the magazine empire's branding and licensing gurus during the 2006 Detroit Superbowl festivities. More on that to come.

Now comes Hennessy. No, not because I need a stiff drink after dealing with a scoundrel, I'm talking about the man, or men, behind the brand: Messieurs Giles and Louis Hennessy of France, of Hennessy cognac. Before I weave the tale, however, a little background. In 1995, I had the opportunity to buy another small, former biker bar on Eight Mile that had been called the Patio Lounge. It had been a blue-collar joint with predominantly white clientele and it already had the necessary cabaret D license. But I had a different vision—I wanted to make it over into Detroit's premier, high-end black club, something no one had yet been able to accomplish. As a white Jewish guy, I figured I was perfect for the job . . . I had the experience and the financing, and I was color blind. I will admit that I did see a lot of green coming my way if the club was done right, but green is the color that makes things grow!

Black topless clubs are a whole different animal. Just as rap and hip-hop reconstituted the music business with a mean, menacing, and infectious blend of word and beat, so followed the black DJ and the "ballers," that is, the self-styled players, who create the atmosphere at the bar I renamed All Star. On a busy night, and most every night is packed, you'll struggle elbow-to-elbow and ass-to-ass just to navigate your way to the men's room, while a deafening volume level dominated by throbbing, staccato drumbeats puts you into a virtual state of delirium. If you're white, and visit, you'll probably suffer a bit of a flashback to black-and-white movies where the natives capture the hunter and trundle him off to a flaming spit somewhere, or stick him in a pot to boil while the dancers gyrate in celebration. I hasten to point out, however, that my sister tends bar at All Star, in spite of the family's pleas to find a nice Jewish guy and settle down. I guess Sis and I share the same genes—we like to be smack dab in the middle of the action, especially when the action is good business. Better than good: If All Star breaks the record for $350 bottles of Cristal served at any club on any given Saturday night, we also sell a hell of a lot of Hennessy. Hennessy cognac, originating from the Hennessy region of France, is the liquor of choice for the black cognoscenti. No self-respecting baller comes into the All Star and orders well cognac, that's for sure.

The funny thing is, even I had no idea how much Hennessy we were pouring, until I got a call out of the blue one day from my manager. "Al, we gotta get ready," Kip, my manager said, a little breathlessly.

"Ready for what?"

"Hennessy is coming to Detroit and he wants to meet you."

"What—you're talking about our liquor distributor?"

"No, no, no," he stammered. "Mister Hennessy, the guy who runs the company!"

"Mister Hennessy?"

"Yeah, let me read the message . . . it's from Monsieur Giles Hennessy of Chateau Hennessy, Provence, France. He's the CEO or something."

"Son of a bitch—well, why is he coming to Detroit?"

"His secretary, the guy who called the club, says All Star is number five in Hennessy sales by the glass in North America. And he wants to meet the owner."

Life is full of surprises, isn't it?

From the lush beauty of France's Hennessy region to the gritty, hard-edged amplitude of Eight Mile, we see that life's spectrum is made full and pleasant in the commonality of good friends, topless dancers, and an excellent, amber libation. I would look forward to meeting Hennessy, where else, but at the club? Hennessy was curious as a cat about All Star, it turns out, as an example of the strange dichotomy of high and low culture as it exists only in America. I suppose that he was also a little curious about Detroit, too. With a national reputation as the Motor City, Motown, and race riots, many people forget that Detroit is, at three hundred–plus years since its founding by French fur traders, one of America's oldest cities. Even fewer know that the French word *détroit* means, in literal translation, "strait," referring to the narrow stretch of the Detroit River that connects Lake St. Clair to the north and Lake Erie to the south while skirting downtown.

The meeting was arranged to take place at All Star on a late weekday evening, when a limo would arrive with Giles Hennessy and his brother Louis, as well as several of his associates who would join us while I sat and chatted with the man. The club was really hopping and I was a little concerned if we'd be able to hear one another. The only requirement they insisted upon for the meeting was that I would make sure a bottle of Hennessy's finest VSOP Reserve would be on the table. What, didn't this guy get enough free Hennessy as CEO? Maybe it was just part of Hennessy's public relations schtick, but I wasn't going to question it.

At the appointed hour, M. Hennessy arrived at All Star and I was ready for him. A table in a discreet corner of the club was set up with the requested bottle and I strode out to meet the man, an impeccably dressed, distinguished gentleman of average stature . . . but it was apparent that he was born of the aristocracy and carried it easily. His manner was both charming and rather formal, and I got a kick out of watching him look around the club as he shrugged off his cashmere overcoat and sat down in a dignified manner.

"So, these eez a very interesting club you 'av here, Meester Markovitz. I must say, I 'av nevair been to a place quite like it."

"Thank you," I intoned. "It's a lot different than it is during the day . . . "

"Because now zee action is happening, non?" he replied with a wink. "I think you will understand I 'av an appreciation for zee nightlife. Perhaps you know that many of your black American entertainers, such as Josephine Baker, 'av found great success in my country."

"I have heard stories about her—topless in a banana skirt!"

"And of course, zee French designed the city of Detroit, and your Cadillac automobile is named after the famous French explorer Antoine de Lamothe-Cadillac, oui?"

"I believe they mentioned that in my social studies class in sixth grade," I added, as M. Hennessy chuckled.

What followed was one of the most fascinating half hours of my life, as my distinguished guest proceeded to ask me all manner of questions about the topless bar business, how I got started, and what prospects I had for becoming fourth, third, second, or even first in Hennessy sales by the glass in the United States. An astute businessman, Hennessy was aggressive about promoting his brand and encouraging my further success along the way. Throughout the meeting, I felt that M. Hennessy was intrigued most by the juxtaposition of a tiny but highly successful club in the midst of a hardscrabble, postindustrial landscape that Eight Mile was then and largely remains today.

At the conclusion of our visit, Hennessy politely thanked me for my hospitality, and reminded me that while Detroit has the All Star, Paris has the Folies Bergère, the famous topless revue that has been in existence since the late 1800s, something he suggested I would enjoy seeing. With that, the Monsieur produced his business card and, elegantly extending it to me between two perfectly manicured fingers, issued an invitation.

"Alan, I should like you to keep my card weeth my number at my private chateau in France, and you weel be my guest at anytime! You may come to go to zee boar hunting and 'av some fine cuisine weeth me, oui?"

"I'd love to!" I replied, delighted.

"Yes, you and your guest, please just give me advance notice of your itinerary and I weel be pleased to see you again!"

"It's been my pleasure."

I escorted M. Hennessy to the parking lot and he nodded to me as his chauffer opened the door for him. I then watched as the black town car disappeared into the motley traffic trundling eastbound on Eight and walked back into the club, looking again at one of the coolest business cards I've ever received and wondering when I might make it to France. I still have that card, and I haven't yet gotten around to making the trip, but Hennessy the Sixth did say anytime. That's one I'm definitely looking forward to.

I later found out that Mr. Hennessy had flown in his own Gulfstream 4 jet to Detroit expressly to meet me—a cost of maybe $10,000 or more—which certainly impressed me. Interestingly enough, he never touched a drop of the Hennessy.

On the other hand, a gentleman I had the pleasure of knowing who did enjoy a drop of Hennessy from time to time—all right, maybe it was more like a couple of fingers—was Coleman Young, the controversial mayor of Detroit from 1973 through 1992—an amazing five consecutive terms in office. During World War II, Young served in the United States Air

Force 477th Medium-Bomber Group, otherwise known as the Tuskegee Airmen, as a bombardier and navigator. As a lieutenant after the war, and foreshadowing his lifelong activism in the civil rights movement, Young participated in the Freeman Field Mutiny in which 162 black officers were arrested for resisting segregation at a base near Seymour, Indiana, in 1945.

Young's involvement with dissident organizations from the Progressive Party to the AFL-CIO and the National Negro made him some powerful enemies, including the FBI, before whom he refused to testify. He also rallied against segregation in the United Auto Workers (UAW). Earlier in this book, I noted that hizzoner was rather infamous in the Detroit suburbs, when after one particularly bruising but successful reelection campaign, Young told all the criminals in Detroit to "hit Eight Mile," presumably toward the suburbs. The actual quote is, "I issue a warning to all those pushers, to all rip-off artists, to all muggers: It's time to leave Detroit; hit Eight Mile Road! And I don't give a damn if they are black or white, or if they wear Superfly suits or blue uniforms with silver badges. Hit the road!" It was played by his opponents as a huge gaffe, but it was emblematic of Young's blunt, honest, shoot-from-the-hip style of politics. Personally, I found Coleman Young to be the kind of guy who said what he meant and meant what he said. Even if he didn't agree with you, you knew where you stood with him. That's more than I can say about most other politicians who say whatever they think people want to hear and change their opinions like some people change hats.

I first met Coleman Young during my early years at The Booby Trap, at Detroit Police Eastern Operations, which oversaw seven or eight East Side precincts. I had gotten to know Commander John Henry, Detroit's Chief of Eastern Operations during the hairy motorcycle gang days when I thought my new club was going to become the epicenter of a war zone. The prompt, aggressive actions of the Detroit Police saved my bacon on more than one occasion, and as always, the brass was curious about the newest topless upstart in their city—especially one operated by a dude still running in hightops, yours truly. John Henry had stopped by one day to chat with me, soon after one of the 911 calls that we made to remove the Renegades cycle gang from the premises. He was friendly and clearly wanted to be helpful, and we exchanged business cards. Later on, he called out of the blue and asked if I could come over to Eastern Operations to chat with the mayor—and could I bring a bottle of something good, say some Hennessy. I calculated this was going to be a friendly, off-the-cuff meeting.

The same day, I showed up with the Hennessy in my briefcase and was summarily ushered into a back office where Coleman Young was kicked back with his feet up on the desk. Commander Henry introduced us, "Mr. Young, this is Alan Markovitz, who owns The Booby Trap."

"How do you do, young man!" the Mayor said, putting his feet on the floor and standing up to shake my hand. "How's business?"

"Business is not bad," I said, smiling, as I was immediately disarmed and put at ease by Coleman Young's easy manner.

"Sit down, sit down . . . I understand you brought a little something?"

"Yeah, I did."

"Well, pull it out—John, get us some glasses in here so we can talk a little and sip a little."

And just like that I was having a drink with the Mayor of Detroit.

"You know," the mayor began, "I don't mind looking at pretty ladies, but the thing is, I can't just walk into your club, Alan, or anybody's club for that matter, because of politics, you understand. But I want you to know that I also understand that you have a right to run your business. And there's a lot of convention business we want to attract to Detroit and they aren't looking for a bingo game when the convention is over. They're looking for the kind of entertainment you provide and they expect to find it."

"I know, Mr. Mayor, I'm shooting for that kind of business."

"Yeah, the businessman, you got it. I know you're trying to upscale the trade and I can appreciate that. We're not looking to harass you, long as you play by the rules. You know some people are looking for any kind of excuse to come down on you, so don't give 'em any."

"I appreciate that."

"Hell, I know you do," the mayor said, with a gruff laugh. "It's easy votes to go after your business, but there's the hard business of bringing Detroit up, and we got to do business if we want to stay in business."

The mayor picked up his glass to take a sip, and put the glass back down on the desk. I instinctively knew the meeting was over. Coleman Young looked at the bottle and, with a wink, said, "You can leave that here. You don't want to be driving around Detroit with open alcohol in your vehicle, now, do you?"

I laughed. "No sir, Mr. Mayor. It was good meeting you."

"All right then," he said, getting up. "I'll call on you again sometime and we can sit down and talk some more. You can keep me up on what's happening in your business. I like to keep up on business in my city!" With a wink and another gruff chuckle from him, I shook his hand and I was gone.

For many years afterward, Young would put a call in to have me meet him, usually at one of the Detroit Police Operations offices, and we would discuss various issues about the city and the current goings-on among Detroit's topless club operators. I don't know if hizzoner had similar tête-à-têtes with other club owners, but I do know that throughout his tenure I never had a problem with police harassment at any of my clubs, and pretty much everyone else also enjoyed conducting business unmolested, so to speak.

Coleman Young had his detractors, sure, but in my opinion he was a pragmatist who spoke his mind. You may not have liked what he had to say, but you sure knew where he was coming from. As far as adult entertainment goes, Young saw the city as an ecosystem that needed to incorporate a diversity of life forms in order to thrive. Topless clubs, as such, occupy a niche that is hundreds, if not thousands, of years old. Not only that, and this is easy for people to forget, we are a legal and licensed business. If you really want to protect society from the negative effects of legal and licensed businesses, then you'd better be prepared to shut down all the bars and liquor producers, outlaw cigarets, take away all the firearms, and then see what you get. I think it would look something like life under the Taliban. Strike a blow for freedom: Visit a topless club near you today.

After Coleman Young became too ill to run for a sixth term in office, some people came to me to talk about a new candidate for mayor, a black lawyer named Dennis Archer. The word was that, like Young, he knew how to do business and he would be good for Detroit because he knew how to reach out through his professional connections, thus bringing much needed suburban investment back into the city. Or, to put it into politically incorrect terminology, Archer was perceived as being "whiter" than Coleman Young and was therefore more amenable to sub-urban realpolitik and business.

I attended what I believe to have been his first fund-raiser, a small event in Detroit's Greektown—there were maybe twenty-five people there. I had a chance to speak with Archer. He was well acquainted with my clubs, telling me that he "understood" the business. He expressed appreciation for my support and said that he hoped he could look forward to more of the same in the future. He seemed like a stand-up guy, and I saw no reason not to throw in. Let me be very clear—in my business, you are stupid if you don't get to know the powers that be or are about to come to power in your city. Archer was looking like a winner, and frankly, if he had been running against a strong opponent, I probably would have contributed to that campaign as well. That's just business and politics, nothing new about it whatsoever. I ended up attending other Archer campaign events and finally helped raise $10,000 for the Archer for Mayor fund.

Flash forward. Archer sweeps into office. I fully expected that I would, at the very least, have an ear in city government—along with an open and honest discourse that would respect both the interests and objectives of the city and my future as a tax-paying contributor to the economic health of Detroit. Sadly, not all politicians are as straight up as good old Coleman Young was. If he liked you or didn't like you, you knew and you knew why. The next time I saw Archer was at a VIP event at the North American International Auto Show at Cobo Hall, in Detroit.

Later, during the Archer administration, I suffered terrible police harassment that almost cost me my business when Trumpps was raided and virtually all the gentleman's clubs on Eight Mile took a gigantic nosedive as our patrons fled and were slow to return. While it is true that any club operator who engages in blatantly illegal activity is begging to be busted, it's an entirely different story when charges are trumped up, fabricated, or worse, when police are simply sent charging in looking for any minor violation they can sink their teeth into. That's when the police are not enforcing the law, but are being used to play politics. It is reprehensible, but it's reality. It's what politicians do. But I have a feeling that you're not totally surprised . . . are you?

Las Vegas

It's enough to make you want to take your business somewhere else, somewhere where they "get it," somewhere like Las Vegas, for example. Which in 2001 my father and I did, with my dad taking point position on a $2.2 million lot on Hacienda Avenue, where we planned to open a fantastic new club that would rival anything else Vegas had to offer. Think again. Vegas is known for excess, and when it comes to corrupt politicians, there is probably no more vivid illustration of the word "sleazy" than the case of two Las Vegas (Clark County) commissioners named Dario Herrera and Mary Kincaid-Chauncey, who in 2007 were sentenced to prison on convictions of bribery. Bribed by whom? By a now former strip club owner by the name of Michael Galardi, who delivered payola to them in paper bags for favorable zoning, liquor license, and other votes they took to give him an advantage over other strip club operators and erstwhile operators. Interestingly enough, Galardi, who pleaded guilty to other charges stemming from his strip club operations in Vegas, was the one who flipped to the prosecution to convict the very commissioners who had helped him. None the worse for the wear, Galardi was forced only to divest himself of ownership in his clubs by selling them to his father, a highly successful club operator himself, for over $4 million.

Ah, but the plot thickens. What you've just read is fact. And history. Yet the story goes on. When my dad and I hired Las Vegas attorney Matthew Callister to secure a liquor license for the Hacienda Avenue property, the closing was contingent on getting the license. No license, no deal. My father was fronting the project with a clean background and the land was already zoned for a topless cabaret. It was perfect . . . the location was a short cab ride from the famous Las Vegas strip, and The House of Blues and Mandalay Bay were preparing to open their doors nearby, just across Interstate 15. The process of getting the license was expected to be smooth, with approval expected.

But KA-BOOM! Denied! No explanation or reason offered. Our attorney was blindsided, as he had all the votes lined up like ducks in a row. Something had happened seemingly overnight. But, as I have always said, in this business you don't just lie down and accept defeat. You have to fight for your interests or someone will surely stomp all over them. But in the case of City Hall, it's not so easy to fight. So we filed a civil lawsuit against Michael Galardi and the former commissioners who were sentenced in 2007 and named above, along with another commissioner named Erin Kenny and a former board member named Lance Malone, who was a known bag man who delivered cash bribes to his former colleagues. The complaint: We assert that Galardi "sought to obtain a monopoly" over the adult entertainment business in Las Vegas, pure and simple. And if you do that, and the plaintiff presents enough evidence—and bear in mind the burden of proof is lower in a civil than in a criminal case—the plaintiff wins and is entitled to damages equivalent to what profit might reasonably have been made were the project to have gone through.

The third commissioner, Erin Kenny, who testified to accepting $70,000 in bribe money from Galardi (but escaped jail time) and voted against the liquor license, in fact refused to meet with our lawyer, Callister, before the licensing hearing—even though our property was located in her district. Draw your own conclusion.

The main contention of our suit is that the convicted commissioners were known to have taken bribes from Galardi at the same time that my father's application was denied. Yet Galardi's lawyer was quoted in the *Las Vegas Review Journal* on October 14, 2007, as saying that the bribery payments from Galardi to the commissioners were "merely defensive as to stricter regulation by Clark County." Now I ask you, the reader: If you were paying tens of thousands of dollars in bribes to several county commissioners to go soft on regulating the topless business in your town, would you then want them to approve the liquor license of a competitor who could take business away from you? Everything about Michael Galardi and his actions suggest otherwise. The county commissioners also had no persuasive reason to deny my father the license he requested for his properly zoned property. Come on—Las Vegas is going to start banning topless bars because they might corrupt the image of Las Vegas?

The fact of the matter is that where there's money, there's always the possibility of corruption. The more money, the greater the potential for corruption. Human beings will always try to get away with whatever they can, which is why we have laws and lawyers. Then again, those with money can afford to use laws and lawyers to their benefit by bending, breaking, or rewriting the law. All you can do in my business is be prepared to step up and spend whatever it takes to protect against those who would do you harm. It ain't cheap, but it is necessary.

BACK TO THE FUTURE

As Detroit prepared for its biggest party ever, Super Bowl XL on February 5, 2006, I prepared The Flight Club for an equally outrageous blowout. The Pittsburgh Steelers were clashing with the Seattle Seahawks and The Rolling Stones would rock halftime. Anticipating a flood of testosterone-geeked high rollers and partiers of every stripe—from students to corporate CEOs—I had arranged an entertainment schedule designed to appeal to one and all. Tera Patrick, the sultry brunette porn starlet of the moment, would be doing a series of shows at the club as well as signing and selling copies of her popular videos . . . alongside a rotating harem of 300, count 'em, 300 of the hottest honeys ever to stalk a topless stage.

Anticipating a capacity crowd, I'd made sure the bar was stocked with every kind of premium pour you can name: Jagermeister, Goldschlager, Hennessy, Remy, Absolut, and Grey Goose, single malts and 18-year-olds and Pucker and schnapps and . . . hey, the list goes on and on. Along with five dozen barrels of brew, several thousand olives, and bartenders who had spent the previous month doing wind sprints in the Andes, I calculated that we would be ready for anything.

The chief task was getting people to The Flight Club, so I had put out a small fleet of vans and limos to canvass downtown Detroit, all around Ford Field, as well as the major hotels around town to pick up and deliver partiers door-to-door from open till close. Downtown is about twenty miles from Inkster, via I-94, but the lack of top-end gentleman's clubs in the city itself all but guaranteed a full house. Besides, every hotel room in a thirty-mile radius was booked solid, and in the sweet spot between city and suburb, many of the hotels full of football fans were within five or ten miles of my location.

As expected, the Superbowl was a party without parallel. You could barely walk from one end of the club to the other without bumping off bosoms like a pinball. Even with close to three decades in the business, I was having as good a time as a twenty-one-year-old who had had his cherry busted and was given the keys to a new Corvette convertible on the same night. It didn't hurt that we were racking up receipts of almost fifty grand a day.

I lost count of how many faces from the old days, as well as new faces and celebrities, passed through my doors in the three days that constituted the core of the rip-roar. But maybe the most interesting, and significant for me, was a visit from Jeff Stoller, head of licensing and brand management for the Penthouse group. Jeff had come in from New York to do a little business. Penthouse had organized an exclusive, celebrity-studded bash of its own downtown—and, like everyone else, Stoller wanted to have a good time. He had heard about The

Flight Club from his well-traveled friends and associates and wanted to check out the operation for himself.

It turned out that we had a lot in common in terms of "production values." My ambition to build and operate a gentleman's club on par with or even better than anything found in New York was not lost on him. And I think he was impressed that I had pulled it off on a challenging section of Michigan Avenue, literally miles from any other anchor destination or location. From my perspective, I was intrigued with the possibilities of allying myself with an established brand in order to extend my reach into other markets with new clubs. I have long been aware of the importance of branding and licensing in today's global consumer society. Everywhere you look, from chain brands like McDonald's and Kentucky Fried Chicken up to The Hard Rock Café and The Ritz Carlton, the strength of a brand name lies in meeting consumer expectations with a certainty of quality wherever in the world you encounter that brand.

After getting bruised in my battle with Boeing over their "747" brand, I was forced to reinvent my aviation-themed club under a new moniker. The Flight Club, I had realized by 2006, had become a powerful local brand, albeit with one single location. But among those I talked to from outside Detroit who have visited, I often heard the highest form of praise a customer can give to an establishment: "I tell my friends, when you're in Detroit, you've gotta visit The Flight Club. It's the best gentleman's club in town!"

Further driven by the number one rating nationally given by individual consumers who vote on topless clubs, at TUSCL.com, I began to really appreciate the value of using branding to help assure the success of multiple clubs. The more clubs that one could successfully open and operate, the stronger the brand value and hence a greater valuation for the brand name itself in addition to the physical assets and financial performance of clubs under the brand name. A successful, powerful brand name creates opportunities for great synergy; just look at companies such as Pierre Cardin, Gucci, and others that have packaged and promoted goods made by hundreds, or even thousands of other manufacturers, under their own brand names—ringing up sales in the billions of dollars annually.

Why couldn't the same thing be accomplished in the field of gentleman's clubs? It seems that Jeff Stoller had the same idea, was already pursuing arrangements with other topless club owner/operators, and wanted to discuss the possibilities of opening up a Penthouse club in Detroit. I was interested, so we started talking. I had been eyeing a prime location back on Eight Mile, the site of a dilapidated club that had most recently been running under the name City Heat. Enough time had elapsed since Eight Mile had gone radioactive from the police raids and protesting community groups that the shake-out was long over. The grandfathered cabaret license was just begging for someone with enough cash and savvy to resurrect the location.

Making the buy had been a no-brainer. It was 2006. It had been almost a full decade since I had left Eight Mile behind. I had the perspective of time, the added experience, and the cash to do the deal. I made the offer on City Heat at asking price, $2.5 million, and knew that no matter what I called it, it would be successful. I would do whatever necessary to assure that outcome—it looked like I'd need to pour in another $2 million to bring the club up to my standards. In this case, that meant turning the existing layout—a two-story building with a basement and the second floor as an apartment—into a two-story club. To do so involved eliminating the basement. You can now see where that cash was going to go.

So, would it be The Flight Club, or Flight Club II? I was getting a lot of advice from my team to extend the brand, build the brand. But I was also nagged by the consideration that while The Flight Club is a powerful brand in the Detroit area, could I extend it regionally, or nationally? I was at a point in my game that I had to decide if I'd be happy with owning a couple three clubs—be the classic big fish in a small pond—or look forward to competing on a larger scale, and maybe do so without the name recognition that comes in so handy.

To go big, I wanted to tie in with a big name in the industry if I could. The one that first came to mind was Scores, the New York gentleman's clubs that have long defined the big leagues in my industry. I have always regarded New York clubs as the ultimate of adult entertainment. Scores, like Penthouse, is also aggressively seeking profitable licensing deals with experienced club owners around the country. But as they say, in business and in personal relations, nothing can replace a good face-to-face. I hit it off with Jeff Stoller, and to my mind, the Penthouse name and reputation more aptly dovetails with my approach to gentleman's entertainment. Scores is obviously more sports-oriented in both its name and its association with professional athletes and those who follow pro sports.

Finally, you've got to make up your mind. It's been said that those who are most successful in business are quick to make decisions and slow to change their minds, and conversely, that those who are least successful are slow to make decisions and quick to change their minds. I think there's a lot of common sense in that. If you dither too much, it's easy to get confused and lose sight of the essential quality of any given decision or deal. But if you trust your instincts, you know when something feels right and you pounce. The only wild card is that many times you've got to have enough patience to wait until conditions are right or the right opportunity presents itself.

I now have the property and the alliance. My new club on Eight Mile has been designed to dominate, and with the Penthouse name, I will be positioned to extend my success in Detroit to other cities such as Atlantic City, Philadelphia, and Miami, where deals are already in the works. I guarantee you that when you come to my new Penthouse club on Eight Mile your senses will be knocked for a loop. And the same thing will be true when you visit The Flight Club, which has recently undergone a $300,000 renovation to make sure that we keep our number one national ranking.

Breaking Eggs to Make the Omelet

The reality of doing a complete teardown of the old City Heat property and building a completely new, customized club has been a certified bitch and three-quarters.

To give you some idea what it's like to be me, imagine the following scenario. You've ponied up your $2.5 mill for the location and the license. But that only gets you a seat in the theater of Municipal Abuse: Detroit city officials ain't about to roll over and let you scratch their bellies while you go to work on the plans and building permit that they issued—signed, sealed, and dated!

Why wouldn't a city want to encourage the creation of an addition to their tax base, the resurrection of a previously derelict piece of property, a place of employment for fifty to a hundred hospitality workers, and perhaps another two hundred or more entertainer positions? Because the city doesn't really like adult entertainment—unless you're a gigantic casino operation. Casinos can be extorted to pay vast sums of cash to acquire city property because the city will be able to extract hundreds of millions of dollars from gaming. I'm not quite on that scale; therefore it's a little easier to punk me around. But in reality, the city is doing me a favor. The more difficult the city makes it for topless operators to exist, the greater the value of the clubs of those persevering enough to build them.

Arguably, going into a topless club versus visiting a casino at least guarantees that you get what you pay for—food, drinks, and personal entertainment at fixed, although premium, prices. Go to a casino, and you could win some money, but the house always wins. You're more likely to walk out with a big hole in your pocket. You walk out of a topless club after a fine meal and a half dozen couch dances and you'll be smiling and dreaming about the experience for days, or weeks, to come.

The next time you see a news story about police busting a topless club or community organizers bashing one because of a purported negative influence on local housing values, or public morals, consider this: people in urban neighborhoods do not put bars on their windows and doors in order to keep patrons of nearby topless bars from breaking in and assaulting or robbing them. They do it because there is real crime in the neighborhood: shootings, robberies, and assaults by criminals who are dealing drugs or defending drug turf and/or gangs committing gang-related violence. Why doesn't the city spend its resources vigorously attacking real crime? Because it's typically easier to score political points rousting NIMBY (not in my backyard) businesses. If you're a city dweller and the unfortunate victim of a personal or property crime, call 911. Then, sit around and wonder why it will often take thirty minutes to an hour to get a patrol car, when cops busting topless bars have the ability to organize news media to arrive at the scene at the exact same time they do the raid . . . while a couple of blocks down the local Subway shop is like an armed camp with two-inch-thick Plexiglas windows. Who's minding the store, here, anyway? Have the lunatics finally taken over the asylum?

By and large, I have little time for sour grapes. There is too much opportunity out there and too much potential profit for me to waste time whining. I'd much rather consolidate my gains, sustain my growth, and look for new ways to improve my performance. Let the city fathers and mothers waste tax-payer dollars harassing adult clubs. And on the other side of the spectrum, I'm just as glad that the complexities and chal-lenges of opening and running a topless establishment have kept corporate America from sinking its claws into one of the last bulwarks of entrepreneurial opportunity in America—a vast, still untapped potential that will, in time, surely become a brand manager's dream.

It took a lot of sweat equity to hammer the business in Detroit into what it is today. When I began back in the early 1980s with The Booby Trap, I was still running around in Con-verse high tops and groping, no pun intended, for the best way forward. At that time, the adult entertainment industry was primed for explosive growth . . . but no one really saw just how that was going to happen. It came about, in part, because I was unhappy with how much cash I was forking over to get danc-ers to dance. It also came about because I could clearly see that there was a pent-up demand for a clean, well-appointed, upscale environment so that white-collar customers could enjoy what their blue-collar brethren had long enjoyed without the frills, or amenities. Not that white-collar guys are snobs, but it's a lot more conducive to do business in a clean, upscale environment. There are some topless clubs still out there, doing good business by the way, that resemble something out of the middle ages or perhaps a fleshy freak show, but some people are looking for that sort of thing.

As advanced as The Booby Trap was for its time, it simply was not designed to compete with today's glitzy mega-clubs that generate multimillion-dollar grosses. And, for a mega-club to exist, in order to pull the volume of high-spending clientele that keeps a hundred or more dancers on rotation, the performers had to shift their thinking and begin kicking up a portion of their earnings. In return for paying tip-out, or stage fees, or whatever you want to call it, dancers helped to finance a much better moneymaking machine. Everyone has benefited from this revolutionary re-jiggering of the topless club model.

But, as you now know, they did not come along willingly. Even though they were making money hand over fist by the mid 1980s as I moved them off-stage and put them first on boxes and then aluminum stands, allowing them to sell three- or four-minute dances for $5, then $10, they did not want to give up that hourly wage.

Tycoon's and then Trumpps finally provided the full-blown incentive to go to a total independent contractor model . . . they were making so much money that they couldn't walk away! When other clubs saw what I was doing, they wanted a piece of the action, too. So, everybody upgraded to couches, if they could, or did their best to create a more "posh" atmosphere that was conductive to VIP rooms.

The Topless Bottom Line

Exotic Dancer Publications is the de facto trade association for topless and nude clubs in America. They put on an annual convention in Las Vegas that is a must visit for club operators, managers, and vendors to the gentleman's club market. In their 2007 Media Kit, ED relates the following:

There are 2,500 topless clubs in America with gross revenues exceeding $7.5 billion. Topless clubs entertain an estimated 1,000,000 customers every day and employ 350,000 workers to serve them. Topless clubs serve more alcoholic beverages (and, I would add, at a higher average price) than any other type of nightclub and are open more days and hours than any other type of nightclub. Of particular significance, topless clubs pay more state and local taxes than any other type of nightclub and receive less corporate branding than any other type of nightclub.

The way I see it, topless clubs are the Energizer Bunny of bars and nightclubs. No matter what the general state of the economy, to put it in the words of the commercial for the batteries sold under that brand name, they just keep going and going and . . . going!

Unless we degenerate to fascist rule in America or suffer a religious-cultural backlash on the order of the Taliban in Afghanistan, or the mullahs of the Middle East, I predict that topless entertainment will further evolve into the mainstream. Though America was founded by the Puritans, and although there remains a to-be-reckoned-with Christian conservative movement that seeks to reverse what they see as a dangerous erosion of "family values," I firmly believe that Americans possess a righteous amount of mind-your-own-business independence along with a certain, and healthy, lustiness. Call it a lust for life and a lust for the freedom to enjoy something that has existed since ancient times: wine, women, and song.

Or, as I have often said, "Bring on the dancing girls!"

The main reason any business stays in business, or thrives, is demand. Undoubtedly, the demand for the close proximity of nearly naked beautiful women, along with premium cuisine and libations, is there . . . and is not going away until testosterone is outlawed. The next ingredient for runaway success is so simple that many topless club operators miss it entirely. That ingredient is quality. The more beautiful ladies you have, the more customers you will get. But without sumptuous and stunning surroundings, the ladies won't come, and neither will the big spenders. Every single element from building design and appointment, from the signage to the kitchen to the bar to the lighting to the servers, and managers and valet parkers—everything has to be top-notch. Or, to put it in customer service parlance—everything about your club must exceed expectations. You must always be playing your "A" game and always thinking and doing that which will set you apart as the best of the best. But not every operator is willing to do that. It's easy for some guys to get lazy, because even a topless club that's down at its heels can still rake in a lot of money. But that's not the way I'm wired. I do whatever it takes to literally trump the competition because I absolutely love what I do. I am playing not just against the competition, I am also playing against myself, continually assessing and reassessing what I can do to improve my game. In short, I'm a perfectionist. If you're not number one, you're number two, which is just a nice way of saying you're the first loser. It also doesn't hurt that I have around twenty-five years of experience in a very tough business, which goes a long way.

Also, at this point in my career, I've learned how to find, hire, and promote the best managerial talent available, some of whom own a piece of my various clubs. There is certainly no greater incentive to create success than to have a personal financial stake in the business. And, as I expand, I obviously cannot be everywhere at every moment. I have to be able to count on my people to keep everything humming—and, frankly, I also like to be able to take some time for myself to do other things that excite me and give me satisfaction.

After nearly three decades in the land of topless splendor, I have often been asked what I would do if I had to start my life over from scratch. If I couldn't be in the gentleman's club business, I'd have to say I would be in a NASCAR racer going more than two hundred miles per hour around a beautiful oval track. It's not a fantasy, though. Because I've been financially successful, I've actually had the experience driving in the ARCA and Winston West series races on some of the best tracks in America. I'm proud to say I got there the way any other driver does it: I ponied up and trained at the Buck Baker race school under professional driving instructors until I was good enough to earn my stripes and qualify to enter and field a car at many tracks throughout the country, from Pikes Peak International Speedway in Colorado to Lowes Motor Speedway in Charlotte, S.C., and Bristol Motor Speedway in Tennessee, among others.

Unfortunately, to be truly great in racing you've got to start young, like Tiger Woods in golf. Maybe if my dad had stuck me in a go-kart when I was five and let me cut my teeth on real track competition, I could have made the pro ranks at nineteen or twenty, grabbed a major sponsor, built a fantastic team, and run with the big dogs in the Sprint Cup and beyond. If you're good enough—and I know that if I didn't have the early experience, I sure as hell had the drive—you can make millions in the racing game. I know that I would have been so pissed off if I didn't win that I would have worked my butt off until I became good enough to go all the way to the top. Even so, with my racing experiences mostly behind me, I have had the satisfaction and the thrill of going pedal to the metal in the groove with some of the best drivers out there.

Another consideration for giving up racing, however, is that with my topless empire growing, my other partners wouldn't want to lose a seasoned CEO to a violent end. Although racing has enjoyed many safety innovations along the way, it remains that no one is truly invulnerable. With the standard of quality that I set, along with my reputation for taking my clubs to number one in their respective markets, let's just say that I think it's better if I stick around.

It's easy to look back when you've become successful and feel like it was all preordained, or fate, but at the beginning I never dreamed the business would become what it has. I really was just a kid, but I knew in my bones that I could take topless entertainment in a different direction from where it was at the time. It was really a huge chance I was taking, even with the confidence and cash my dad and Sol Milan contributed. Wow— to buy what had been a seedy biker bar, and then to turn that into something as presumptuous as an adult version of a TGI Fridays! I had vision, all right, but it wasn't 100 percent and we had some big peaks and valleys at the beginning, some very rough patches. But I persevered—there was no freaking way I was going to let my dream slip through my fingers.

If I really had a do-over, rather than my dream of driving full-time in the Sprint Cup series, I would probably be more fiscally conservative than I was the first time around.

Perhaps that sounds a bit boring, but if you're going to take it to the top in business, you'd better build up a big war chest—

as much cash liquidity as you can sock away—because I don't care what kind of business you're in, there are times you'll be riding high and times you'll be face down on the mat gritting your teeth and wondering how you're going to survive.

You must expect and plan for tough times. There's no better example of that lesson than the massive sub-prime credit crisis the big investment banks have been going through since 2007. Everybody was making so much money writing no-money-down, no-documentation loans and then slicing and dicing the debt up into a multitude of confusing packages that were sold and re-sold along with other types of debt that, after a while, even the banks themselves didn't know who owned what, or who owed what to whom. What they came to find out, however, was that when a seemingly endless rising tide of property values crashed, and hundreds of thousands of people couldn't make their newly adjusted and exorbitant mortgage payments, they were the fools caught holding the bag. Folks whose homes were suddenly worth less than what they owed the banks either went bankrupt or simply walked away from their properties. In the good old days, you had to pay 20 percent down to get a mortgage, you knew who your lender was, your lender knew you, and you were both committed to making the thing work. You really had made an investment, and, having done so, you would be more likely to save money, to spend conservatively, and to be damn sure you made your monthly payments because losing your house was simply not an option.

The complacency that led investment banks to get strung out on a limb while they were making money hand over fist is the same thing that screwed the Big Three automakers.

Toyota and Honda and BMW didn't just materialize out of thin air with high-quality vehicles and steal half of Detroit's beautiful post-war monopoly—they showed up forty years ago and nibbled away relentlessly year after year after year—while Detroit did nothing! They earned the confidence of consumers by building automobiles with solid reputations for quality, while Detroit kept churning out vehicles that rusted through and were generally guaranteed to totally crap out at 100,000 miles. Were they freaking blind?!? No! The answer is, everybody was making plenty of moolah with things running just the way they were . . . so why rock the boat with some stupid vision thing?

The Topless World of Tomorrow

Just as I advocate business people to hedge against adverse economic conditions in the future with a big rainy day fund, I also, without hesitation, recommend that investors take a good look at the long-range profit potential of topless entertainment. For the entrepreneur, it can be an extremely risky venture with a steep, sharp learning curve. They just don't teach you in business school what it takes to get an adult club off the ground without immediately crashing and burning. You pretty much have to learn the business hands-on, so to speak, or from the bottom up, as I did when I went to work at La Chambre. If you don't know what you're doing, you will get ripped off by thieving parasites of all varieties, and, for those of you who believe that topless entertainment is the abject exploitation of women, all I have to say is this: you try managing fifty or a hundred competitive and strong-willed ladies who are more often than not drinking copious amounts of alcohol on the job. If you let them, they will walk all over you in their stiletto-heeled dancer platforms until you are no longer breathing . . . I kid you not.

They can and will whine, wheedle, demand, manipulate, and fight—literally tooth and nail—with all their feminine wiles as well as tricks they have picked up from traveling kung fu masters to get what they want. Mind you, I am not saying that there are not honest, kind, decent, hardworking, and responsible women working as topless entertainers. There are. But trying to separate out the different personalities that often inhabit each individual dancer is work for a dozen clones of Sigmund Freud.

As long as my dancers show up on time, do their stage rotations, mind their manners, and leave at the end of each of their shifts, I am a happy camper. The DJ is my cow wrangler and tip-out collector, who will confirm and back up everything you have just read about how to handle dancers. And, if your dream is to be a topless club DJ so you can meet all those hot ladies, take note. One of my best DJs, who has been with me for over a decade, when asked about dating the talent, has this to say: "Keep one hand on your family jewels and the other on your heart, because one crazed dancer will relieve you of both in a New York second if you don't watch yourself. My advice is, don't go there!"

Remember—topless entertainment is a business. Don't buy a club—which, by the way, will run you anywhere from $2–$3 million minimum these days—with the notion that it will be your personal playground. Unless, of course, you have a personal fortune to play with, because the old joke about aviation goes double for topless clubs. As I mentioned earlier, "How do you make a million dollars in aviation? You start with ten million!" Get the picture?

That being said, a topless bar in the right location, and run like a business, can be like your own personal ATM with unlimited withdrawals. If you get a good topless bar fine-tuned, you can then do what aggressive businessmen have always done; leverage your success into another, and then another, and then yet another establishment. The day is finally dawning when banks are willing to make loans to solid operators, and corporate expansion is slowly but surely squeezing out marginal operators. In the same way that gambling had its origins out in the middle of the desert in Nevada, run by shady characters and out-and-out mob guys like Bugsy Siegel, yet has matured into a totally mainstream, multibillion-dollar industry run by the likes of Kirk Kerkorian or Steve Wynn, so too goes the topless game.

Rick's Cabaret International, headquartered in Houston, and VCG Holdings are two publicly traded companies that collectively own and/or operate a couple of dozen premium topless clubs between them—and both have been growing strongly as reflected in total revenue as well as return on investment.

Steven Gart, an analyst with Nickel Investment Capital, put it this way in 2007 in an MSN article on both firms: "We view Rick's Cabaret as an underfollowed, undervalued growth play in the gentleman's club industry." He added that Rick's "deep acquisition pipeline combined with the company's ability to deliver respectable organic growth at existing clubs should yield continued strong results in the future." That's stock marketese, for sure, but Gart goes on to summarize the topless trade as akin to a "well-run restaurant chain with slightly different entertainment. If you get the customer in there with a few hundred dollars, he is going to spend it."

Add that assessment to figures such as VCG's projected gross revenues of $60+ million in 2008 and $90+ million through the end of 2009 and you begin to get a true picture of where gentleman's entertainment is really heading. I have seen the future and I am now moving strongly in the direction of corporate event and market planning, glossy advertising and promotions, and ten or twelve more clubs, five to seven years down the road. Whether it's me and Penthouse extending our reach through brand building, or perhaps more Flight Clubs (a registered trademark, by the way) in other cities, there remain tremendous opportunities to rehabilitate, reenergize, and rebuild flagging topless clubs and turn them into highly attractive entertainment destinations. Whether I end up creating topless equivalents of Bellagio or mass-market topless à la Hooters—without the T-shirts, obviously—there will be good, wholesome exotic entertainment for as far into the future as the eye (and more importantly, the mind) can see.

The key to all of this, by the way, is that my industry is providing LIVE entertainment. Penthouse realized a number of years ago that with magazine revenues becoming stale and unlimited Internet erotica from mild to truly wild available on the cheap 24/7, their brand had to diversify, and fast. There is still no substitute for bricks and mortar, the vivid and tantalizing experience of walking from the bright sunlight into a posh, discreetly lit club and being able to talk to and interact with beautiful, live women. You simply cannot do that "virtually."

The biggest challenge, however, in expanding such an intensively hands-on business is replicating the seasoned talent and formulating and perfecting the streamlined systems for keeping the individual clubs under control. It's the perfect case of the iron fist in the velvet glove: You need people who understand finesse, diplomacy, and how to motivate the staff, but they've also got to be damn tough, because as I have pointed out repeatedly, this business will spin out on you faster than a Jag on black ice if you don't know how to handle it.

Take the bartender, for example. Just a booze slinger and a register ringer, right? Not quite. The bartender in each of my clubs is wholly responsible for each and every cash and credit transaction from every single customer in the club during his shift. He is a critical control node—you've gotta pick the right guy—or gal—for the job. He's someone you can trust, but also someone whose performance is verified against the head count of cover charges for the shift—the assumed or average per customer spending rate, and certain other hard numbers that can be weighed in order to assure that nobody is skimming the cash flow. The truth is that in even the most tightly controlled club or bar business, there are hundreds of ways for "leakage" to occur. You have to expect it, account for it in your overall performance, and constantly work to minimize it. It's all part of the cost of doing business.

I had to learn most of this from scratch in the early days. But then again, that's where my old neighbor, employer, mentor, and then partner Sol Milan entered the picture. Whatever business you choose to go into, my advice is to find an already successful and experienced partner in order to minimize the mistakes that you will make on the way up. It's the old sourdough bread equation. You break off a little bit of the sourdough from your first batch before you bake it in order to start up the next batch of sourdough for the oven. I also had my father at the beginning, the importance of which cannot be underestimated. He had been successfully running his TV and electronics repair business for over thirty years when I was obliged to tap him for a cash infusion to get The Booby Trap up and running. He brought to the table far more practical business sense than I even realized at the time and helped me keep both feet on the ground.

As successful as I have been, looking back, I realize that the middle class in America is where almost all small business took root and blossomed. All the huge brands today, at one time, were the ideas and dreams of those who were able to scrape together the resources to make a go of their own enterprise. Some folks made it by creating a mom-and-pop pizzeria, and others—like the Ilitch family of Detroit or Tom Monaghan—did the same thing, but they parlayed one or two stores into thousands of franchised units. It was a formula that worked wonders for McDonald's before them and has continued to spread and thrive all over the developing world. But today, unfortunately, it's a different story for the middle class, or rather, what's left of it. My father was able to start and run a thriving small business in electronics, but today, with globalization and the consolidation of mega-corporations that produce and sell millions of products that are not even designed to be repaired—where is the hope and opportunity for mom and pop?

I'll tell you where. Instead of opening up his own shop, today my dad would have gone to work at Circuit City, or Radio Shack or a Best Buy, locked into an $8- or $10-an-hour job with little or no hope of growth beyond perhaps becoming a floor manager. There are plenty of low-paying service jobs for the simple reason that we no longer manufacture much of anything in America anymore! Cheap labor for commodity products is every big corporation's holy grail. What we're left with is, yet again, service jobs, construction, retail, and agriculture as more and more engineering and technical jobs are easily outsourced to the Far East. Unless you can figure out an angle to make your own personal fortune in America, you are being increasingly squeezed from both sides—good white-collar and decent blue-collar jobs are becoming increasingly difficult to find.

As has always been true, you have to constantly be in the process of improving your education—whatever field you're in. But with out-of-state or even in-state college tuitions for four-year degrees pushing toward $60,000 to $100,000, you can see why many of us who aren't twenty-two and female often wish that we had a nice pair of boobs so we could go work in a topless bar somewhere! At least there's no hefty up-front tuition. Between energy prices that seem to have nowhere to go but up, a crumbling national infrastructure, a health care system based purely on profit rather than people, and a trillion-dollar debt for the war in Iraq that is roughly the equivalent of a $25,000 credit card balance for every single living American—well, let's agree that the middle class is squarely on the endangered species list, at best.

In my life, I've been very lucky. I became entranced by the experience of walking into my first topless club and, galvanized by the lure of riches, I was fortunate enough to open my own club early in the genesis of topless entertainment in America when there was vast opportunity for rapid growth. You've noticed, no doubt, that I generally refer to the essence of my business as "topless" rather than to rest on the arguably classier crutch of "gentleman's club" or "show bar" to describe any one of my establishments. The label "topless" is what it is—polarizing in many ways, as for some it evokes distasteful images of gritty street corners strewn with the glass of smashed liquor bottles or, to others, simply shouts, "Beautiful topless women inside—along with ice cold beer and dirty martinis! Come and see 'em, boys, they'll knock your socks off!"

It's what men want and are willing to pay for, and nowadays it's what a lot of women will pay for, too, coming inside with their men in order to enjoy the experience and thus supercharge their amorous escapades at home.

I've been lucky, all right, in that I've survived two shootings as well as a murder-for-hire plot, numerous expensive lawsuits defending my right to purvey topless entertainment to the masses, and the efforts of self-righteous, out-of-control authorities who sent the whole topless business into such a state of shock in the early 1990s that my very survival was gravely in doubt. I have lived and breathed that rarefied air of cigaret and cigar smoke mixed with body spray, hairspray, perfume, cologne, and the pheromones of throngs of topless dancers to the extent that it is a permanent part of the chemical matrix of my brain. I truly believe that just by walking into one of my clubs I can sense the unique mood and profit potential on any given day or night to within a few bucks of the actual till.

Because I have persevered and have been willing to reinvest many of my profits into enhancing and expanding the quality of my product, I have been rewarded with even greater returns. I have been able to indulge in driving NASCAR and have had the ability to invest in my own private jet, along with a couple of partners who count their holdings in the billions rather than the mere millions. It has been a complete kick in the head to be able to jet down to Palm Beach or the Caymans in order to enjoy the fruits of my labors. I have likewise been able to treat my closest friends, and particularly family, to some richly deserved perks as well. One of my fondest memories was when I surprised my father by buying for him and delivering to him a completely restored shiny black 1957 Chevy Bel Aire, which was one of his all-time favorite cars and in which he now enjoys tooling around in his retirement in Florida. (He'd owned one just like it in his salad days.)

And yeah, I'm a gear head too, I must confess. My first Ferrari was that bloodred Testarossa I bought back in the eighties, but I've got to tell you the new Ferrari 360 Modena I drive now blows the Testarossa away. Of course, I just had to have a Rolls Royce, too, and a few years back I acquired an '04 Phantom that was built by BMW—it even had a James Bond-style compartment in the rear doors for a bumbershoot—that's umbrella in English, mate—that one could pull out in the event of a drizzle. But ultimately, I got bored with the Rolls and unloaded it. When you finally get to the point in your life that you can have the toys you've always dreamed of, they suddenly become less important to you. I recently read that the CEO of the Boeing company, who makes enough to afford to fly his own private jet, instead went out and bought a small Cub single-engine airplane that flies two people at around 100 mph—perfect for experiencing the joy of going low and slow over a green summer countryside. The cost of that Cub, at around $120,000, is less than the cost of a single fill-up of jet fuel for one of his company's 777s. Funny how one's priorities change, isn't it?

Besides doing what I do best, which is building and operating the finest topless clubs in America, if not the world, I enjoy investing in real estate and doing various property deals as opportunities arise or are presented to me by friends, family, and associates.

The more you're out there bumping elbows with other successful business people, the more you learn, the more opportunity you find, and the more success you acquire. I am more motivated than ever by the challenge of competing, and winning, in the race to build America's finest portfolio of premium gentleman's clubs.

But for all the success I've had, and all that I'm privileged to enjoy, from a wonderful fiancée to the kindness and counsel of my father in both business and in life, there is one thing for which I am most grateful, beyond anything—and that is my good health. It's so easy to take one's health for granted and it's so easy a thing to lose, whether by accident or neglect or bad habit. Having been shot twice, I am acutely aware of how your entire existence can change radically in a matter of seconds. I am also aware of how supremely lucky I was not to have died from the bullets that slammed into my chest and then into my face, fired by a crazed dancer and a crazy cop, respectively. I am fortunate in having had terrific doctors and surgeons and responsive and skilled trauma specialists in Detroit and Ann Arbor, who worked quickly to minimize the catastrophic effects of gunfire on my body.

When the Greek shipping magnate Aristotle Onassis was old and infirm, it is said that he remarked that he would gladly give up every penny of his vast fortune if he could only have back his robust health and a chance to live his life over again. But, as in a Greek tragedy, it was then too late. In the business of beautiful women and erotic entertainment, it is easy to foster the illusion that all sweet fruits of youth are forever in one's grasp. And for now, they are, for me and for those of us who have our health and the strength of heart to enjoy our gifts. Never say never, but also never think that poor health won't steal away from you those gifts that are now yours. Good health is the greatest gift of all, to be treasured, nurtured, and protected. With it, the enjoyment of all things is possible. With good health, one may endure all the trials and tribulations of life . . . all the better to savor life's triumphs. On this, not the last page of my life but the beginning of what I hope is my best chapter yet, to you the reader, I raise a toast. L'chaim! To life!

And, as always . . . bring on the dancing girls!

YOU ARE INVITED

I would be a poor host indeed if I didn't take the opportunity to invite you to visit one of my clubs, especially if you've never been to a gentleman's club before. For those of you who have, the point is moot, and I'll be looking forward to seeing a lot more of you in the clubs I currently operate and those that I will be opening in select locations in the future.

For those of you who have not visited a gentleman's club before, you are in for a truly unique experience. There is something electric in the air in a place where beautiful, nearly naked women are allowed to cavort. Let me provide you with the dictionary* definition of that word:

ca • vort
1: to leap or dance about in a lively manner
2: to engage in extravagant behavior

Merriam-Webster's Collegiate Dictionary (11th ed.)

I could have used the word "dance," obviously, but I think what you'll find is that there is an extra dimension of expression in my clubs, the very element I have worked awfully hard for over twenty-five years to achieve. The French call it the joy of life—*joie de vivre*. As for the element of extravagance, you'll simply have to see for yourself what my clubs are like. From the women to the atmosphere to the food to the overall level of service, I guarantee you a superlative gentleman's club experience. Whether you're a healthy, red-blooded guy, or a woman who is curious as to what all this "gentleman's" club stuff is about, I encourage you to come. I am often found in my various establishments and I would be very happy to meet you, and most definitely to entertain you.

You are invited!

The Flight Club
29709 Michigan Avenue
Inkster, MI 48141
734.641.2400 or Toll Free 866.641.2400
TheFlightClub.com

The Penthouse Club
20771 W. Eight Mile
Detroit, MI 48219
313.541.7000
PenthouseGentlemanClub.com

All Star
14541 W. Eight Mile
Detroit, MI 48235
313.342.7944

The Penthouse
3001 Castor Ave.
Philadelphia, PA 19134
215.423.6000